The Accidental Ecosystem

The publisher and the University of California Press Foundation gratefully acknowledge the generous support of the Richard and Harriett Gold Endowment Fund in Arts and Humanities.

The Accidental Ecosystem

PEOPLE AND WILDLIFE IN
AMERICAN CITIES

Peter S. Alagona

UNIVERSITY OF CALIFORNIA PRESS

University of California Press
Oakland, California

© 2022 by Peter S. Alagona
First Paperback Printing 2024

Library of Congress Cataloging-in-Publication Data

Names: Alagona, Peter S., author.
Title: The accidental ecosystem : people and wildlife in American cities /
    Peter S. Alagona.
Description: Oakland, California : University of California Press, [2022] |
    Includes bibliographical references and index.
Identifiers: LCCN 2021035766 (print) | LCCN 2021035767 (ebook) |
    ISBN 9780520386310 (cloth) | ISBN 9780520397880 (pbk.: alk.
    paper) | ISBN 9780520386327 (ebook)
Subjects: LCSH: Urban animals—United States—History.
Classification: LCC QH541.5.C6 A532 2022 (print) |
    LCC QH541.5.C6 (ebook) | DDC 577.5/6—dc23
LC record available at https://lccn.loc.gov/2021035766
LC ebook record available at https://lccn.loc.gov/2021035767

Manufactured in the United States of America

31 30 29 28 27 26 25 24
10 9 8 7 6 5 4 3 2 1

I dedicate this book to my son, Saul—surfer, slugger, mathematician, zombie slayer—who has spent much of his childhood listening to me chirp and squawk and hoot and howl about urban wildlife. There's nobody else in the world with whom I'd rather share my nest.

Contents

Preface

One bright winter day several years ago, I packed up my things, changed my clothes, hopped on my bike, and headed home from work. It was a Friday, and I thought I deserved an early start to the weekend. I had just put the finishing touches on my first book, which had consumed almost a decade of my life, and I was ready for something new. For now, though, I was content to take the afternoon off.

The bike path heading home leads out of my campus, past a beach, alongside a freeway, across wetlands, and then around several small farms before winding its way through sleepy suburbs and into a bustling downtown. About a mile from my office, the path meets up with Atascadero Creek. *Atascadero* is a lovely word for an unlovable place. In Spanish it means something like "quagmire," and this sad little stream lives up to its name. Unnaturally straight, it parallels a gravel road, looking less like a creek than like a canal. Long sections have been lined with concrete to control flash floods. On most days, though, it flows lazily, with tepid pools as black as asphalt and murky runoff trickling over slimy green rocks.

Fifteen minutes into my ride, I crossed a bridge over the creek and turned east between a subdivision and a golf course. That was when, about a hundred yards in front of me, something unusual loped across the path. It was the size of a small dog, but it had a tiny round head, big pointy ears, cartoonishly oversize haunches, and paws that, from a distance, looked as flat and wide as dinner plates. As I coasted forward, I ticked off a list of suspects: Deer? No. Raccoon? No. Skunk? No. Coyote? Probably not. Dog? Maybe. House cat? It was too big, but it *had* moved like one.

When I reached the spot where I thought I had seen the critter, I stopped my bike and peered into the bushes. There, sitting no more than fifteen feet away from me, was a bobcat—stout and full grown, with a plush speckled coat, bright green eyes, and trademark tufted ears. This cat was in its prime. Staring back at me, it looked as big as a lion, though I knew that most bobcats weigh less than twenty pounds. We locked eyes for several seconds, two mammals in the ancient act of sizing each other up.

I'd seen bobcats in the wild twice before. The first time was just after daybreak, on a crisp fall morning, along the shore of an alpine lake in the High Sierra. That mottled gray cat blended perfectly into her granite backdrop. The second time was on a warm summer evening, on a ranch in the hills above Monterey. This second cat, with tawnier fur to match her golden brown surroundings, paused on a grassy hilltop and glanced over her shoulder at me before disappearing into the brush.

Despite my previous encounters with bobcats—or perhaps because of them—this third one came as a surprise, and then as a revelation.

I was surprised because I had always pictured bobcats only in the kinds of wild places where I'd seen them before. I was even more surprised to learn that my sighting was nothing special. With a range that spans temperate and subtropical North America, bobcats thrive in a dizzying variety of habitats, from Florida's Everglades to Quebec's North Woods to Mexico's Sonoran Desert. They prefer to avoid people, but because most of their favorite foods, including rodents and other small mammals, don't, bobcats often end up in or around suburbs. Many of my friends and colleagues had seen them before in my hometown. Apparently, I was one of the last to know they were there.

The revelation came next. I had spent the previous decade studying endangered species, creatures that, almost by definition, most people never get to see. And yet here was this wild predator—as bold and beautiful and fearsome, from a certain point of view, as any Kodiak bear or Bengal tiger—prowling the Southern California suburbs. In the days that followed, I began to think a lot more about wildlife in cities. You can thank that bobcat for this book.

I also realized that I had reproduced a larger pattern. For decades, most scientists and conservationists shunned urban areas and the creatures that inhabited them, focusing instead on rarer species in more remote areas. People who cared about wildlife considered cities artificial, destructive, and boring. There was little to be learned from such places, and even less to be salvaged or nurtured within them. Only recently had wildlife advocates become interested in urban areas. It took them, like me, a long time to start looking. But when they finally did, also like me, they were amazed by what they found.

In the years after my encounter with that bobcat on the bike path, whenever I told anyone I was studying urban wildlife, what I got in response, without fail, was a story. What made that encounter so remarkable, I came to learn while writing this book and listening to all of those stories, was not that it was so unusual but that it was so common. My goal in the pages that follow is to explain both how we got to this point and what it means that just about every resident of every American city now has their own wildlife story.

Acknowledgments

Most books have one person's name on the cover, but the truth is that writing a book, like raising a child, takes a village. In my case, writing a book about wildlife in cities required an entire city's worth of friends, family, students, and colleagues. I am indebted to all of them in ways both big and small.

First, I thank my family for their love and support, especially my mother, Judy, whose interest in and enthusiasm for my work has been one of the few constants in my life.

I'm fortunate to have a group of fellow travelers whom I consider family in all but name. Some of these people are students or colleagues, but many are also close friends with whom I've worked, played, and grown up over the years, and whom I still call on a regular basis to vent, rant, rage, laugh, cry, lament, or ask advice. On this project, I benefited from dozens of conservations with Kevin Brown, Scott Cooper, Robert Heilmayr, Jessica Marter-Kenyon, Jennifer Martin, Alex McInturff, Tim Paulson, Gregory Simon, Ethan Turpin, Brian Tyrrell, Lissa Wadewitz, Bob Wilson, and Marion Wittmann.

At the University of California, Santa Barbara, several brilliant and (fortunately for me) patient colleagues, including Jeff Hoelle, Patrick McCray, and Jim Salzman, offered sound advice along the way. The members of the California Grizzly Research Network—especially Andrea Adams, Sarah Anderson, Elizabeth Forbes, Elizabeth Hiroyasu, Bruce Kendall, Molly Moore, and Alexis Mychajliw—were a source of both support and inspiration. Several undergraduate students, including most notably Bailey Patterson, assisted me with various aspects of this project.

I owe an enormous debt of gratitude to a far-flung constellation of friends and colleagues who offered their insights, connections, and advice at key moments. These include Mark Barrow, Dawn Biehler, Wilko Hardenburg, Melanie Kiechle, Emma Marris, Beth Prett-Bergstrom, Andrew Robichaud, Scott Sampson, and Louis Warren. Special thanks to everyone who funded, organized, or participated in the "Environments and Societies" colloquium at the University of California, Davis, the "Biodiversity and Its Histories" conference at Columbia University, and the City/Nature Summer Institute at the University of Washington. Sarah Newell found the robin's nest I describe in the coda.

More than two dozen experts on urban wildlife and related fields generously offered their time and insight, including several who met with me and my students or took me out into the field to see their work firsthand. Thank you to Cameron Benson, Jennifer Brent, Tim Downey, Cait Field, Dan Flores, Joel Greenberg, Liza Lehrer, Ron Magill, Seth Magle, John Marzluff, Michael Miscione, Ellen Pehek, Eric Sanderson, Paul Sieswerda, Jeff Sikich, Richard Simon, Peter Singer, Anne Toomey, Mark Weckel, and Marie Winn.

I send out a special thanks to my developmental editor, Eric Engles, who helped me whip an unwieldy first-draft manuscript into shape; Thayer and Jane at Ink Dwell studios for providing the interior artwork that gives this book its look and feel; my brilliant copy editor, Juliana Froggatt; and Stacy Eisenstark and other staff at

University of California Press for lending this project their expertise, professionalism, and enthusiastic support.

Finally, I thank that bobcat from the preface, along with all of the other creatures who taught me so many important lessons during my research and writing process.

Introduction

This book is about an ecosystem that was never supposed to exist.

Since the first cities emerged in the Middle East several thousand years ago, every great thinker who has studied them, from Plato to Voltaire to Jane Jacobs, has agreed on one thing: cities are for people. A handful of hardy wildlife species have always thrived in urban areas, but most were driven out as cities grew bigger and denser. Domesticated animals once roamed city streets in great numbers, but most of these too were eventually removed or brought under control, herded into the countryside or ushered into human homes. By the mid-twentieth century, fewer animals than ever before lived in the world's most developed cities. This arrangement started to seem natural, and there was every reason to believe it would continue.[1]

Then, beginning around 1970, people living in cities in Europe, North America, parts of East Asia, and elsewhere noticed a strange new trend. Wild animals that had not been seen there for decades— or in some cases ever—were showing up in the least likely of urban

1

environments. Conservationists called these creatures flukes, or described them as the last gasps of a natural world choked by smog and buried under concrete. Yet the sightings continued. Soon, hardly a week was going by without a report of a new species in a new city. By 2020, no one who had seen a deer graze on a suburban lawn, an alligator plunge into a golf course pond, a hawk devour a pigeon in an urban park, a bear pluck apples from a neighbor's tree, or a seal sunbathe on a busy dock could deny that cities were filling up with wildlife.

Even as wildlife populations inside cities have thrived, outside cities many have collapsed. Since 1970, global wildlife populations have declined by an average of 60 percent. North America has lost 30 percent of its birds. Some iconic species once considered secure, from giraffes to elephants, are now threatened. Vast swaths of wildland habitat have been cleared, graded, ploughed, or paved. At least one million species are in danger of extinction.[2]

Why have so many cities—the most artificial and human-dominated of all Earth's ecosystems—grown rich with wildlife, even as wildlife has faded from most of the rest of the world? And what does this paradox mean for cities, people, wildlife, and nature on our increasingly urban planet?

The Accidental Ecosystem tells the story of how American cities filled with wildlife. It argues that although cities were not built with the goal of attracting wild animals, they have become rich wildlife habitats—or even weird wildlife refuges—because of decisions people made often decades ago and mostly for other reasons. The recent explosion of wildlife in American cities is one of the greatest ecological success stories since the dawn of conservation, but it happened largely by accident. Only over the past generation have scientists, conservationists, planners, and civic leaders throughout the United States begun to study, grapple with, and appreciate cities as fertile ecosystems housing diverse multispecies communities. But bringing these animals back was the easy part. The hard part, and the real work ahead of us, is living with them now that they're here.

·   ·   ·   ·   ·

Ecologists and conservationists were slow to grasp the changes that brought so much wildlife to so many American cities. Over the past few decades, however, as interest in urban wildlife and ecosystems has grown, two schools of thought have emerged. Let's call these two groups the skeptics and the cheerleaders.

According to the skeptics, cities are mostly agents of destruction. Cities replace diverse native creatures with a smaller number of tough exotic species that can multiply in the company of humans, sometimes rising to the level of pests but not contributing much to the world. Even beyond their boundaries, cities gobble up resources, laying waste to natural habitats. As this process unfolds, our planet grows more uniform and less interesting. Urban wildlife may be useful for educating the public and raising its support for conservation in more pristine areas, but cities and most of the creatures that inhabit them are of little ecological value compared with what they destroy.[3]

The cheerleaders respond that cities are novel ecosystems, which provide crucial services—such as pollination, storm protection, and water filtration—for the people who live in them. Cities house diverse wildlife, including hundreds of endangered and migratory species. Creatures that prosper in cities are marvels of adaptation and resilience worthy of our respect. Since urban environments are harbingers of the future on a planet increasingly shaped by human action, we should embrace them, learn from them, and cultivate them in all their weedy glory.[4]

This book—which concludes that we should value and foster urban wildlife, even when living with it poses real challenges—draws insight and inspiration from both the skeptics and the cheerleaders. Instead of taking a side, it tells the story of how we got to a point where we can have such a debate, and what this debate says not only about wildlife but also about us.

·   ·   ·   ·   ·

Any book about urban wildlife must begin by defining two terms—
urban and *wildlife*—both of which are slipperier than they may at
first seem.

Cities exert a lopsided influence on local and global ecosystems.
By 2020, only around 2 percent of the earth's ice-free land surface
was covered with urban areas, but many cities were booming, particularly in Africa and Asia, and together they already housed more
than 56 percent of the world's human population. In the United
States, around 83 percent of people lived in urban areas, including
nearly 95 percent of residents in California, the most urban U.S.
state. Cities occupy a small fraction of our planet's land base, but
because they contain so many people, they consume vast quantities
of resources and produce immense volumes of waste.

Yet what counts as a city has changed over time. As late as the
1940s, the U.S. Census defined *urban* as "compris[ing] all territory,
people, and housing units in incorporated places of 2,500 or more"
residents. In 1950, the Census Bureau introduced the term *urbanized area,* which now includes any contiguous zone with a population of at least 50,000 and a density of 1,000 or more residents per
square mile. The bureau defines a metropolitan statistical area as a
larger region containing at least one urbanized area, plus its surrounding county and any outlying counties that meet certain crite-
ria. Researchers outside the bureau have developed other ways of
defining cities, for example by using satellite imagery to map the
proportion of built and paved land versus green space in an urban
region.[5]

For wildlife, it is best to think of the term *urban* as representing a
continuum. Downtown, people are everywhere, most surfaces are
paved, and only a few, hardy wildlife species linger for very long.
Suburbs contain fewer people per square mile, tend to be leafier, and
offer greater opportunities for creatures that can avoid the hazards
cities pose while tapping the riches cities offer. On the outskirts, in
areas known as urban-wildland interfaces, diverse species benefit
from a Goldilocks combination of refuge and resources. An urban

satellite area may be dozens or even hundreds of miles from its parent city, but the two places are intimately connected. A dam built to supply a distant metropolis with water and power, for example, both shapes the city and transforms the watershed. Some places that few people consider urban, including tourist magnets such as Yosemite Valley, also possess many of the features typically associated with cities, from trash dumps to traffic jams. Finally, there are urban waterways. We tend to equate cities with land, but from New York Harbor to San Francisco Bay to the Florida Everglades, urbanization has rearranged aquatic habitats on a massive scale, even if these changes can be hard to perceive for a bipedal primate.

This book focuses on vertebrate wildlife, including birds, mammals, fish, and a few reptiles. Insects, arachnids, and other diminutive creatures play important supporting roles in urban ecosystems. Yet they play only bit parts in this story, because of limited space and because we still know so little about them, including trends in their populations over time. The pages that follow also contain relatively little about some of the most familiar urban wildlife species. Squirrels make an early debut, but crows, pigeons, rats, skunks, opossums, and raccoons remain backstage. Most of the starring roles in this drama go to creatures like bald eagles, black bears, and sea lions—large and charismatic species that few would have expected, fifty or a hundred years ago, to thrive in urban spaces. Their presence in some modern American cities reminds us both how little we knew about them decades ago and how much more we still have to learn.

There are some things we may never know. One of the great ironies of ecological science is that we know so little about the places where most of us live. For decades, most ecologists ignored urban wildlife, missing opportunities to collect baseline data and monitor growing populations. Over the past generation, however, our understanding of urban ecosystems has grown in leaps and bounds. But because scientists got such a late start, there are many questions about the past that we lack the data to answer in a statistically satisfying way. There are a few exceptions to this rule, most notably regarding birds, which legions of admirers have followed in cities for more than a century. But birds are a special case. This book combines historical and scientific records with interviews and field observations to assemble a story of change over time.

When you start talking with people about urban wildlife, one thing becomes clear. People who encounter these animals—which, these days, means almost anyone who lives in a city—invariably make meaning of the experience. Clichés portraying urban animals as diseased menaces, criminal gangs, swarthy immigrants, gritty hustlers, faithful servants, good neighbors, upstanding citizens, icons of resilience, or wellsprings of hope have always said more about the people expressing them than they do about the creatures they claim to describe.

Consider the example of native versus exotic species. Exotic species are, after habitat destruction, the second-greatest driver of global biodiversity loss. Distinguishing between natives and exotics sometimes makes sense, particularly for newly introduced species. In cities, however, this distinction often breaks down. If cities are novel ecosystems, the oldest of which in North America date back only hundreds of years, then although some species may have adapted to living in them, no species is native to them in any deep ecological or evolutionary sense. Cities exist in regions with native species that may pass through or settle down in developed areas. Cities also contain newcomers, some of which cause problems, but others of which have found benign or even beneficial niches. Drawing a bright line between those that belong and those that don't, based solely on their ancestors' places of origin, raises the specter of xenophobia. It is unwarranted and—since one of the goals of studying urban wildlife is to engage a younger, more diverse constituency for conservation—it is unwise.[6]

The story of wildlife in American cities has unfolded differently in different places. One common theme is that in every place there have been winners and losers. Although cities may be sanctuaries for some creatures, they are traps for others. This book focuses mainly on the winners, species that possess some quality—such as fecundity, flexibility, or fearlessness—that has enabled them to flourish in urban environments. But for every species in this book that has thrived, many more not covered in these pages have dwindled in or disappeared from our cities. Managers charged with protecting struggling creatures in pockets of urban habitat have some of the toughest jobs in conservation. Coexisting with wildlife means not only celebrating the charismatic species that most people like but also treating common species that most people don't like humanely, while giving those that are struggling the space and resources they need.

The time has come to start making more and better decisions with all of these creatures in mind. Some forward-thinking people and places are already doing so, and it is crucial for the rest of us to join them. As the stories that follow show, issues that affect wildlife also affect people, and decisions made in one city influence what happens in other cities and regions, including in far-off nature preserves and wilderness areas. The choices we make today will affect wildlife and shape ecosystems—in cities and beyond—for generations to come.

1 Hot Spots

Ecologists love nature reserves: places where people are visitors, wild animals roam free, and ecosystems still seem, at least on the surface, relatively intact. Yet, in an era when humans are transforming almost every aspect of the natural world, such places are increasingly the exception, not the rule. For a different way to understand wildlife in the twenty-first century, you don't need to travel to some distant mountain range or remote wilderness area. Instead, take a free, twenty-five-minute ride on the Staten Island Ferry.

Heading south from the Whitehall Terminal in lower Manhattan, the ferry plies some of the most urban waters on our planet. To the north loom the Financial District's skyscrapers, including the fraught monolith of One World Trade Center. To the west stand the Statue of Liberty and Ellis Island. To the east sit the partly artificial landmass of Governors Island and beyond it the Port of New York and New Jersey's giant Red Hook shipping terminal.

Look closer, though, at the leafy hills of Brooklyn's Greenwood Cemetery, or out past the Verrazano-Narrows toward Lower Bay and the Atlantic Ocean, and you will see the traces of a once-great ecosystem. Look even closer—down into the milky blue waves for the humpback whales and harbor seals that, in recent years, have returned to these waters after long absences, or upward at the gulls, terns, and ospreys circling in the sky overhead—and you may catch glimpses of its partial return (see figure 1).

Prior to European contact, the place we now call New York City teemed with life. The island of Manhattan alone, according to the ecologist and author Eric Sanderson, contained an estimated fifty-five distinct ecological communities, more than a typical coral reef or rain forest of equivalent size. Its meadows, marshes, ponds, streams, forests, and shorelines housed between 600 and 1,000 plant species and between 350 and 650 vertebrate animal species.[1]

Early visitors and settlers marveled at New York's wildlife. David Pieterz de Vries, writing around 1633, counted "foxes in abundance, multitudes of wolves, wild cats, squirrels—black as pitch, and gray, flying squirrels—beavers in great numbers, minks, otters, polecats, bears, many kinds of fur-bearing animals." Others complained of chirping birds and croaking frogs so loud that it was "difficult for a man to make himself heard." Yet this racket was a mere inconvenience. According to the seventeenth-century politician and businessman Daniel Denton, New York's rich land and temperate climate ensured the "Health both of Man and Beast."[2]

Compare colonial New York to Americans' current benchmark for wild nature, Yellowstone National Park. Congress established Yellowstone, the world's first national park, in 1872, to protect its scenery and wildlife and to attract tourists to an area that, unlike New York, had few other economic prospects. Yellowstone is now a United Nations Biosphere Reserve and World Heritage Site. Drawing more than four million visitors annually (roughly the same number of people who live in Manhattan and Brooklyn combined), it is one of America's greatest wilderness wonderlands. It is also one of the few areas in the Lower 48 US states that retain their full suite of native fauna—from wolverines, grizzly bears, and lynx to bighorn sheep, mountain goats, elk, moose, pronghorn, and bison.

Yellowstone may be a paradise for ecologists—since 1970, it has accounted for more than one-third of all the published peer-reviewed articles based on research conducted in the national parks—but it is no picnic for most of the creatures that actually live there.[3] With its frigid winters, short growing seasons, and rocky, acidic, nutrient-poor soils, the park can be a tough place to live—especially compared to the rich, temperate, and sheltered landscapes and waterways that once defined the area we now know as New York City. Prior to the nineteenth century, almost all of the big wild species in Yellowstone also inhabited places that were wetter, milder, more productive, and richer in resources. In such areas, these creatures often had larger populations and required smaller home ranges to meet their needs. Most of them remain in the park today not because it is their ideal habitat but because people have protected it and because they have few other places to go. Yellowstone remains a land of immense natural value. Yet it is so important not because nature endowed it with biological diversity but rather because people chose to protect it.

The numbers say it all. Prior to European contact, Manhattan, an island of just twenty-three square miles, contained roughly the same number of species as now live in Yellowstone National Park, a vast region of mountains, valleys, forests, and prairies covering some thirty-five hundred square miles. This means that the Manhattan of yesteryear housed around 150 times more plant and animal species per land area than the Yellowstone of today. If European settlers had wanted to save North America's wildlife instead of getting rich from harvesting it, they would have built a great city in northwest Wyoming and set up a national park at the mouth of the Hudson River.

There are several reasons why New York contained such a riot of life. For two and a half million years, glaciers sheared its cliffs, rounded its hills, tilled its soils, and polished its bedrock, leaving a varied landscape. Located at the boundary between the mid-Atlantic

region and New England, it was a biological crossroads where northern and southern species overlapped and mingled. It also straddled contrasting habitats, in a place where salt water met freshwater and land met sea. Nutrient-rich runoff from the Adirondack Mountains flowed into a vast estuary where it circulated with the tides, fertilizing plants and feeding animals while supplying sediment for mud flats, wetlands, and beaches.[4]

Humans also had a crucial role to play. For thousands of years, the Lenape people and their predecessors hunted, gathered, and fished in the area. They stewarded and shaped the land, setting fires to clear brush, stimulate plant growth, and create wildlife habitat, while moving seasonally to harvest resources and find shelter. Archaeologists used to think that the coastal Lenape, like their inland Algonquian relatives, relied on staple crops such as squash and maize. Yet more recent work suggests that, in the area that became New York City, natural resources were so abundant that the prosperous locals had little need for crops. Though gardens were common, they supplied less than 20 percent of the calories people consumed. The rest came from their ecosystem.[5]

The Dutch, who arrived in New York in 1609 and settled in 1624, also found the area to their liking. With its timber for shipbuilding, fish for catching, furs for trapping, and whales for harvesting just offshore, it contained the raw materials to fuel an early modern capitalist economy. These settlers quickly grasped that the area's central location, inland river access, and deepwater port could make it an ideal site for gathering resources and trading with indigenous and European partners. New York soon emerged as a center of North American and trans-Atlantic commerce. By the time of the first U.S. census, in 1790, it had become America's most populous city.

·   ·   ·   ·   ·

New York may seem exceptional (New Yorkers certainly think so), but it is far from unique in its ecological richness. Many of the biggest cities in the United States are located on sites that, prior to their founding, were unusually biologically diverse and productive compared with their surrounding regions. They were also crawling with wildlife.

Several factors explain this pattern of overlapping ecological richness and urban growth. Some cities emerged on the sites of indigenous settlements that were well positioned to access food, water, and other resources. In California, for example, beginning in 1769, Spanish-speaking priests, soldiers, and bureaucrats established a chain of missions along the coast and in nearby valleys. These colonial outposts were built next to indigenous communities, which benefited from their sites' agreeable climates, diverse fish and game, staple food plants such as oaks, and year-round access to freshwater, a rarity in much of that arid region. After Mexico achieved independence in 1821, pueblos formed around the old missions, later becoming farming towns and eventually cities. California's four biggest cities—Los Angeles, San Diego, San Francisco, and San Jose—all share these indigenous, mission, and pueblo roots.

Los Angeles deserves special mention because of its well-documented ecological history. When the padres founded their missions at San Gabriel and San Fernando, they had no idea that just fifteen miles away and a century later, farmers, oil workers, and eventually paleontologists would discover one of the world's greatest troves of fossils, covering the past fifty thousand years. Formed from the same deposits that fueled Southern California's early twentieth-century oil boom, the La Brea "Tar Pits" have produced more than three million fossils, including the remains of around two hundred vertebrate animal species. A list of the entombed includes extinct behemoths like Columbian mammoths and giant short-faced bears, as well as current stalwarts like skunks and coyotes. These creatures were there for a reason. The Los Angeles Basin offered a mild climate and diverse habitats that supported a spectacular profusion of wildlife. Even after most of the basin's megafauna disappeared, by the end of the last ice age, it remained a kind of American Serengeti. Los Angeles, like New York, was a hotspot of biological diversity.

Even where indigenous communities were small or absent, American cities tended to develop in areas that provided settlers with easy access to rich natural resources. Some cities developed right on top of those resources, whereas others emerged close enough to serve as supply hubs. Others formed in strategic locations where their residents could gather or process resources from vast regions. Montreal and Saint Louis started as fur-trading posts; Denver served as a transit point and supply depot for mining in the nearby Rockies; Chicago became America's greatest nineteenth-century boomtown by raking in the West's bounty of timber, beef, and grain.[6]

Many large American cities developed on sites with access to water for transportation. Harvesting natural resources doesn't do you much good if you don't have a means to bring them to market. Most of this country's oldest and biggest metropolises sprouted up by the seashore, and more than half of all Americans still live within fifty miles of an ocean coastline. Protected estuaries with high ground for building and deep water for shipping have worked well as city sites. Cities not located on coastlines are often connected to them by navigable inland waterways—Pittsburgh and Minneapolis are obvious examples.[7]

Coastlines and rivers corridors are not only favored spots for cities; they also tend to attract a lot of wildlife. This is especially true for river mouths and deltas, which pack diverse habitats into small areas, are highly productive, and provide crucial pathways for migrating fish, marine mammals, and birds. Cities like Sacramento and New Orleans now occupy many of these soggy landscapes.

A reliable source of potable water was often a crucial factor in determining the location of a settlement. Consider the example of Phoenix, America's fifth-largest and second-driest major city. Some two thousand years ago, the Hohokam built canal systems, farms, and thriving villages along the Salt River. Later native peoples repurposed much of this infrastructure, creating vibrant societies of their own. An 1867 account of the valley described "a sparkling stream the year round, its banks fringed with cottonwood and willow; the land level and susceptible of irrigation. The evidences of a prehistoric race were everywhere in evidence." A carpet of annual grasses, providing "a most excellent fodder for stock," covered the higher ground. This water and forage attracted diverse wildlife, including hundreds of migratory bird species, aquatic animals such as beavers, and grazers like elk and antelope, not to mention the wolves, pumas, and jaguars that hunted them. The desert city of Phoenix now sprawls over this once lush and well-watered landscape.[8]

Other cities developed on sites that are often inconveniently wet. Miami is blessed with access to vast wetlands, forests, and the only coral reefs in the contiguous United States. But it is cursed with water lapping at its borders on four sides: to its east is the Atlantic Ocean, to its west is the Everglades, from the sky above comes the wet subtropical weather that makes it America's second-rainiest big city, and below is porous limestone that is filling up with salt water as the sea level rises. Houston grew into a major metropolis after the Great Galveston storm of 1900 drove Gulf Coast development inland. Decades of reckless construction then left what is now the country's fourth-biggest city vulnerable to a series of floods, culminating in 2017 with Hurricane Harvey. Wetlands that had been converted into reservoirs and later into subdivisions filled with water, pushing thousands of snakes, alligators, raccoons, and other creatures into suburban neighborhoods and reminding Houstonians, at least for a few days, that they still lived in the bayou.[9]

Even many cities that appear to have no good ecological reason to be where they are still often seem to be located in oddly biodiverse areas. Las Vegas's very existence depends on vast quantities of water and power from the Colorado River and cheap desert land provided by the US government. Few places so emphatically stand for the plastic antithesis of wild nature, yet Las Vegas has an astonishing natural history unlike that of any other big city in the United States. Its name, in Spanish, refers to the lush meadows that once blanketed its valley floor. It has a drier climate than Phoenix, but prior to its development, the Las Vegas Valley had some of the most reliable freshwater sources in the Mojave Desert, courtesy of the nearby Spring Mountains. Clark County, where Las Vegas is located, contains 18 ecological communities and at least 233 protected species or species of concern, including some that exist nowhere else, making it a neon-red hot spot of biological diversity.[10]

All of this adds up to a striking pattern: in the United States, major cities are disproportionately located on sites with high natural levels of biological diversity. As of 2020, fourteen of the fifty largest US cities occupied areas of "very high" biological diversity, even though such areas made up less than 2 percent of the US land base. These areas serve not only as homes for resident animals but also as stopovers for traveling creatures. Many birds migrate on paths known as flyways, which parallel mountain ranges or follow river valleys or coastlines. At least forty of the fifty largest US cities are located within the narrow bands of North America's seven major flyways. More than 260 species of birds migrate through Manhattan, for example, making Central Park a celebrated, if unlikely, bird-watching destination.[11]

This pattern extends beyond the United States, though it applies less in some regions than in others. Throughout the world, big cities contain disproportionate shares, given their land areas, of the total biodiversity in the countries where they are located. In Europe, the continent with the best-studied urban ecosystems, cities house at least 50 percent of most countries' species, even though they rarely cover more than 30 percent of the land. This pattern probably does not hold for most of the tropics, but even there one can find tantalizing examples of the overlap between biodiversity and urbanization, in places like central Mexico and the Atlantic coastal forest of Brazil.[12]

Scholars have been slow to grasp this phenomenon. Until the past couple decades, most ecologists ignored cities, preferring to work in the Yellowstones of the world. Sociologists described future city sites as blank slates. Economists saw in these sites only raw materials or strategic trading posts. Anthropologists emphasized the indigenous cultures of future city sites over their ecosystems, as if the two were unrelated. And historians stressed the unlikely locations of some cities, as well as the eccentric personalities and chance events that led cities to flourish or decline. Geography, they were all quick to point out, is not destiny.

Yet geography does matter. Attributes such as protected coastlines, navigable rivers, potable freshwater, varied habitats, and raw materials were often found in areas of high biological diversity and productivity. These features sustained large numbers of wild creatures, provided the resource bases on which native cultures flourished, and attracted Europeans who built settlements, some of which grew into great cities.

.   .   .   .   .

City sites started with abundant wildlife, but they didn't stay that way. Cities have complex effects on the landscapes and waterscapes where they develop. As they grow, they add to local biodiversity by importing species and by creating new habitats that attract others. But they also harm native species by harvesting large numbers of useful animals, killing undesirable ones, and destroying or rearranging entire ecosystems, both near and far. These forms of ecological damage characterized even the early days of American urban life, beginning in the seventeenth and eighteenth centuries, and then accelerated in the nineteenth century with industrialization, globalization, and urban population growth. Fertile ecosystems that had attracted settlers decades earlier cracked and buckled. These processes unfolded at different times in different places, but by the second half of the nineteenth century, areas in and around many American cities, which had once been among the most biologically diverse and productive places on the continent, had lost much of their native wildlife.

The loss of wildlife in densely settled areas of North America was part of a larger process that had begun centuries earlier in Europe. By the late medieval period, hunters had depleted wild game across much of Europe, leading wealthy landowners to create private preserves and issue oppressive decrees that imposed severe penalties on violators. Food species such as deer and aurochs (a type of large wild cattle) and fur-bearing mammals like beavers and foxes disappeared from many places. Deforestation leveled the habitats of woodland species, and predator-control efforts cleared the countryside of wolves, wolverines, bears, lynx, and jackals.

Aquatic species also suffered catastrophic losses. Prior to 1000 C.E., most of the fish consumed in Europe were local varieties—such as pike, perch, and trout—found in freshwater streams or coastal seas. In the centuries that followed, the Norse, English, Scottish, and Dutch reached farther into the North Atlantic, netting enormous hauls of cod, mackerel, and menhaden. These protein-rich food fish, easily preserved by salting or drying, transformed economies, connected distant regions, and fueled population growth, creating a feedback loop that increased demand. By the mid-nineteenth century, most of the great North Atlantic fisheries had collapsed. Populations of marine mammals and seabirds also plummeted as hunters sought out their eggs, skins, blubber, and meat.[13]

By 1600, the European onslaught had washed ashore in North America. Beavers' plush pelts, strong and pliable enough to withstand the felting process, attracted French, British, and Dutch trappers and traders, funded a diverse indigenous workforce, fueled a globalizing economy, and forged new political alliances. Soon, trappers started bringing other pelts to market: fox, raccoon, mink, fisher, deer, and eventually bison and Pacific sea otter. The fur trade did not cause any species to go extinct, but in their rush to thwart competitors and supply urban markets, trappers and traders cleared vast regions of North America.

The wild creatures that remained found themselves confined to dwindling and deteriorating ecosystems. Loggers and farmers followed the trappers, felling, hauling, and milling trees and clearing fields for crops and livestock. Wild creatures considered threats to economic progress were blacklisted, persecuted, and driven into the most remote corners of their ranges. Northeastern forests were among the first ecosystems to feel these pressures on a large scale. Between 1600 and 1900, New England's tree cover dropped from more than 90 to less than 60 percent of the land area. Some species that thrived in more-open landscapes benefited, but those adapted to living in forests saw their numbers plummet.[14]

Lakes and streams were hit even harder than forests. Logging and farming muddied once clear waters, organic runoff fed algae blooms, and dams blocked migrating fish. Industries like tanning flushed nutrients, metals, and chemicals into streams. Untreated sewage flowed freely. Wetlands were drained and estuaries filled. Coastal pollution choked marine life, forcing fishers to travel farther in search of healthy stocks and giving local residents pause about consuming food harvested from toxic waters.

Things were little better at sea. Migrating fish, like salmon, were obliterated in many areas. By the late nineteenth century, marine mammals—once abundant in the waters around Boston, New York, Seattle, and San Francisco—were all but gone. Atlantic gray whales, walruses, northern elephant seals, and sea otters vanished from entire regions. Southern right whales, California sea lions, gray seals, and several fur seal species hung on throughout their ranges, but in deeply diminished numbers. Although much of this devastation unfolded outside urban areas, demand for marine animal products, from fish for eating to whale oil for lighting street lamps, increasingly came from cities.

By the late nineteenth century, the populations of dozens of wildlife species in the United States had crashed compared to their precolonial sizes, with some reaching all-time lows. Many of these species would eventually return to cities like New York, but only after a long period when domesticated animals ruled the urban wild.

2 The Urban Barnyard

It was a scene out of the nineteenth century in the heart of twenty-first-century New York. Just before noon on October 17, 2017, a young bull—dark brown and shaggy, with floppy tan ears—escaped from a slaughterhouse near the corner of Sixteenth Street and Fourth Avenue in Sunset Park, Brooklyn. Unwilling to accept his fate, the bull burst his confines and bolted, heading east into the fashionable neighborhood of Park Slope, with its stately brownstones, bougie coffee shops, and overpriced vegan eateries. He soon found his way into Prospect Park, a 526-acre patch of green space in the middle of the borough. For the next three hours, a bull ran loose in Brooklyn (see figure 2).[1]

Considering all of the bad things that could have happened—a trampling, a kicking, a car accident—the episode unfolded with little consequence. A toddler received a black eye when mother and child darted out of the bull's way, but no other injuries were reported. Grainy video, shot from a helicopter, shows the bull trotting across a basketball court. Minutes later, he paused on a ball field to gaze, through a chain-link fence, at a herd of cell-phone-toting primates.

One local called the situation "hilarious and amazing." Another described himself as in "total culture shock." A third, who had lived in the neighborhood for forty years, claimed never to have seen cattle there before. "Raccoons, yes," she said, but "cows, no."[2]

This was not the first time in recent memory that a bull had wandered the streets of New York. A year earlier, another bull had broken free and briefly toured Queens. By the time the authorities captured him, cheeky locals had dubbed him Frank and were calling for a pardon. The comedian Jon Stewart and his wife Tracey, a prominent animal welfare activist, stepped in, arranging for Frank to be given a checkup at a nearby animal hospital and then sent to a bucolic sanctuary upstate. Nowadays, cattle that escape from the few remaining slaughterhouses in New York City rarely end up back on the line.[3]

The sight of a bull on the streets of a major American city turns heads today, but this was not always the case. During the eighteenth and nineteenth centuries, American cities had little wildlife, but they had plenty of animals. City dwellers needed eggs, milk, and meat for their tables, lard for their soap, and hides for their shoes, jackets, belts, and saddles. They had to convey their goods and themselves. Before the era of supermarkets and factory farms, livestock were boarded, fed, worked, slaughtered, and eaten in cities, sometimes in the same home. Churches, factories, and storefronts were interspersed with barns, stables, and pastures. Since the numbers of working animals in American cities rose along with their human populations, most urban dwellers had daily contact with a diverse cast of barnyard creatures that provided food, power, materials, fertilizer, transportation, and, increasingly, companionship. It was not until most of these domesticated creatures were removed from cities that most wild creatures would have a chance to return.[4]

.   .   .   .   .

In 1800, only 6 percent of Americans, or around 324,000 people, lived in cities. This is about as many as live today in Lexington, Kentucky, or Stockton, California. These scattered towns were small, cramped, dusty, and treeless. Not surprisingly, some of America's most influential thinkers wrote unflatteringly about their country's budding urban centers. Thomas Jefferson, for example, saw no contradiction in praising the virtues of an agrarian society while scorning the cities where his beloved farmers sold their products. In 1787, Jefferson scoffed that the "mobs of great cities add just so much to the support of pure government, as sores do to the strength of the human body." Writing to James Madison a few months later, he went further: "When we get piled upon one another in large cities, as in Europe, we shall become corrupt as in Europe, and go to eating one another as they do there."[5]

Charges of cannibalism aside, Jefferson had little to worry about at that time. It wasn't until the Civil War, which sparked a manufacturing boom in the Northeast and Midwest, that the United States really began to urbanize. By 1900, almost 40 percent of Americans lived in cities, and the country's urban population was doubling every twenty-five years. Some cities grew even faster. The population of New York City increased seven-hundred-fold, from around 5,000 in 1700 to 3.5 million in 1900, making it the world's second-largest city, after London. Between 1840 and 1900, Chicago grew from a frontier settlement of 4,500 people, known as the Mudhole of the Prairies, to a metropolis of 1.7 million souls. As late as 1847, San Francisco wasn't even San Francisco. It was Yerba Buena, a run-down mission and mothballed Hudson's Bay Company fur-trading post perched on a windswept peninsula along Mexico's remote northwestern frontier. By 1900, its population had reached 342,000, more people than had lived, a century earlier, in all American cities combined.

If one had to choose a flagship species for this nineteenth-century urban environment, it would undoubtedly be the horse. James Watt, who patented a revolutionary version of the steam engine in 1775, coined the term *horsepower* as a measure of work equal to thirty-three thousand foot-pounds per minute, the amount of effort one could expect from a strong draft horse. In Watt's time, horses were living machines, laboring in workshops and factories alongside steam engines, water wheels, and other mechanical contraptions. Horses were also an essential mode of transportation, at least for those who could afford to use them. As cities grew, armies of horse-powered vehicles—including carts, street cars, and ferries—accelerated the pace of urban life, connecting far-flung districts, fueling suburban growth, and segregating neighborhoods by class, race, language, and ethnicity.[6]

Pigs were also common in nineteenth-century cities. Opinions about these plump brutes, according to the historian Catherine McNeur, reflected one's place in society. Elites tended to see them as walking sewers, vectors of disease, and symbols of American backwardness. Yet for poor people and immigrants, pigs were more than just symbols: they were one-stop factories, garbage cans, and recycling bins, clearing the streets of refuse long before humans stole their jobs as trash collectors. When times got tough, such as during the War of 1812 and the depression that followed, pig owners could slaughter and eat their hogs, selling the excess body parts to processing plants on the squalid outskirts of town. Piggy banks, indeed.[7]

Cows have lived in cities as long as people have. Medieval and early modern European towns reserved common areas for grazing dairy cows. This tradition continued in American cities until after the Civil War. Between 1870 and 1900, dozens of cities passed ordinances prohibiting open grazing, but cows remained in urban barns and backyards well into the twentieth century. In Seattle, as late as 1900, one-quarter of the households in the city center owned cows.[8]

Dogs played different roles in nineteenth-century American society than they do today. Prior to the 1800s, most dogs in households were working animals: hunters, herders, mushers, guards, and exterminators. But this was a small proportion of their total population. Most dogs lived outside and had no clear owner. Known as "tramps," a derogatory label that applied to footloose people as well as canines, stray dogs wandered American cities begging for handouts and scavenging through trash in the company of pigs, goats, rats, and humans. Some dogs wore collars, suggesting that they had owners, but even most family pets slept outside and spent their waking hours roaming free.[9]

The sheer number of creatures in this urban menagerie was astounding. By 1820, New York City had at least 20,000 pigs and 130,000 horses. Estimating the numbers of dogs, cats, chickens, goats, turkeys, and geese is more difficult, but accounts from the time suggest that they were everywhere. So were the infrastructures that supported them. An 1867 Sanborn Insurance Map of Boston identifies 367 stables. Around three-quarters of these wooden structures were more than one story tall, making them the rickety livestock parking garages of nineteenth-century cities.[10]

Urban animals consumed a seemingly endless supply of food. A horse ate around three tons of hay and sixty-two bushels of oats annually. A cow required at least two acres of land on a typical town common. After local ordinances confined them to barns and backyards, each cow had to be fed at least thirty pounds of hay daily. Pigs and dogs often scavenged for their meals, but they also stole food and begged for handouts.

What goes in must come out. A heavy draft horse expelled around seven tons of manure each year. Feces piled up in the streets, clogged gutters, attracted legions of flies, and were shoveled into great heaps of "street dirt" that baked on hot days, froze in the winter, and oozed in the rain. Yet this stuff proved valuable. Urban gardeners had long collected it as fertilizer for their plots. By 1800, cities were signing exclusive contracts with firms that gathered manure, separated it by quality, and sold it. In Manhattan in 1842, thirty cents could purchase a fourteen-bushel cartload. By 1860, the Long Island Railroad was shipping more than one hundred thousand of these cartloads to nearby farms each year.[11]

Like manure, animal carcasses were hazardous but valuable. By 1850, butchers in New York were slaughtering as many as 5,000 sheep, 2,500 cows, 1,200 calves, and 1,200 hogs per week. Urban animals also succumbed to abuse, neglect, exposure, exhaustion, disease, old age, and injuries, which were all too common on chaotic nineteenth-century streets. Little went unused. Rendering plants melted down bones, fat, and offal to make soap and tallow; factories used bones to make toothbrushes and buttons; builders used horse-hair to bind plaster; and refineries used blood and bones to purify sugar. Tanneries, among the dirtiest animal-processing facilities, used chemicals and manure to cure hides.[12]

The most common complaint about animals in the city was their odor. Nineteenth-century cities stank. Sometimes, as in the Great London Stink of 1858 and the Great Paris Stink of 1880, this stench assumed apocalyptic proportions. Prior to the triumph of germ theory in the 1880s and 1890s, Americans associated foul odors with miasmas, or "night airs," which they believed carried diseases from rotting organic matter to human bodies. In crowded cities racked by outbreaks of cholera, yellow fever, typhoid, and other dreadful diseases, offensive smells seemed like mortal threats. The renowned British sanitarian Edwin Chadwick spoke for the nervous masses in 1846 when he wrote that "all smell is disease."[13]

Few places could reek as much as a stagnant water body on a hot day. In New York City, a toxic cocktail of chemicals and organic waste ran unfiltered into ponds, rivers, and bays, where it sloshed back and forth with the tides. In 1862, spring runoff failed to flush six months' worth of waste from the Chicago River, leaving the city's residents to contend with "the blood and entrails of more than eighty thousand head of fat cattle and of four hundred thousand hogs, besides the sewage." Water seemed to be a minor ingredient in this frothy stew. Thousands of residents signed a petition complaining about the "foul poisonous stench," and the *Tribune* labeled the polluting businesses "offenders against humanity and manufacturers of disease."[14]

Urban residents also understood that animals could transmit diseases directly, even if they didn't know exactly how. We know today that livestock share dozens of diseases with humans. Many of these did not yet have names in the nineteenth century, but they spread easily in crowded, unsanitary conditions.

With so many threats and frustrations related to domesticated animals in urban spaces, conflicts inevitably arose over where they were kept, how they were used, and who could own them. The opposing sides divided along class lines. Poor and working-class people who depended on animals for their livelihoods and sustenance clung to them, while wealthy and powerful people argued that modern cities had no need and no place for tens of thousands of working animals.

Debates about domesticated animals reflected broader anxieties about the social order. When reformers railed against urban animals, they were expressing their worries about urbanization, industrialization, and immigration. They said they wanted to help, and they believed they were doing so. Yet their solutions often hurt those who were already hurting, while ethnic stereotyping and scapegoating gave progressive reforms an oppressive edge. The legal apparatus applied to these animals and the state violence inflicted on them— including portraying them as nuisances and treating them as expendable—sent clear messages about who belonged in the city and who didn't.[15]

Working animals faded from American cities for several reasons. Horses were essential and ubiquitous, but it gradually became clear that they were not a viable solution for the needs of modern cities. They were too skittish, too dangerous, too prone to injury and disease, and too unreliable in emergency situations, such as when responding to a fire. Machines powered by electricity and fossil fuels—including steam engines, motorcars, and trains—took many of the jobs horses had filled. In 1930, the Horse Association of America reported that the use of motorized cars and trucks alone had cut the number of horses in the United States by 77 percent, from what would have been an estimated 6.5 million in the absence of these machines to 1.5 million.[16]

Unlike with horses, debates about the place of pigs in cities were loud, emotional, and sometimes violent. When, beginning in the 1820s, New York City attempted to phase out its free-roaming pigs in favor of human street sweepers, the pigs' owners fought back. Anti-pig forces pressed their case further during the cholera epidemics of 1832 and 1849. These tensions exploded during the "Piggery War" of 1859, which killed nine thousand hogs and destroyed three thousand pens and one hundred boilers. In 1866, the city banned free-roaming pigs, but some residents continued to resist this law into the 1890s, staging acts of civil disobedience or keeping their hogs hidden.[17]

Cows remained in most cities longer than pigs, but their association with immigrants also made them targets. In the days after the Great Chicago Fire of 1871—which burned more than 2,100 acres, destroyed 17,500 buildings, and killed at least 300 people—newspaper reports claimed that a cow owned by Catherine O'Leary, from the city's Near West Side, had started it by kicking over a kerosene lantern in a hay-filled barn. An investigation cleared the O'Learys of guilt for the incident, which burned thousands of shoddy wooden structures in a city whose officials had failed to implement building safety codes. One of the reporters who wrote the key story blaming the O'Learys later admitted that he and his colleagues had made it up. Yet this myth, fueled by anti-Irish bigotry, persisted. Cows were increasingly seen as dangerous denizens of urban areas. But because they supplied a heavy, perishable, and indispensable fluid commodity, milk, they remained in American cities in considerable numbers until the 1920s, when refrigerated boxcars and buggies made daily milk delivery cheap, safe, and convenient.

Dogs were a different story. Fear of rabies, arguably the most terrifying infection of the time, prompted leash and muzzling laws for pets, as well as violent campaigns against stray dogs. In response to the rabies scare of 1848, for example, Philadelphia, Boston, New York, and other cities launched a "Great Dog War," which was really a dog massacre, featuring sharpshooters, bounty hunters, vigilantes, and children wielding clubs. Yet unlike pigs, dogs had diverse and powerful supporters, from hunters and breeders to businesspeople and politicians. Over time, the dog debate thus shifted from *whether* to *how* dogs should live in cities. Even as most other domesticated animals faded from the urban scene, dogs remained.[18]

By the early 1900s, what it meant to be a dog in American cities was changing. Early suburbanites started neutering and spaying their dogs, bringing them inside at night and during the winter, feeding them special foods, taking them to veterinarians, breeding them, founding kennel clubs, walking them on leashes, training them, sleeping with them, and even burying their bodies in pet cemeteries, where the epitaphs on their gravestones identified them as cherished family members. From rootless tramps, symbols of moral decay and social disorder, dogs were turning into icons of the nuclear family. Dogs became less like wayward adults and more like precocious children at the very moment when Victorian society was inventing the modern concept of childhood.[19]

Civic groups helped guide this transition. In 1866, the American Society for the Prevention of Cruelty to Animals (ASPCA) formed in New York. It attracted former abolitionists, women's clubs, temperance societies, and church groups, many of whose members worried not only about animals but also about the corrosive moral effects of animal cruelty on the men and boys who perpetrated it. By 1874, ASPCA-affiliated societies had formed in twenty-five of the thirty-seven US states that existed then, many with the legal authority to care for stray animals, investigate charges, issue citations, and even make arrests.[20]

It took several decades, but the Victorian-era urban barnyard eventually vanished. After the Civil War, veterans brought their practical battlefield skills and experiences—including those related to medicine, health, and public administration—back to their hometowns. Some got jobs working for state and local agencies, such as New York City's Metropolitan Board of Health, established in 1866, where they wrote and enforced public health codes. Experts soon fanned out across American cities, drawing "stench maps," documenting dangerous facilities, and tagging sites for cleanup. At the outset, most such agencies had little power, but their authority grew as cleanliness, and the sense of order it represented, became a kind of civic religion. By 1920, even New York, once known as the "dung heap of the universe," was becoming a model sanitary city.[21]

The decades that followed were unique in American history. In 1920, for the first time, more than half of all Americans lived in cities. But although these cities had more people, they had fewer animals, wild or domesticated, than at any time before or since. This era of animal-poor cities defined how most Americans think about what a city is, or at least what it should be: a clean, modern space designed for and inhabited by people. Yet even as Americans were beginning to see cities as spaces mostly free of animals, changes were under way that would eventually enable many wild creatures to return.

3 Nurturing Nature

On July 4, 1856, the *New-York Daily Times* reported that an "unusual visitor" had turned up near City Hall Park in downtown Manhattan. According to witnesses, this strange creature escaped from a cage, squeezed through a crack in an apartment door, darted down four flights of stairs, dashed across Broadway, bounded into a park, and climbed a nearby tree, attracting throngs of fascinated onlookers and causing an uproar in one of New York's busiest neighborhoods. The rogue beast in question was a plump eastern gray squirrel.[1]

The squirrel that dashed for her freedom on Independence Day drew so much attention because, as odd as it may seem now, in 1856 Manhattan did not have a wild squirrel population. It still had tens of thousands of barnyard animals, but with the exception of pigeons, rats, and gulls, it had few resident wild animals. Over the coming decades, urban scholars, planners, and designers would help modernize American cities. Their goal was to make cities cleaner, greener, and healthier for people, but in the process of doing so, they also created the conditions under which some wildlife, including eastern gray squirrels, could return.

Eastern gray squirrels are so common in so many places today that it is difficult to imagine most American cities without them. Native to eastern and Midwestern forests, eastern grays are hardy, fertile, long lived, omnivorous, and famously comfortable around people. They are also a keystone species, feeding dozens of predators and tending the forests they call home by caching millions of nuts and seeds. Eastern gray squirrels are small creatures that have big impacts.

Eastern grays were widespread in eastern North America prior to European contact, but their populations crashed during the seventeenth and eighteenth centuries. Deforestation leveled their habitats, and hunting—for food, for fur, and because people considered them farm and garden pests—killed tens of millions of them. By the late eighteenth century, they were rare enough to be kept as exotic pets. In 1772, Benjamin Franklin, saddened by the loss of this quintessential American species in the wild, went so far as eulogize one kept as a pet and named Mungo, who had survived a trans-Atlantic journey only to die in the jaws of an English hound. Eastern grays remained popular pets for many decades, which explains what one was doing in 1856 in a downtown Manhattan apartment.[2]

Eastern grays reappeared in cities such as Philadelphia and Boston during the 1840s. According to the historian Etienne Benson, residents of these cities introduced squirrels to "beautify and enliven" their new public parks and squares. Yet most early introductions failed, because these cities still had too few parks and trees to support viable populations of most arboreal animals.[3]

Unsure about the wisdom of living with squirrels, people debated what eastern grays contributed to society and how humans should treat them. Detractors viewed them as pests. Their supporters argued that having these attractive and industrious little creatures as neighbors inspired people to be kinder, gentler, and more charitable toward all of God's creation. The naturalist Vernon Bailey concluded

TOW-AWAY
NO PARKING
ANY TIME
Blah Blah Blah BLAH

that eastern grays were "probably our best-known and most loved native wild animals, as they are not very wild and, being very intelligent, accept and appreciate our hospitality and friendship." To be a good urban animal, in Bailey's eyes, was to be smart, friendly, and relatively tame.[4]

By the early 1900s, eastern grays were making a comeback. As the country's agricultural heartland migrated to the Midwest, forests reclaimed abandoned farms throughout the Northeast, enabling squirrels to return to the region's rural areas, while lower-density housing developments and tree-planting programs created leafy new suburban habitats. People reintroduced eastern grays into places where they had long ago disappeared, and shipped them to far-flung locales where they had never lived before. Eastern grays soon appeared on the West Coast from San Francisco to Los Angeles, abroad in Britain, Italy, and South Africa, and even on remote islands like the Azores, the Canaries, Bermuda, and Hawaii (see figure 3).

.   .   .   .   .

The conditions that enabled eastern grays to thrive in American cities took shape over more than a century. Beginning around 1860, urban scholars, designers, and planners set out not only to transform American cities but also to teach Americans what a modern city should be. They advocated diverse ideas over many decades but all had a few things in common: they embraced ecological metaphors, they used plants as tools, and they envisioned urban environments largely devoid of animals.

The leading urban scholars, designers, and planners of the late nineteenth and early twentieth centuries were all reacting, in one way or another, to what they saw as the iniquities of the Victorian city: its crime, squalor, poverty, diseases, volatility, oppressive congestion, and suffocating stench. They wanted to remake cities as clean, controlled, orderly spaces for people. In doing so, they responded to and helped direct a range of tectonic social changes, including shifts in population, immigration, technology, industrialization, consumption, and suburbanization.

Each of these changes brought with it problems and possibilities. For Marxists, the root of Victorian-era urban problems lay in the reorganization of labor and capital that emerged with the Industrial Revolution. For the growing corps of civil servants, urban problems resulted from bureaucratic challenges, including a lack of funding and civic capacity. For more romantic critics, the problem was the city itself. Rural life, they argued, fostered moral character, family bonds, traditional gender roles, and bodily health, whereas urban life did something close to the opposite.[5]

One solution to these problems was to get people out of the city. During the first few decades of the twentieth century, increased access to mass transportation, via horse and later electrified railcars, enabled city dwellers, many of whom had grown up in rural areas, to access the countryside more easily. It also fueled the growth of bedroom communities in early suburbs. But these were mainly for the well-to-do. Since most urbanites lacked the means to move into or even visit the countryside, planners began to think about how to bring the country into the city.[6]

A leading figure in the movement to transform cities was Frederick Law Olmsted. Born in Connecticut in 1822, Olmsted rose to become the most famous landscape architect in American history, and one of the most prolific, designing many of the country's best-loved parks. Olmsted believed that parks served a range of civic functions. They improved public health by providing clean air and opportunities for exercise. They reminded city dwellers about the wonders of nature. They instructed visitors on the value of engaged democratic citizenship. They uplifted the spirit. They boosted property values. And they offered outlets for social tensions that might otherwise boil over.[7]

Whereas Olmsted's vision focused on discrete projects, like parks and campuses, Ebenezer Howard laid out a broader vision for whole cities. Howard turned to writing and design after moving from

England to the United States, then failing as a farmer in Nebraska. Inspired by the anarchist movements of the 1890s, he sketched out elaborate plans for what he called "garden cities." Organized into concentric circles and radiating spokes, Howard's sketches included central parks, urban cores, and outlying townships separated by farms and linked by rapid transit. His plans took the form of physical layouts, but his goal was to reconnect people with nature, with one another, and with themselves. Garden cities were places where people could exercise their personal freedom while participating in voluntary, independent communities.[8]

During the twentieth century, some urban thinkers shifted from nature-based designs to ecological metaphors. In 1925, the sociologist Robert Park argued that cities were like ecosystems, exhibiting "life cycles" of growth and decay. For Park, planners were conservationists whose job was to nurture urban resources while allowing nature to take its course. The firebrand social critic Jane Jacobs agreed. Beginning in the 1960s, Jacobs argued that cities were for people, pure and simple. Yet, in a 2001 interview reflecting on her life's work, she said that she thought about cities in terms of "biomass, the sum total of all flora and fauna in an area. The energy, the material that's involved in this, doesn't just escape the community as an export. It continues being used in a community, just as in a rainforest the waste from certain organisms and various plants and animals gets used by other ones in the place."[9]

According to Jacobs's contemporary, the Scottish-born landscape architect Ian McHarg, urban planners must not only employ clever metaphors but also work within the physical constraints of actual ecosystems. In *Design with Nature* (1969), McHarg walks readers through his meticulous process of mapping landscapes, evaluating their hazards and resources, and then following ecological principles to design green communities. McHarg pioneered the "polygon overlay" approach, which arranges spatial data sets in stacked layers and is the basis for the geographic information systems that scholars and planners use today to map landscapes. His work has left its imprint on fields from environmental impact analysis to ecological restoration.[10]

Olmsted, Howard, Park, Jacobs, and McHarg offer but a few examples of the extraordinary range of ideas and approaches produced during the first century of American urban planning. Yet virtually all of this field's most celebrated figures had one thing in common: they left out the animals. These thinkers were aware of animals' ecological roles—Olmsted, for example, knew that birds and rodents could help regenerate denuded forests—but the idea that cities were vital, diverse, and dynamic wildlife habitats eluded every one of these major figures in urban planning and design.

In retrospect, this makes sense. Wild animals were mostly absent from American cities throughout the nineteenth and early twentieth centuries. The urban thinkers who worked during this formative period thus saw few reasons to include wild animals in their theories or designs. And since nobody expected that much wildlife would ever return to urban areas, there was little need to plan for the challenges and opportunities of living with them. Search as you may, you will find almost nothing about wildlife in the canon of American urban planning before 1960.

.   .   .   .   .

Ideas advanced by early urban planners played out on the ground first and most obviously with parks. Before the Civil War, public green spaces like City Hall Park, site of the Independence Day squirrel incident, were rare. The biggest green spaces in most cities were town commons used for grazing cattle. There were also cemeteries, but most were on small plots of land that grew more crowded over time. This changed with the first sprawling, pastoral cemeteries. In 1831, the Massachusetts Horticultural Society established the Mount Auburn Cemetery in the Boston suburbs of Cambridge and Watertown. In the years since, Mount Auburn's 174-acre rolling, wooded campus has become not only a sprawling graveyard but also a public park, historical landmark, experimental garden, and celebrated arboretum.

The first modern city parks appeared a few decades later. In 1858, Olmsted and his partner Calvert Vaux won a design competition to create the plan for what would become Central Park. When the pair first toured the site of the proposed park, they found hardpan soils, rocky outcrops, murky bogs, and razed forests, as well as homes, farms, dumps, tanneries, ramshackle factories, utopian hamlets, and the free Black settlement of Seneca Village. Recalling the condition of much of the site prior to its redesign and redevelopment, Olmsted expressed a sense of revulsion common among elites of his time. "I had not been aware that the park was such a very nasty place," he said. "In fact, the low grounds were steeped in the overflow and mush of pig-sties, slaughter-houses and bone-boiling works, and the stench was sickening." Olmsted and Vaux's famous Greensward Plan envisioned a pastoral scene of woods and meadows that would invigorate, inspire, and instruct its visitors. The site's human residents would be forced to leave, but nature, or at least a certain kind of nature—tame and largely devoid of animals—would thrive.[11]

Inspired by visionary projects like Central Park, other cities were soon competing to hire the most prestigious firms and commission the best designs. Many of these projects extended beyond single sites to include parkways, park systems, and even city plans. Olmsted's firm, which remained the most active and influential such outfit for several decades, designed parks in Boston, Brooklyn, Buffalo, Chicago, Louisville, Milwaukee, and Montreal, as well as plans for Stanford University, the University of California, Berkeley, the University of Chicago, and portions of the US Capitol grounds.

Like most park planners, Olmsted was enamored of nature. Many of his firm's projects produced bucolic landscapes reminiscent of both natural savannas and the countrysides of western Europe, with their woodlots, ponds, gently rolling hills, and graceful shade trees. Other projects featured more-dramatic landscapes typical of the

American West. At sites from Niagara Falls to the University of Washington, his firm emulated or emphasized the grandeur of wild nature, celebrating an idealized western frontier at a moment when the actual frontier was fading into legend.[12]

Olmsted's plans required a tremendous amount of time, effort, and money to make these sites appear natural. He erased traces of previous human residents, shunned most artificial structures, and resisted vulgar attractions such as zoos, amusement parks, and even playgrounds. Yet this was a sleight of hand. In his quest to mimic nature, Olmsted moved tons of earth, rerouted waterways, laid footpaths, built bridges, and planted hundreds of thousands of trees.

Trees, at least in such large numbers, were a new feature in most American cities. Most early modern cities had few street trees. During the eighteenth century, pundits mocked the idea of planting street trees, residents viewed trees as nuisances, insurance companies refused to provide fire protection for houses with trees nearby, and politicians rejected tree planting as a frivolous expense. In 1782, the Pennsylvania State Legislature even passed a bill ordering that all street trees in Philadelphia, the country's largest city, be removed. This operation was never completed, thanks in part to a grassroots effort, led by the physician, educator, politician, and social reformer Benjamin Rush, to establish an insurance company that offered policies to homeowners whose houses stood next to trees.[13]

By 1850, attitudes toward street trees were shifting. Reformers argued that they improved public health and boosted real estate values, and designers instructed cities to plant trees in new town squares and along boulevards and parkways. By the 1880s, trees were an indispensable feature of modern urban life and planting them an expression of civic pride. The urban forests that grace so many American cities today, from Atlanta to Seattle, all date from this period.

This was same time when modern zoos, natural history museums, and botanic gardens started appearing in cities around the country. The wealthy donors who founded these institutions hoped they would instill senses of both wonder toward the natural world and responsibility for it. Theirs was an imperialist, paternalist, and often racist vision, but people flocked to these places anyway. The advent of the eight-hour workday, and later the weekend, gave city dwellers more leisure time, and rising wages gave them more disposable income to spend on their days off. But they also went because they yearned to reconnect with a natural world from which they felt alienated, they were drawn to the romance of the frontier, and they were fascinated by displays of the spectacular and exotic.

Victorian-era zoos, gardens, and museums aimed to educate and inspire their visitors, but they sent mixed messages. Zoos and museums presented their patrons—most of whom had no chance of ever seeing a lion, a tiger, or even a bear in the wild—with a thrilling experience in a grand setting. Yet these institutions also made it clear that wild animals belonged in wild places. The only place for a wild animal in a city was confined in captivity or stuffed in a diorama.

Around this time, cities began establishing preserves on their outskirts. Among the best known of these is the system of Cook and Lake County forest preserves that forms a giant green crescent around Chicago. In 1913, after more than a decade of work by forest and open-space advocates, the Illinois State Legislature passed the Cook County Forest Preserve District Act. Its purpose was to safeguard "the flora, fauna, and scenic beauties within such district, and to restore, restock, protect and preserve the natural forests and such lands together with their flora and fauna, as nearly as may be, in their natural state and condition, for the purpose of the education, pleasure, and recreation of the public." Today, these counties manage around one hundred thousand acres of preserves, rich in the kinds of wildlife that are rarely found either in Chicago's urban core or on Midwestern farms.[14]

Other cities acquired more-distant sites to supply water for their residents, creating protected spaces that became de facto nature reserves. New York began its quest for upstate sources after a series of cholera epidemics, including one in 1832 that killed 3,516 people, or around one in fifty New Yorkers. Doctors would not identify a clear link between polluted water and cholera until 1854, when the British physician John Snow showed that water from a polluted well was spreading the disease in London. In their suffering, however, parched cholera victims cried for water, strengthening a long-standing belief that New York City had outgrown its polluted and depleted local sources. In 1842, the city completed its first rural reservoir, on the Connecticut border about twenty-two miles to the north. Others went online in the Catskills in 1915 and in the Delaware River Watershed in 1950.[15]

A pattern emerged across the country as cities sought permanent sources of freshwater, sometimes reaching to lakes and streams hundreds of miles away. The fates of these distant watersheds may not seem relevant to wildlife in the city, but these places and creatures are connected in many ways. Cities imposed strict conservation measures on some waterways to prevent contamination even as they dammed, drowned, diverted, and dumped in others. Access to faraway water sources allowed many cities to trash their local streams even as their residents imported millions of gallons of water to irrigate their lawns and gardens. These changes affected creatures in all of these environments, including some migratory bird species that experienced the entire gamut of urban influences on their long journeys.

By World War II, cities throughout the United States had built parks, planted millions of trees, created forest preserves, and established sanctuaries around crucial water sources. This combination of factors led to a kind of greening in and around many urban regions. This allowed creatures like eastern gray squirrels, once reintroduced, to thrive in the very same cities from which their native populations had been eliminated a century or more earlier. In the decades that followed, these changes would enable a host of other creatures, including some that were new to these areas and some that are far bigger and tougher to live with, to make their own inroads and comebacks. Eastern grays were among the first wild animals to return to the hearts of American cities, but they would not be the last.

4 Bambi Boom

In August 1942, nine months after the United States entered World War II, Walt Disney Productions debuted its sixth feature film at Radio City Music Hall in midtown Manhattan. Building on the success of earlier releases—like *Snow White and the Seven Dwarfs* (1937), *Pinocchio* (1940), and the modernist classic *Fantasia* (1940)—this new film's trailer boldly declared that "the world's greatest storyteller brings the world's greatest love story to the screen." "*Bambi*," the announcer continued, "proves that love can be loaded with laughs."

After a disappointing first box office run, six postwar rereleases made *Bambi* one of the most lucrative films of its era. As late as 1966, it remained the fourth-highest-grossing movie of all time. By 1989, when Disney started distributing it on home video, *Bambi* had generated more than ten times as much revenue as the second-most-famous film released in 1942, *Casablanca*.

Bambi was more than a lighthearted story about goofy critters, spring flowers, and young crushes. It was one of the most influential films ever made, with cutting-edge animation and a multilayered narrative that drew from long-standing ideas about nature, society, and American culture while opening the door to new genres of animal-themed movies and television shows. *Animal Planet, March of the Penguins, Finding Nemo,* Shark Week, *Planet Earth:* all of these built on the foundation, and capitalized on the success, of *Bambi.*[1]

Bambi was a film with depth, ambition, and politics. It combined naturalistic with impressionistic artwork and featured lovable young animals with bobble heads and saucer eyes, drawn to resemble human infants. Babies need parents, but with a generation of men fighting abroad and women working on the home front, social conservatives worried that the American family was under threat. By placing the characters in nuclear, male-dominated clans, Disney reassured his viewers that traditional gender roles and family structures were natural and thus would survive the war. Taking his father's place as the Great Prince of the Forest, Bambi embodied the "circle of life" theme common in later Disney productions like *The Lion King* (1994). Humans, who were prone to acts of cruelty like hunting and of carelessness like setting fires, were not part of this circle. If a person could kill an innocent animal, then how far was he from killing another person or even starting a war? "It is Man," Bambi's father declares in the movie's most memorable line. "We must go deep into the forest."[2]

When *Bambi* first hit theaters in 1942, the white-tailed deer, on which Disney based the main character, was what we would now call a threatened species. Native Americans had harvested them for millennia, maintaining their populations by using fire to create the forest clearings and edges that white-tails favor. Nobody knows how many white-tails lived on this continent prior to European contact, but by 1930 their population had dropped an estimated 99 percent, from as many as thirty million to as few as three hundred thousand. To produce the initial drawings for Bambi, Disney sent one of his artists all the way to Baxter State Park in Maine for six months. When this proved insufficient, he had two white-tails shipped twenty-six hundred miles from Maine to California to serve as models.[3]

By the time of *Bambi*'s release, however, white-tailed deer had begun to recover. They were reintroduced to some areas where they had been eliminated. Laws restricting hunting—by the location, season, number of animals a hunter could take, and sex of the animals that could be killed (bucks were prized, while does were spared)—protected them. With most of their natural predators gone—wolves, pumas, and bears had been eliminated in most of the eastern United States—there was little to slow their rapid rebound.[4]

White-tails quickly regained their status as the most common wild ungulates, or hoofed animals, in North America. As early as 1950, some biologists believed that the population of white-tails had reached pre-European levels, up one-hundred-fold from the number just two decades earlier. White-tails could soon be found living in forty-six US states—mostly east of the Rockies, whereas their close cousins, black-tails and mule deer, are more common west of the Rockies—not only in the rural areas where they had once thrived but also in the country's booming suburbs (see figure 4).[5]

White-tails were not alone. Their success as one of the first and most visible members of a new wave of wildlife flowing into urban areas was part of a bigger story. Within a few decades of *Bambi*'s release, the film's entire cast—including rabbits, skunks, opossums, and owls—began appearing in greater numbers in and around American cities. Some had always lived on the outskirts of cities, but they multiplied during the postwar era. Others returned to areas where hunting and trapping had decimated their populations decades earlier. Still others appeared where people had never seen them before. A host of additional species—raccoons, foxes, coyotes, bobcats, hawks, and others—would soon join them. Instead of taking the Great Prince's advice to "go deep into the forest," these creatures sought out the very places that, according to Walt Disney, they were supposed to avoid.

Bambi alone did not cause any of these changes. It did, however, help shape popular ideas about nature at a moment when wildlife was beginning to recover from the onslaught of the eighteenth and

nineteenth centuries. Before World War II, city dwellers created the conditions that made this possible by building parks, setting aside reserves, planting trees, passing conservation laws, and reintroducing lost species. After the war, two additional, related factors—the growth of leafy suburbs and the decline of hunting in and around these new communities—enabled more wild creatures, of more kinds, to make cities their homes.

.   .   .   .   .

The first "streetcar suburbs" sprouted up near American cities in the late nineteenth century. Planned around commuter rail stations served by horse-powered and later electric streetcars, they featured parks, commercial centers, tree-lined streets, and tidy, Craftsman-style homes. These early suburbs provided a growing middle class with both the convenience of the city and the calm of the country. An early example was Oak Park, near Chicago, where suburban growth kicked off in 1872 after the town constructed its first railroad depot. Over the next several decades, its residents, including the famous architect Frank Lloyd Wright, built an extensive streetcar system, a bustling downtown, and dozens of architectural landmarks.[6]

Between 1920 and 1930, suburbs grew twice as fast as the country's central cities. Some expanded much faster. Shaker Heights, outside Cleveland, grew by 1,000 percent, while Beverly Hills, near Los Angeles, grew by 2,500 percent. Beginning in 1929, however, the Great Depression slashed birthrates, access to loans, and purchasing power. Between 1928 and 1933, new home construction plunged by 95 percent, leaving a housing shortage that would last beyond World War II.[7]

After 1945, four factors—new roads, zoning laws, government-backed mortgages, and the postwar baby boom—ignited the housing market, creating vast suburban regions around the country's tightly packed older cities. The developers who pioneered these postwar suburbs, at sites like Levittown in New York and Lakewood in

California, turned the complex artisan craft of home building into a mass production process reminiscent of Henry Ford's automobile assembly lines. These two industries, in fact, worked together. Cars fueled a fantasy of unlimited mobility, while the suburban tract home promised freedom, prosperity, and independence. These dreams seemed within reach. In 1947, a World War II veteran could purchase a new Levittown home for less than $7,000, the equivalent of around $83,000 in 2020. By 1951, the Levitt and Sons firm had built 17,447 homes, or an average of 12 per day.[8]

Most scholars have taken a dim view of these early postwar suburbs, noting that they managed to be both the most segregated and the most monotonous human habitats in our species's history. They also gave men freedom but tended to isolate women. As late as 1960, developments like Levittown issued "covenants" excluding nonwhite buyers from purchasing homes. Densely packed into geometric layouts with few trees, uniform green lawns, and acres upon acres of concrete and asphalt, these were hostile places for most living things. Postwar suburbs gobbled up farmland, displaced rural communities, polluted waterways, paved over habitats, decimated wildlife, obliterated historical sites, and devoured incalculable resources while forcing their residents to depend on cars, roads, and fossil fuels—all in the name of a hollow consumer culture that promised bricks and mortar but delivered mostly plastic.[9]

Postwar sprawl was not inevitable. In the United Kingdom, for example, at least until the deregulation of the 1980s, government officials exercised more control over land-use planning, and they contained sprawl to a far greater degree than in the United States. Here, however, suburbs emerged as the defining urban form. By 2000, for the first time in any country's history, more than half of all Americans lived in communities that were neither truly rural nor truly urban.[10]

Postwar suburbs were, by just about any measure, ecologically bleak. Yet, for the most part, they were not carved from pristine nature. Most were built on flat, open areas that farmers had cleared decades earlier to grow food for nearby cities. Early suburbs replaced farms on New York's Long Island, along Chicago's western fringe, and around dozens of other American cities.[11]

One of the clearest examples of farms giving way to sprawl was in Los Angeles. From 1910 to 1955, Los Angeles was the United States' top-grossing agricultural county, producing everything from wheat and cattle to vegetables, fruits, and nuts. Crisscrossed by the world's largest network of streetcars, early twentieth-century Los Angeles had an urban geography similar to that of other American cities, with one major exception. Downtown thrived for a time, but the L.A. Basin lacked a single urban core, instead containing at least a dozen major towns. Each of them was too far from the next closest one to reach it comfortably on foot, but all were within what would soon become a short drive.[12]

Cars turned L.A. from a region of small cities and large farms into a vast suburban metropolis. As early as 1915, L.A. had one car for every eight residents, compared to the average national ratio of one to forty-three. By 1930, single-family dwellings constituted more than 90 percent of L.A.'s housing stock, compared to around half of the stocks in New York, Chicago, and Boston. The nation's first high-speed divided road, the Arroyo Seco Parkway, linking downtown L.A. to Pasadena, opened in 1940, paving the way for California's freeway-building bonanza. By 1963, when its last streetcars were decommissioned, Los Angeles was more of a suburban region than a city in the traditional sense. Today, concrete and asphalt blanket tens of thousands of acres of what was, not long ago, some of the world's most productive farmland.[13]

As suburbs spread outward from older city centers, they encroached further on more natural areas. Aquatic habitats—including lakes, streams, and wetlands—were among the first and hardest hit. In Southern California, development altered or obliterated two-thirds of the region's coastal wetlands. Many became harbors, ports, parks, or subdivisions. Although these changes began in the nineteenth century, the most ambitious projects were completed after World War II.

In San Diego, for example, the massive Mission Bay project, launched in the 1940s, converted a tidal marsh into the country's largest aquatic park. In Los Angeles, the Marina Del Rey project, which broke ground in 1953, turned the Ballona Creek estuary into the world's largest small-craft artificial harbor.[14]

The Army Corps of Engineers and the US Bureau of Reclamation also reengineered the streams that fed these wetlands. With developments encroaching on nearby floodplains, the corps and other agencies funneled unruly creeks and rivers into concrete storm drains. Glorified gutters—such as the one that entombs the Los Angeles River and was made iconic by the 1991 dystopian film *Terminator 2: Judgment Day*—shielded nearby communities from floods. But they ruined riparian habitats, devastated wildlife, destroyed open space, depleted aquifers by reducing water infiltration into the soil, and flushed billions of gallons of freshwater into the ocean.[15]

In the 1970s, new developments, particularly in the Sunbelt and western states, pushed farther into native habitats. These places would become ground zero for conflicts over wildlife, open space, and suburban sprawl. An advancing front of suburbs crept up brushy hillsides, onto mountains near public lands, and into previously marginal areas like mud flats and sand dunes. Construction along this urban-wildland interface, which has continued in the decades since, has placed more homes in the paths of fires and mudslides and put more rare species at risk.[16]

Yet the same suburban developments that have destroyed so many habitats and threatened so many species have unintentionally and unexpectedly benefited others. Industrial farms can be among the most hostile environments for wildlife, and creatures that wander onto them encounter a range of hazards—from heavy machinery to guns, traps, pesticides, baited poisons, and a lack of places to hide. In areas where neighborhoods replaced farms, some creatures moved in or started commuting, feasting on suburban food and water by night and taking shelter in wilder places by day. By the 1970s, the urban-wildland interface had become a conduit for enterprising wildlife, including a range of species that were recovering their numbers or expanding their ranges, like white-tailed deer.

.   .   .   .   .

Suburban growth had another unanticipated consequence—a widespread decline in recreational hunting—that enabled some wildlife species to grow their numbers even further in and around cities.

When the United States was a mostly rural country, many of its residents depended on hunting for some portion of their food or livelihood. By the late nineteenth century, with the country's wildlife in steep decline, wealthier and more urban hunters, who killed animals for sport rather than nourishment, called for strict limits on subsistence hunting and for bans on the sale of wild-caught game. Several states responded with new hunting and fishing laws, but these were often controversial and poorly enforced. Congress addressed this situation with the Lacey Act of 1900, which outlawed the transport of wildlife taken in violation of state laws. In 1911, the US Senate ratified the world's first wildlife treaty, the North Pacific Fur Seal Convention. Dozens of state and federal laws that were passed during the Progressive, New Deal, and postwar eras built on these foundations.[17]

The system that emerged, known as the North American Model of Wildlife Management, has seven principles: Wildlife is a public resource. Its use is governed by state, federal, and international laws. People can use wild animals for purposes permitted under these laws. It is illegal to sell most animals captured in the wild. Lawful access to wildlife is open to anyone, without preference or prejudice. Wildlife management should be based on science. And wildlife users help fund conservation by paying fees to enter refuges and by purchasing hunting and fishing licenses.

The North American Model enjoyed fifty years of success. From 1920 to 1970, during the golden era of "hook and bullet" conservation, resources flowed into programs designed to enhance hunting and fishing, and many wildlife populations rebounded. After 1970,

however, the North American Model started to crack. A new generation of conservationists, many of whom had grown up in cities and
suburbs, pushed for programs that did not just serve a rural hunting
and fishing clientele but rather advanced the broader goal of conserving biological diversity. They viewed some traditional wildlife-man-
agement approaches, like controlling most predators, as wasteful and
ineffective, and they championed bills like the Wilderness Act, the
Marine Mammal Protection Act, and the Endangered Species Act.
Unsatisfied with their progress, in the 1980s many defected from
wildlife management to form the new field of conservation biology.

Around the same time, the number of recreational hunters in the
United States started to plummet, a trend that has continued to this
day. In 1972, 29 percent of adult Americans—nearly one in three—
polled by the General Social Survey reported that they or their
spouse had hunted at some point. By 2006, this had fallen to just 17
percent, a decline of more than 40 percent in thirty-four years. From
1991 to 2006, the number of active hunters in Illinois and California
declined by half, and in Arizona, Colorado, Kentucky, Utah, and
West Virginia it fell by more than one-third. According to the US
Fish and Wildlife Service, between 1991 and 2016 the number of
hunters nationwide dropped by about 2.6 million, even as the country's population over the age of sixteen grew by 64.7 million.[18]

This decline in hunting resulted, in large part, from suburbanization. Hunting has a notoriously high barrier to entry compared with
other outdoor activities like hiking, bird watching, or even fishing.
People without a hunting tradition in their family are unlikely to pick
it up. Rural residents are more likely to have hunters in their families,
but when members of those families move to urban areas, the skills,
equipment, and interest required to hunt often fail to pass from one
generation to the next. Since most cities and suburbs have laws
against discharging firearms in public, urban growth can make hunting more costly and time consuming. In Massachusetts, for example,
by 2012, shooting restrictions had made at least 60 percent of the
state off limits to hunting. And in areas where hunting participation

fades, public opinion often turns against the sport, with nonhunters viewing it as unfair and inhumane.[19]

For more than a century, hunting has been one of wildlife managers' most important tools. Seasons, bag limits, and other rules have enabled them to revive depressed wildlife populations. Once a population recovers, hunting and fishing can keep it at a moderate and sustainable level—even as these activities raise money for other conservation efforts. Recreational hunting and fishing were thus linchpins of the North American Model of Wildlife Management at a time when these pursuits were broadly popular, when most wildlife professionals and enthusiasts participated in them, and when almost all remaining wildlife lived in rural areas.

The decline of hunting has had an enormous impact. As fewer hunters enter the ranks, funding for wildlife management has failed to keep up with needs. Chronic shortfalls mean that regular maintenance tasks get neglected and major projects get postponed, scaled back, or cut. This makes hunting less attractive and robs managers of crucial tools. Populations of fertile, opportunistic species like white-tailed deer may grow unchecked, while others that could benefit from efforts to restore or conserve habitat suffer. Private groups, from nonprofits to pest-control firms—with their own motives, agendas, and business models—assume more of the work, jeopardizing the idea of wildlife as a public trust.[20]

Even if hunting had not diminished as an American pastime, however, it would be of little help for managing wildlife in urban regions. With the discharging of firearms prohibited in most cities, some people have taken up bowhunting. But shooting an animal like a deer with an arrow, which often results in a long, bloody chase, can be gruesome and dangerous in populated areas, provoking even more pushback against hunting. The US Department of Agriculture operates a sharpshooter program to cull deer, but it's not very popular, for many of the same reasons. Trapping in cities also tends to be controversial, because regulations are often unclear, particularly on private property, and because many people consider it cruel. None of these were concerns a century ago, when the populations of many woodland critters were at all-time lows, most of the remaining wildlife lived in rural areas, and cities were still relatively compact—but all of this changed with the advent of postwar suburbs.

.   .   .   .   .

Back in 1942, Walt Disney did not imagine that white-tailed deer, or any of the other members of *Bambi*'s cast, would become common residents of American suburbs. Over the next few decades, however, as new laws protected wildlife, suburbs matured into lush habitats, and hunting declined as a pastime, deer (and other wild animal) populations in and around American cities grew to unprecedented levels. Instead of going deeper into the forest, white-tailed deer moved into populated areas, heralding a new era of urban wildlife.

Initially, many people welcomed this sea change, but they soon recognized that it came with challenges. Unchecked deer populations could overwhelm their habitats, gobbling up vegetation, degrading forest ecosystems, spreading diseases, and causing thousands of automobile collisions. In recent years, deer populations have leveled off in many areas and even declined in some. Yet many people who live with these animals still agree that, in their quest to recover and maintain deer populations, the wildlife managers of the twentieth century produced too much of a good thing. Despite these concerns, city dwellers across the United States have continued to create the conditions that attract species like white-tailed deer into their backyards.[21]

5 Room to Roam

During the 1980s and 1990s, conflicts over the protection of endangered species and their habitats were roiling the American West, from the forests of Washington and Oregon to the deserts of Nevada and Arizona. In few places was there more at stake in these debates than in Southern California, home to both dozens of endangered species and some of the country's priciest real estate. In 1991, the Building Industry Association of Southern California made a sobering, if self-serving, prediction. If the US Fish and Wildlife Service listed a little bird called the California gnatcatcher as endangered, this would "lead to more confrontation, to hopelessly deadlocked habitat conservation programs, and to significant economic hardship. Litigation would be inevitable. Efforts to weaken the Endangered Species Act itself . . . would only gain momentum."[1]

These remarks came as a surprise to many Southern Californians, most of whom had never heard of a California gnatcatcher. Under four inches long and weighing less than two-*hundredths* of a pound, with a call that sounds like the squeaky chatter of a bottlenose dol-

phin and dull gray plumage that blends into its brushy surroundings, the gnatcatcher was an unlikely subject for such a high-profile
dispute. Yet efforts to protect it would thrust both this bird and
this region—long known for its powerful developers and devotion
to private property—onto the front lines of endangered species
conservation.

The gnatcatcher debate came two decades into a long era, beginning around 1970 and continuing through today, when American
cities built on the legacies of earlier urban park preservation efforts
to protect thousands of new open spaces and nature reserves.
Supporters argued that setting aside these areas lessened the impacts
of suburban sprawl, maintained the quality of life for nearby residents, safeguarded watersheds, and conserved endangered species.
Their efforts proved controversial, but their successes secured permanent spaces for wild creatures to roam in many of America's biggest urban areas.

.   .   .   .   .

The roots of the gnatcatcher conflict stretch back to the middle of
the twentieth century. After World War II, Southern California's
population boomed, growing from 5.7 million in 1950 to 17.5 million
in 1990 and 21.6 million in 2010. Developers raced to build housing
for this fast-growing market. Early projects featured modest tract
homes designed for middle-class families. Within a few decades,
however, many residents discovered that their little bungalows and
tract homes were sitting on million-dollar lots. By the 1980s, much
of coastal Southern California—outside of its parks, national forests,
and military bases—had been developed. Most early postwar projects
replaced old farms, but builders eventually pressed into more natural areas. Vast swaths of low-lying evergreen vegetation called coastal
sage scrub happened to cover some of the most sought-after parcels,
which were suddenly in high demand for development but seemed
to have little value for anything else.

In a state with some of this country's highest peaks and lowest deserts—as well as the tallest, oldest, and most massive trees on earth—coastal sage scrub is a homely sight. Knee to head high, with a light silvery green tint, it consists mainly of tough, drought-tolerant shrubs that, when viewed from above, seem to drape the ground like a scratchy wool blanket. During the spring, coastal sage scrub, which is home to an assortment of rare species, can burst forth with a riot of yellows, blues, purples, and oranges. But for most of the year, its most common perennial plants—sagebrush, buck-wheat, brittlebush, coyote brush, yarrow, lupine, and the occasional succulent—seem almost dormant, cowering from the very ocean breezes and cloudless skies that have attracted so many people to this sun-drenched region.

California gnatcatchers, whose range extends into Baja, Mexico, were probably never very abundant even within their coastal sage scrub habitat. In 1898, a young Joseph Grinnell, who would later serve as the founding director of the Museum of Vertebrate Zoology at the University of California, Berkeley, described gnatcatchers as a "common resident in a few limited localities." In their landmark 1944 tome, *The Distribution of the Birds of California*, Grinnell and his successor as director, Alden Miller, noted that although gnat-catchers were "locally common," their range already had been "some-what reduced" during the previous twenty years, and their future was far from assured. Gnatcatchers were losing ground even then, but few people noticed or cared.[2]

For the next forty years, it was open season on coastal sage scrub. Builders uprooted it, graded it, and turned it into manicured yards, parking lots, and ball fields. New laws, including the California Environmental Quality Act of 1970 and the California Coastal Act of 1976, protected some coastal sage scrub areas, but builders contin-ued to whittle away at them as scattered towns and cities merged into a two-hundred-mile-long megalopolis. By 1990, coastal sage scrub was one of the most threatened ecosystems in the most bio-logically diverse US state.

Assessing the damage was surprisingly difficult. In a region with more than seventeen million people, few had thought to study coastal sage scrub or its inhabitants. Many of those who had done so were consultants whose job was to help developers comply with, or if necessary skirt, the law, not advance scientific knowledge or share their data. Estimates varied, but most experts agreed that only a couple thousand gnatcatchers remained north of the US-Mexico border.[3]

Southern California had lost between 50 and 90 percent of its coastal sage scrub, but this region still contained as many as 450,000 acres of it in the five counties—Los Angeles, Orange, Riverside, San Diego, and Ventura—where gnatcatchers lived. Since these were among the most prized areas for future development, and because 80 percent of coastal sage scrub was on privately owned land, any attempt to protect gnatcatchers would collide with the region's pro-growth agenda.[4]

Under pressure from all sides, legislators in Sacramento responded by amending the California Endangered Species Act to create a program known as Natural Communities Conservation Planning (NCCP). Under the revised law, scientists, politicians, and other stakeholders would work together to conserve habitat while allowing construction to continue in other areas. They would achieve this, in part, by imposing fees on new developments, which would fund land purchases, transfers, and easements in sensitive and threatened habitat areas.[5]

By 1993, the NCCP process, announced with fanfare just two years earlier, had stalled. Conservationists wondered whether it was distracting from other efforts to protect endangered species. Politicians worried about the economic consequences of setting aside vast tracts of land. Builders questioned whether participating would really enable them to move forward on their projects without further roadblocks. And officials on the ground were still waiting for directions from their bosses about how to implement the sweeping new NCCP law.

Three key events jump-started the process. The California Resources Agency published guidelines for NCCPs, providing instructions on how to proceed. The US Fish and Wildlife Service listed the California gnatcatcher as a "threatened" species, signaling that if the state process failed, the federal government would step in. And the secretary of the interior, Bruce Babbitt, threw his support behind California's efforts, promising to honor state-approved plans that complied with federal laws. In 1996, California approved its first NCCP, in Orange County, and in 1997 and 1998 the state approved additional plans in San Diego County. According to Babbitt, this was "an example of what must be done across the country if we are to avoid the environmental and economic train wrecks we've see in the last decade."[6]

Over the next quarter century, NCCPs would expand to cover most of urban Southern California south of Los Angeles. By 2017, these plans encompassed 1.84 million acres in twenty-nine cities, including more than 958,000 acres of nature reserves—an area larger than Rhode Island. Another six plans, covering eleven cities and 2.25 million acres, were in the works. California's NCCP process created a permanent place for wild species and native ecosystems in one of the country's most urban regions. It harnessed a multibillion-dollar construction industry on behalf of wildlife conservation, and it did so in the name of a dusky gray bird that weighs about as much as a quarter.[7]

·   ·   ·   ·   ·

Momentum for setting aside open spaces and nature reserves in urban regions grew gradually. As suburbs marched toward the horizon, they did so unevenly, leapfrogging one another, bumping up against holdout farms, water bodies, and public lands, hugging freeways, and leaving undeveloped areas scattered between them. Many lingering green spaces seemed destined for development. The suburbs themselves, meanwhile, were growing leafier but also more urban. As their roads filled with cars and their skies clouded with smog, their semirural flavor soured, and many of their human residents started to feel that these neighborhoods were losing the very qualities that had drawn them there.[8]

Suburbanites soon began agitating for measures to protect their quality of life. They passed zoning ordinances and set design standards limiting building heights, capped dwelling densities, restricted parking, and curbed construction. They also cited environmental factors—such as flood risk, wildfire danger, circumscribed water supplies, and public health concerns—as limits to growth. In recent years, these tactics have been criticized as drivers of high housing costs and attempts to exclude poor people and people of color from mostly wealthy and white suburbs, and some are now even being rolled back. As awareness of the costs of these anti-growth measures has grown, one of the few growth-limiting approaches that has aged well is the protection of open space.[9]

The San Francisco Bay Area led the way in the open-space movement. Since the mid-nineteenth century, conservationists there had worked, with some success, to create urban nature parks. During the 1960s and 1970s, local, state, and federal governments augmented the Bay Area's scattered public lands to form a sprawling open-space network. Mount Tamalpais State Park in Marin County, the chain of East Bay Regional Parks in Alameda County, Mount Diablo State Park in Contra Costa County, and several dozen parks in Sonoma, Napa, San Mateo, Santa Clara, and Santa Cruz Counties were all established or expanded during this period.[10]

The federal government, with the prodding of local activists and politicians, led the way in three of the Bay Area's most ambitious initiatives. The Golden Gate National Recreation Area, established in 1972, combined new and existing sites like Muir Woods into a single unit of the National Park System. Today, Golden Gate—which includes 37 sites covering 80,000 acres, with 130 miles of trails and 1,200 historic structures—is the country's most-visited national park. Also in 1972, after two decades of debate, Congress created the Don

Edwards San Francisco Bay National Wildlife Refuge. Billed as the country's first urban wildlife refuge, Don Edwards sought to protect the remaining marshes along San Francisco Bay's southern shoreline while restoring salt ponds and other areas to a more natural state. Although its existence was initially motivated by ecological concerns and development pressures, this refuge now protects endangered species, hosts educational programs for local schools, and buffers low-lying cities from high tides, storm surges, and sea-level rise. Today, Don Edwards is part of the seven-unit, forty-four-thousand-acre San Francisco Bay National Wildlife Refuge Complex.[11]

By 2007, the Bay Area contained the country's largest urban open-space network. Only about 750,000 acres, or 17 percent, of this 4.5-million-acre region was covered by buildings and pavement. The other 3.75 million acres remained undeveloped, including about 1.8 million acres of farms and ranches, 725,000 acres of water and wetlands, and 500,000 acres of forests and woodlands. Within forty miles of San Francisco, some two hundred parks, preserves, and open spaces formed a network of public lands larger and more diverse than Yosemite National Park.[12]

Los Angeles, a city long known for its lack of public space, followed the example of its northern neighbor. The push to preserve land in the Santa Monica Mountains, which extend from Malibu in the west to Hollywood in the east, was, like many of the efforts in the Bay Area, a response to proposed developments. Beginning in the 1950s, local developers and politicians announced plans to flatten mountaintops for new subdivisions, construct freeways over the range, build a nuclear power plant, fill several canyons with garbage, and then cap these dumps and top them with golf courses. During the 1960s and 1970s, local activists like Sue Nelson and Jill Swift advanced the cause of land protection. Their big break came in 1978 when the powerful San Francisco congressman Phil Burton included the Santa Monica Mountains in his omnibus parks bill. Today, the Santa Monica Mountains—a "patchwork park" with dozens of federally owned parcels interspersed with state and county parks, easements, and private lands—covers 154,000 acres, making it the world's largest urban park.[13]

In other parts of the United States, older parks were repurposed, updated, expanded, or converted to achieve new goals. Beginning in the 1970s, conservationists aiming to expand the Chicago area's regional network of forest preserves struggled with complex politics, multiple interest groups, and an indifferent public that seemed to know more about the threats facing Brazilian rain forests than those facing local species and ecosystems. In the mid-1990s, however, a consortium of more than 250 Chicago-area agencies and nonprofit groups rallied under the banner of the Chicago Regional Biodiversity Council, known to most in the area by the oxymoronic name Chicago Wilderness. By 2017, the alliance had undertaken more than five hundred projects related to its Green Infrastructure, Biodiversity Recovery, and other programs. Ten percent of the greater Chicago area is now in some form of park or reserve.[14]

A different story has unfolded along the banks of the Trinity River in north Texas. Since the nineteenth century, a litany of ill-advised schemes has attempted to harness, tame, or develop a twenty-mile strip of floodplain that bisects Dallas. Political bickering and frequent floods stymied most of these projects. After World War II, developers again began eyeing this area, but most of their plans failed too. Now it seems that the river is destined for a different future. Bond measures in 1998 and 2006 provided funds for the city to purchase much of the floodplain, and as of 2018 it was engaged in a planning process to improve flood protection and recreational opportunities while conserving thousands of acres of wildlife habitat, including the country's largest urban hardwood forest.[15]

Some cities have reclaimed old infrastructure as nature reserves. One of the best examples is the Fresh Kills landfill on Staten Island. Fresh Kills, which gets its name from the Dutch word *kil*, referring to a creek or tidal inlet, opened in 1948. Chosen for its proximity, access, and layer of impermeable clay soil just below the surface, it soon became New York's main waste disposal site, receiving up to twenty-nine thousand tons of trash daily. Locals always resented Fresh Kills as a health hazard, blight, and insult from condescending inner-borough residents. In the 1990s, the city adopted a new system, in which each borough would manage its own waste. Fresh Kills closed in March 2001, then briefly opened again to receive debris after 9/11 before beginning a $300 million closure, capping, and redesign process.[16]

Fresh Kills is now the world's largest landfill-to-park project. Set to open in phases over the next quarter century, it will be New York City's largest park when completed. At 2,200 acres, or around 3.5 times the size of Central Park, Fresh Kills will constitute 40 percent of the parkland on Staten Island. In its early years, wellheads stationed around the site will capture enough methane from decomposing waste, at peak production, to heat thirty thousand homes. Already, wildlife is returning. Birds—from grasshopper sparrows, bobolinks, and meadowlarks to ospreys and bald eagles—flock to the site's rolling meadows and eleven-mile shoreline. Foxes are common, beavers have returned after a two-hundred-year absence, and the first coyote arrived in 2012.[17]

State and federal policy changes have also helped drive many metropolitan conservation efforts. Between 1964 and 1986, Congress passed around two dozen pieces of major environmental legislation, and many states followed suit, enacting their own similar statutes. These laws applied to a wide range of conservation issues, including protecting wildlife and habitats.

One of the most important of these laws was the Endangered Species Act (ESA) of 1973. Under the United States Constitution, local jurisdictions including cities and counties handle land-use planning, whereas the states have most of the authority over the wildlife within their boundaries. The federal government provides funding, manages wildlife on federal lands, and oversees conservation efforts for specially designated species or groups of species, such as migratory birds and marine mammals. The ESA expanded the federal government's role in wildlife conservation by requiring it to intervene in cases where the states had failed to protect native species. Once a species is listed, the federal agency responsible, either the US Fish and Wildlife Service or the National Oceanic and Atmospheric Administration, must prevent further harm to the species and work with the states and other parties to recover it.[18]

The ESA has played a key role in metropolitan areas across the Sunbelt and the West. In the years after California founded its NCCP program, more than a dozen urban areas in these regions launched similar habitat conservation efforts under the ESA. Some of these started because the protection of a single species, like the California gnatcatcher, threatened to halt development or infrastructure projects, and several evolved into larger regional plans covering dozens of species. Habitat conservation plans would eventually cover urban areas across the Sunbelt, from Bakersfield, California, to Austin, Texas.

In 1997, for example, the Fish and Wildlife Service listed the cactus ferruginous pygmy owl as endangered at the northern tip of its range, in the desert around Tucson. Developers sued in 2006, stripping the species of ESA protections, but the case soon ended up back in court. By then, community leaders in Tucson were working on a habitat conservation plan like the ones already created for San Diego and Orange County. In 2016, after 600 hours of meetings, 200 technical reports, and input from more than 150 scientists, Pima County, where Tucson is located, completed its Sonoran Desert Conservation Plan. The plan aims to protect 44 animal species and conserve 116,000 acres of habitat in exchange for development permits on another 36,000 acres.[19]

Some city and county planning agencies also passed guidelines or promoted certification systems meant to encourage more wildlife-friendly designs within new suburban developments. To qualify for certification, developments were required to include habitat conservation or restoration elements, open-space access provisions, stormwater management systems, low-impact night lighting, and resident education programs. Many also promised to use more-sustainable construction materials and cluster buildings close together to minimize the development's ecological footprint.[20]

Suburban open space and conservation areas proved to be rich habitats not only for the rare and endangered animals they were meant to protect but also for much other wildlife, including many longtime residents and some species that had long ago disappeared from those areas or had never dwelled there before. As had been the pattern in so many American cities in decades past, parks, open spaces, and conservation areas that had been set aside for other reasons enabled a range of wild creatures to thrive, including many that were never considered in planning processes or meant to benefit from having these areas preserved.

Glittering new parks and preserves weren't the only urban habitats that changed rapidly during the 1960s, 1970s, and 1980s—or the only kinds of spaces that became more available to enterprising wildlife. During this period, crime, racism, white flight, deindustrialization, and disinvestment hit some American cities hard. In older industrial cities like Detroit and Baltimore, dilapidated buildings rotted, brown fields sat empty behind chain-link fences, and vacant lots grew wild with weedy vegetation.[21]

We don't have an apt word in English for these neglected and abandoned areas. In a 2017 documentary film, the British geographer Matthew Gandy borrowed a German word, *brachen,* which Berliners use to describe the in-between spaces left behind after the devastation of World War II. Over time, these empty lots and rubble piles filled with life, symbolizing Berlin's rebellious spirit when most of its residents were confined within the city's walls, becoming cherished public spaces, and serving as subjects of study for the first generation of self-identifying urban ecologists. The word *brachen* itself refers to fallow fields, left unattended by accident or necessity to grow wild and free, perhaps for use on another day.[22]

The brachen in America's urban cores—many of which are too polluted, too small, too isolated, or too overgrown with noxious weeds to provide much habitat—will probably never be as valuable for wildlife as suburban nature reserves. Brachen also tend to be short lived. Even in Berlin, development pressures are now placing the city's beloved brachen at risk. Nevertheless, these in-between spaces still provide refuges for hundreds of species of wandering wildlife, and many communities have worked hard to improve their condition, sometimes even converting them into permanent nature reserves.[23]

For one of the best examples of a rehabilitated American brachen, take a walk along the Bronx River. As late as the 1980s, this corridor was a dangerous dumping ground. Over the next two decades, community groups partnered with New York City's Department of Parks and Recreation to launch a massive grassroots cleanup effort. By 2003, they had removed seventy cars and an estimated thirty thousand tires from the Bronx River and its shores. Alewives attempting to spawn now swim upstream, coyotes frequent its woodsy banks, and even a few beavers have returned. When will the first black bear find its way into this once-gritty corner of New York City?[24]

. . . . .

Gnatcatchers still live in Southern California's coastal sage scrub. Creating the reserves that enabled them to hang on required hard work, comprise, and more than a little coercion. Today, these open-space areas are among the region's most popular, used by hundreds of thousands of people for exercise and recreation. They are also popular with wildlife. Protecting the gnatcatcher meant protecting habitats used by hundreds of other species, most of which are not endangered or protected by federal law but still use these reserves as home ranges and migratory corridors. The open-space campaigns that started in the 1960s, and then gained steam with the habitat conservation efforts of the 1990s, ushered in a new phase for wildlife in American cities. Gnatcatchers played a starring role in this drama, even if most of the people who visit the reserves created to protect them still have never seen or even heard of one.

6 Out of the Shadows

On August 26, 1981, a coyote attacked and killed a three-year-old girl named Kelly Keen while she was playing in the driveway of her family's home in the affluent suburb of San Rafael Hills in Glendale, north of Los Angeles. Keen's death was the first human fatality attributed to a coyote in the United States. It was a tragedy at once predictable, preventable, and unprecedented. To understand why, it's useful to take a few steps back and reflect on the long history of people and coyotes.[1]

Coyotes have lived alongside humans for millennia. Thousand-year-old coyote bones appear in middens at Chaco Canyon, New Mexico, an ancient pilgrimage site whose human population could swell to forty thousand during religious gatherings. Coyotes also lived around the grand medieval city-state of Tenochtitlán, which contained a district called Coyoacán, or "Place of the coyotes," home to a sect devoted to them. They played important symbolic roles—related to birth and death, good and evil, and the character of the trickster—in indigenous cultures throughout the Great Plains and American Southwest. Tales about Old Man Coyote, and sometimes his Old Woman counterpart, are the oldest-known human stories from North America.[2]

In 1769, Pedro Fages, a member of the Portolá expedition to Monterey, recorded one of the first European observations of coyotes in Southern California, listing them among the species he encountered while resupplying at San Diego. Coyote populations may have increased during California's Spanish mission and Mexican rancho eras, from 1769 to 1848, as livestock multiplied on the range, providing new opportunities for hunting and scavenging. After the gold rush of 1849, however, ranchers and other settlers set out to rid the state of its predators. Most of the resulting programs focused on rural areas, but some cities eventually joined the campaign. In 1938, for example, Los Angeles launched a coyote control program, which during its first year paid bounties for 650 scalps.[3]

Few species have endured the kind of ruthless onslaught unleashed on America's coyotes. Even today, around 400,000 are killed each year in the United States, for an average of around 1,100 per day. Yet even as chemical poisons, steel traps, and lead bullets were taking tens of millions of their lives, they proved stubbornly resilient. As larger predators like wolves, which had probably kept coyotes in check for thousands of years, faded from the landscape, coyotes pushed outward from their ancestral homelands in the Great Plains and Southwest to every corner of North America.

By 1900, coyotes had surrounded all five Great Lakes and could be found from below the Tropic of Cancer to above the Arctic Circle. By 2000, they had reached the shores of the Atlantic Ocean, as well as the Gulfs of Mexico, California, and Alaska. Today, coyotes live in every Mexican state and at least five Central American countries. In Canada, they inhabit all ten provinces, including Nova Scotia and Prince Edward Island, and two of the country's three territories. Coyotes can be found in forty-nine of the fifty US states. They haven't made it to Hawaii, yet.

Back in California, beginning around 1970, support for predator control programs began to wane, hunting and trapping started to decline, and new laws regulated the use of poisons such as compound 1080. Some rural habitats disappeared, but the suburbs that replaced them often proved more welcoming to coyotes than the farms and ranches that came before had been. By the 1980s, coyotes were showing up more often in more urban areas.

Then came the attack on Kelly Keen. The circumstances surrounding her death remain murky, in part because the Keens had had run-ins with coyotes before. Four years earlier, a coyote had bitten Kelly's then-ten-month-old sister, Karen. The next year, one nipped their teenage brother, John. Was the coyote who killed Kelly the same one that had been terrorizing the Keens for years? Why hadn't officials dealt with a situation that was getting out of control? And why was a toddler playing outside unattended in a place with such clear and present dangers?

Kelly's father, Robert, said that he had called the Glendale Humane Society but its staff set traps that didn't work. It is unclear exactly how the society handled his complaint, but Robert was right that local officials knew little about coyotes and had few effective remedies to offer worried residents.

After Kelly's death, the *Los Angeles Times* quoted some of these same officials making comments that turned out to be false or misleading. The L.A. County agricultural commissioner Robert Howell said that coyotes came to cities to hunt pets. Later research showed that although some coyotes had developed a taste for domestic animals, most subsisted on wild game, roadside carcasses, and plants. Emanuel White, of the Los Angeles Humane Society, said that coyotes had made it as far south as Wilshire Boulevard, but by then they had probably ventured several miles farther south, into neighborhoods like Baldwin Hills and Playa del Rey. The Humane Society's Edward Cubrada said that coyotes were coming to the city because they were being driven out of natural habitats, though the opposite—that the animals were seeking out rich urban habitats—was probably at least equally true.

By the time of Keen's death, reports of coyote-related incidents, most involving pets, had been on the rise in the Los Angeles area for more than a decade. But when they talked or wrote about this, officials, journalists, and even scientists fell back on puns and clichés, calling coyotes "wily" or accusing them of being, in the words of the *Los Angeles Times,* "lazy predators" that seek "easy prey."[4]

If Keen's death saddened many Angelenos, then its aftermath frightened them. In the weeks that followed the attack, trappers under contract with the county captured at least fifty-five coyotes from a one-square-mile area surrounding her family's home. Locals suddenly felt surrounded. With the tragedy still fresh and experts unable to explain the situation or offer solutions, residents lashed out. Foothill suburbs were labeled "coyote ghettos" and coyote packs "gangs." Los Angeles County responded by renewing its war against coyotes with a campaign of trapping, shooting, and "reeducation."[5]

These efforts focused on the coyotes themselves, but managing wildlife is really about managing people. Many coyote-related incidents involved a small number of animals that had become aggressive after being fed. Sometimes this happened when people left out unprotected trash or cat food, but in other cases residents and businesses seemed to be courting danger. In one brazen example, a Malibu Canyon restaurant put out food around dinnertime so that customers and coyotes could dine together under the moonlight, separated by a glass partition. Less than three months after Keen's death, the L.A. County Board of Supervisors passed a long-overdue ordinance that banned feeding skunks, raccoons, opossums, foxes, ground squirrels, and coyotes.[6]

This ban was clearly needed, but the county's larger coyote response was based on little, if any, scientific data. Before 1980, most published research on coyotes dealt with the threats they posed to rural livestock. In the years that followed, a few local agencies and university extension agents conducted studies to inform urban coyote management. It was not until 1996, however, fifteen years after Kelly Keen's death, that the National Park Service in Southern California launched a comprehensive effort to understand coyote ecology, behavior, and population dynamics.

Coyotes were among the vanguard of species whose arrival or increasing presence heralded yet another a new phase in the history of wildlife in American cities (see figure 5). This influx occurred gradually, varied from city to city, and unfolded at different rates for different species. But by the 1980s it was well under way, and incidents like the attack on Kelly Keen drew public attention to it. A flood of questions soon followed: Why were so many wild animals appearing in urban areas? What enabled some creatures to thrive in cities while others dwindled or disappeared? And how should people respond when faced with new challenges presented by urban wildlife? We are still answering these questions today.

.   .   .   .   .

When most people picture "ecosystems," they probably think of forests, deserts, coral reefs, or other natural environments. Yet the influx of wildlife into American cities has made it clear that, in the eyes of creatures like coyotes, cities are ecosystems too. They receive sunshine and rain; they have rocks, soils, and water; they cycle energy, nutrients, and organic matter; and they contain diverse species that interact in complex ways and change over time. In some ways, cities resemble more-natural ecosystems. In other ways, they are fundamentally different from anything that came before them or anything else that exists today.[7]

One of the most obvious ways that cities differ from most other ecosystems is that they are all dominated by a single keystone species. Humans have transformed ecosystems across this planet, but nowhere else, except on some industrial farms, have our actions had as great an influence as they do in cities. The second thing that makes cities unusual is that they are so new. The world's oldest continuously occupied cities, almost all of which are in the Middle East, are only around seven thousand years old. Even ancient Jericho, believed to be the world's oldest continuously occupied settlement, with an archaeological record dating back some eleven thousand

years, appeared an instant ago relative to our planet's four-and-a-half-billion-year history. Life on earth is just beginning to adjust to the strange new environments we call cities.[8]

Adjusting to cities is difficult for many species in part because cities are always changing. Every year, cities spend billions of dollars controlling floods, fighting fires, tending vegetation, and slowing erosion—all activities meant to slow the pace of change—but over centuries they have dramatically transformed. Parts of Jerusalem have been destroyed forty times over the past six thousand years, leaving a layer of debris more than sixty feet deep. In its nine-hundred-year history, Berlin has been sacked, burned, bombed, divided, reunified, redesigned, and redeveloped. San Francisco went from a mission pueblo in the 1820s to a muddy trading post in the 1840s to a booming metropolis in the 1880s to a pile of rubble in 1906 to the center of a vast urban region after World War II. Modern cities crisscrossed by cars and mass transit date back little more than a century, and freeways have existed for only about the equivalent of one healthy human lifespan.

One of the strangest features of cities is that they import many of their resources—water, fuel, materials, and chemicals—and produce waste. Natural ecosystems, by contrast, produce their own raw materials using nutrients in the soil and energy from the sun, and they recycle almost everything they use. Centuries ago, cities harvested their resources mostly from nearby rural areas, and the waste they created flowed outward into the same local surroundings. Today, they extract their resources from locations around the world, and some ship their waste—out of sight and, for most people, out of mind—to distant dumps.[9]

Climate shapes every aspect of ecosystems. Cities are warmer than nearby rural areas—a phenomenon known as the heat island effect—because machines like cars and air conditioners release heat and because roads and buildings absorb and conduct more energy than most natural land surfaces. During the day, artificial materials such as asphalt heat up, then at night they radiate energy back into the air, where it gets trapped by a blanket of pollution. For the same reason, cities have relatively mild winters. This enables creatures from warmer climates to live in them. It also impacts the lives of native species. Plants may flower earlier and enjoy longer growing seasons in cities than in nearby rural areas. Animals that give birth once a year in cooler climates may do so twice or more each year in cities.[10]

Cities tend to receive more rain and snow than nearby places because their dusty air has more microscopic particles on which droplets can form. In most natural ecosystems, falling rain sticks to plants, percolates into the soil, and trickles into streams. In cities, impermeable surfaces—including roofs, sidewalks, roads, and hard-packed dirt—cover between 10 and 70 percent of the land area. This is why many cities, like some rocky deserts, experience flash floods. Cities also move water around, draining some areas while inundating others. All of this replumbing yields a strange result. In wet climates, most species experience cities as desertlike compared to the lusher native habitats nearby, whereas in dry climates, cities may seem like veritable rain forests for species adapted to living in the parched neighboring landscapes.

Streams are among the most degraded habitats in urban ecosystems. Most urban streams have higher high flows and lower low flows than nearby rural streams, but some have weirdly steady year-round flows, in the form of murky runoff from lawns and gardens. Urban streams contain greater quantities of nutrients and chemical pollutants, carry less sediment, have straighter channels with steeper banks, and tend to have fewer species of plants and animals than streams in less-developed areas.[11]

Cities also assault the senses. This can be exhausting for people, and for animals that depend on their senses to navigate, find food and mates, dodge hazards, and avoid predators, it can alter the very nature of their existence.

In 1800, night light was a precious commodity. After twilight, except for the warm, flickering glow of fires, life was mostly dark. The introduction of artificial light, first from gas lamps and later from electric bulbs, drove revolutionary social changes, including the extension of the workday beyond its daytime limits, which helped make industrial capitalism possible. Today, more than 80 percent of people—including 99 percent in parts of Europe, East Asia, and North America—live in areas with enough artificial night light for it to be considered pollution.[12]

The shift from a dark to a bright night has had immense ecological consequences. For creatures like coyotes, which may adopt a more nocturnal lifestyle in cities to avoid people, a little night light can help. Some spiders, bats, lizards, and frogs use night lights as lures to attract their prey. For flying animals that navigate by moonlight, however, including many insects and birds, artificial light increases their risk of collisions and electrocutions and may lead them astray. Coastal cities act as false beacons that divert migrating fish, turtles, and other marine creatures into dangerous nearshore waters. Night light, along with warmer temperatures in cities, may also lengthen the daily active period for mosquitoes that transmit dengue fever, chikungunya, Zika, yellow fever, and other diseases.[13]

Cities are also loud. Some of their noises come directly from machines, whereas others come indirectly from roads, sidewalks, and buildings that reflect sound. Cities produce noises at a wide range of pitches, but in most places, these add up to a constant background hum of less than two thousand hertz. This is roughly equivalent to the combined sound of the entire span from low A to C7, excluding the highest octave, on a standard, eighty-eight-key piano. The volume of a sound is measured in decibels, which form a logarithmic scale, with each increase of ten units meaning that the sound is ten times louder. Most human conversations take place in the range of about 40 decibels, but a busy city street can be closer to 80 decibels, a hedge trimmer may emit more than 100 decibels, and a jackhammer may reach a deafening 120 decibels.[14]

Chronic noise exposure triggers chemical responses in humans that increase our short-term alertness but reduce our long-term health by worsening conditions from high blood pressure to anxiety and insomnia. Noise can also cause stress in nonhuman animals. Noise forces prey species to raise their guard, consuming energy and distracting from other tasks. Birds, insects, and amphibians that communicate by sound may lose their ability to send clear messages, making it tougher to find mates and kin.[15]

Anyone who has walked around a big city on a hot day knows that cities can stink. We humans, with our pitiful sense of smell, have little clue as to how cities alter the olfactory environment that so many other species experience so vividly. Odors are volatilized compounds that animals perceive in their olfactory nerves, and then process in their brains as smells. With their manufacturing, transportation, chemical, food service, and landscaping industries, cities are awash in volatilized compounds. For species that rely on their sense of smell to forage, find prey, evade predators, and communicate, the urban environment can be a tantalizing but also a disorienting and bewildering place.

What makes a species likely to succeed in this urban gauntlet of light, sound, smell, and constant change? In 1996, the same year that the National Park Service began its Los Angeles coyote research, Robert Blair of Stanford University published a landmark paper explaining why some species thrive in these spaces whereas others decline or vanish. Blair's paper has been the subject of some debate in the years since, but it still provides a good place to begin. As a start, he identified three kinds of creatures found in and around cities.[16]

According to Blair, *urban avoiders* are ill suited for city life. Some are specialists: finicky characters that require particular habitats or resources not commonly found in cities. Some are wanderers with vast home ranges or annual migrations. Others may be too anxious or territorial to cozy up with the world's most dangerous primate. Some urban avoiders may be able to eke out a living on the edges of cities by occupying smaller than normal home ranges or by hunkering down in remnant green spaces. More than a few urban avoiders have habits, such as preying on livestock, that bring them into conflict with people.

Urban adapters, Blair's second category, are often most common in places with moderate levels of development, like woodsy suburbs, or along the urban-wildland interface. Urban adapters may commute between wild and developed areas or become more nocturnal in cities as a strategy to live among people while avoiding direct contact with us. Several adapters—like peregrine falcons and red-tailed hawks, which often nest on buildings that resemble cliffs—just happen to have evolved skills, habits, or preferences that both work in natural areas and translate to urban settings. Urban adapters include some of the most charismatic and recognizable wild creatures that people commonly encounter in and around cities, including raccoons, white-tailed deer, water birds like great blue herons, and of course coyotes.

Members of Blair's third category, *urban exploiters,* thrive in cities. Many, such as Norway rats and house sparrows, evolved in Europe or Asia but now live in cities around the world. They tend to be generalists, meaning that they are able to tap varied resources and seem at home in diverse environments. They are often omnivores able to eat a wide range of foods. Urban exploiters such as pigeons are relatively intelligent, meaning that they can solve problems and master new tasks. Some exploiters have high fertility rates, care for their young for long periods, and pass their skills on to their offspring. Temperament also matters. Urban exploiters tend to be mellow enough to live near people but vigilant enough that they don't allow us to get too close. They are often highly social, foraging in overlapping ranges or living in groups with many others of their kind. Over time, some exploiters come to depend on people, shunning all but the most developed habitats.

·   ·   ·   ·   ·

Urban adapters and exploiters may be prepared for life among people, but are people prepared for life among them? In the 1970s and 1980s, when coyotes started showing up more often in dozens of

American cities, residents and officials were unprepared, and many were unwilling to accommodate animals they saw as dangerous interlopers. As one teenager who lost her toy poodle to a coyote told the *Los Angeles Times* in 1980, "Coyotes make me mad. They take care of our rats, which are really disgusting. But I hate coyotes." The same year, the Yale social ecology professor Stephen Kellert found that, among US survey respondents, coyotes ranked twelfth from the bottom on a list of "most liked" animals, above cockroaches, wasps, rattlesnakes, and mosquitoes but below turtles, butterflies, swans, and horses. The most-liked animal was the dog, which is so closely related to the coyote that the two can mate in the wild and produce fertile offspring.[17]

In his 2010 book *Some We Love, Some We Hate, Some We Eat: Why It's So Hard to Think Straight about Animals,* the anthropologist Hal Herzog wrote that "the way we think about other species often defies logic." This is not to say that our ideas about animals are arbitrary, but rather that the ways we think about them are shaped as much by history, culture, and psychology as by physics, chemistry, or biology. In the absence of this social context, people's ideas about and actions toward other animals can seem nonsensical, hypocritical, or downright weird.[18]

Animals are often presumed innocent or guilty—and thus treated with respect or contempt—based on the baggage our culture, through art or literature or tradition, has forced them to carry. An animal's inherent or perceived qualities also matter. We tend to give the benefit of the doubt to creatures that are big, that we think are cute, pretty, majestic, or humanlike, that seem to embody admirable qualities such as grit, entrepreneurship, or good parenting, or that at the very least leave us alone. Yet such perceptions rarely reflect a species's real behavior or ecology. Many people see rats as disgusting or dangerous, even though most rats pose little threat to most people most of the time. Cats, meanwhile, seem friendly and cuddly despite being ferocious predators and disease-ridden ecological wrecking balls.

Mass and social media play especially important roles in shaping perceptions. When large and charismatic wildlife species started showing up in many American cities more frequently in the 1970s and 1980s, around the time of Kelly Keen's death, newspapers and TV shows often adopted one of two tones: irony or sensationalism. Ironic images and stories emphasized how surprising it was to see wild animals showing up in supposedly civilized areas. Sensationalistic stories emphasized conflicts between people and wildlife. They often used military metaphors about wars and battles or echoed the paranoid, racist, and xenophobic tropes of the day, comparing wildlife to undocumented immigrants, gang members, criminals, terrorists, and "super predators."

These images were circulating in the media during an era when the proportion of Americans with firsthand experiences of wild places was flattening or even declining. During the 1970s and 1980s, consumer products and better infrastructure fueled the growth of outdoor sports, including nonhunting wildlife activities like bird watching and photography. Yet technology, which enabled so many people to enjoy the outdoors, also began inserting itself into these same people's encounters with nature, first mediating and then replacing them. Video screens allowed Americans to spend more time watching virtual creatures and less time interacting with actual animals. Animal-themed visual media exploded in popularity, while zoos and museums struggled to attract patrons. Between 1995 and 2014, even the National Park system saw its annual per capita visitation slide by 4 percent.[19]

It is not surprising, therefore, that the people who encountered wildlife in cities often reacted by treating these animals like the caricatures they read about in the news or saw on TV. For many, creatures like coyotes looked like either cuddly pets or bloodthirsty killers. Neither image was accurate, of course, but both had real-world consequences.

When people who viewed coyotes with suspicion saw them in urban areas, often the first thing they did was call the police. Involving the police tended to turn a nonproblem into a problem or make a bad problem worse. Yet moving away from a law-enforcement-based approach has been difficult.

As late as 2015, New York City, which saw its first coyote twenty years earlier, was still often approaching these creatures as outlaws. That April, the New York Police Department, responding to an early-morning 911 call reporting a coyote in Riverside Park on Manhattan's Upper West Side, deployed tranquilizer guns, patrol cars, and helicopters. The ensuing three-hour chase ended when officers failed to corner the fugitive canine. When questioned about the costly and time-consuming incident, the NYPD contradicted a statement previously issued by the Department of Parks and Recreation saying that the city would no longer pursue coyotes that did not appear to pose a threat. It turned out that the two departments did not have a written agreement spelling out this policy. NYPD officers were not trained on how to deal with coyotes, but it was up to them to decide how to respond. The result was predictable: the same excessive force that has plagued modern policing in general was mobilized to combat a wild animal that presented little if any risk.[20]

Over time, some cities and their residents adjusted to their new reality of living with coyotes. Jurisdictions with ample budgets, supportive residents, and helpful institutions like zoos and museums developed research, education, conservation, and citizen science programs. Some parks and police departments started working together to develop new policies and practices, limiting the use of force and trying, with some difficultly, to respond only to genuine emergencies. One of the key messages wildlife officials stressed was that the decision to launch a response should depend on an animal's behavior—whether it appeared injured or sick or was acting aggressively—and not its mere presence.

As such messages have percolated, attitudes have evolved. In New York, as people have become more accustomed to living with coyotes, fear has given way to tolerance and even a tenuous kind of acceptance. In some neighborhoods, individual coyotes have become mascots with names, backstories, and social media accounts. Few people actually trust coyotes, and most people don't want them prowling around their backyards, schools, or playgrounds, but many communities have shown a growing willingness to embrace their furry neighbors.

As early as 2008, studies from suburban New York showed that most residents appreciated coyotes, enjoyed having them around, and even "found the likelihood of injury from a coyote acceptable." But people's willingness to live alongside coyotes in their communities dropped quickly when incidents occurred, suggesting that tolerance for them remained fragile. Overall, however, the longer most people lived with urban wildlife like coyotes, the more they viewed these creatures not as threats but as natural and beneficial members of multispecies urban communities.[21]

·   ·   ·   ·   ·

Coyotes have received a lot of attention in both Los Angeles and New York, but Chicago is, without a doubt, America's early twenty-first-century coyote capital. A few coyotes had reached Chicago's outskirts by World War II, but it wasn't until the 1980s and 1990s, after years of slow migration and population growth, that many more people started regularly seeing them in the city. Today, Chicago is home to an estimated two thousand coyotes living among three million people, many of whom have undergone a familiar pattern of surprise and fear followed by growing awareness, understanding, and acceptance.[22]

The person most associated with the remarkable story of Chicago's coyotes is the Ohio State University biologist Stan Gehrt, who started studying these animals in 2000. Of the hundreds of coyotes he has followed, one stands out as having taken city life to a new extreme. In February 2014, Gehrt trapped and collared an adult male coyote in the Bronzeville neighborhood, just south of downtown. Dubbed coyote 748, he soon came to be known as the "ulti-mate urban animal."[23]

GPS data from coyote 748's collar showed that he had an established territory. Having adopted a nocturnal lifestyle, he emerged from his den each evening to hunt and forage along the Lake Michigan shore in Burnham Park, by the Chicago River in the South Loop's industrial yards, and on the weedy embankments of the sixteen-lane Dan Ryan Expressway. Coyote 748 was cautious, deliberate, and consistent—qualities that served him well in this most urban of habitats.

In April, however, his behavior changed. He started confronting neighborhood dogs—some of which were on leash—and their own-ers, most of whom had grown to accept coyotes in their midst but feared that this particular animal was becoming dangerous. GPS data confirmed that 748 was involved in several confrontations, fit-ting a common pattern in which a rash of incidents in a community all turn out to involve a single coyote. Was 748 sick or injured? Had he found a new source of food, causing him to lose his fear of humans and grow bolder? Or was something else going on in his life that made him change his behavior?

Gehrt soon discovered the answer: 748 had become a father. He was raising his litter of pups on the top floor of a parking garage next to Soldier Field, home of the Chicago Bears football team, a domes-tic arrangement that would make any new parent a little paranoid.

Over the next month, Gehrt and his colleagues hassled, hazed, and harassed 748—using noisemakers, chasing him on foot, and fir-ing a paintball gun at him. He and his mate remained in their home territory, but they moved their den to a safer site and the conflicts subsided. It was a successful operation: a miniature rewilding project in which concerned residents, instead of calling in the troops, alerted a biologist with a deep knowledge of a species and its ecosys-tem to a potential problem before it got out of hand. The biologist responded by assessing the situation, determining the source of the problem, and then reminding an individual coyote that humans and their dogs were better left alone.

Unfortunately, the ultimate urban animal lived only a few more months. On June 15 he was found in a parking lot near the stadium, 25 percent lighter than he had been the previous winter and having sustained the kind of traumatic blunt-force injury that often results from an automobile collision. Chicago Animal Control euthanized him the following day. His pups remained healthy, however, and Gehrt wrote in his incident report that he expected the family to stay in the area. Coyote 748, Gehrt concluded, "will be replaced soon by another adult coyote."

7 Close Encounters

In July 2014, Greg Macgowan, a middle-aged dad from Oak Ridge, New Jersey, about thirty miles northwest of Manhattan, posted a three-minute YouTube video that sparked a two-year saga five decades in the making. The clip begins, like a low-budget horror film, with Macgowan outside his home, holding a shaky camera, and calling out tensely to his wife. He's searching for something. About thirty seconds in, he starts shouting: "There it is! There it is! That is a bipedal bear walking across the street! A bipedal bear! Walking towards me! I am walking backwards!"[1]

A dark figure soon comes into grainy focus. Its size, pace, posture, and gait are so humanlike that it is not immediately clear whether this is a bear imitating a person or a person imitating a bear. Standing upright on short, bowed legs, face forward, arms bent, it strolls down a neighbor's driveway, crosses a street, cuts through the yard of an abandoned house, and then disappears into the wooded neighborhood beyond (see figure 6).

So began the beautiful, bizarre, heartbreaking tale of "Pedals," New Jersey's suburban Sasquatch. Over the next two years, Pedals, an adult male black bear, captured the hearts of thousands of people who encountered him in their neighborhoods, watched his videos, reported on his adventures, debated his condition, fretted about his well-being, adopted him as a mascot, and wielded him as a weapon. If animals that look or act like humans tend to attract outsize attention, then Pedals was bound for fame. But he also became a lightning rod because he strolled into New Jerseyans' lives at moment of great change in the history of America's wildlife, and in particular that of its bears.

New Jersey has not always been a great place for bears like Pedals. Despite being nicknamed the Garden State, it has long conjured images of grimy cities, traffic-choked highways, and urban sprawl. As late as 1970, New Jersey contained fewer than two dozen wild black bears.[2]

That was then.

Today, New Jersey is home to around 5,000 black bears, a 227-fold increase in half a century. With about 1 bear for every 1,800 people, New Jersey is now both the most densely populated state for humans (more than 1,200 per square mile) and the most densely populated state for bears (around 0.57 per square mile). To put this in perspective, Alaska, which is home to an estimated 30,000 brown and 100,000 black bears, contains only around 0.2 bears per square mile. You have a better chance of bumping into a bear outside Newark than you do outside Fairbanks.[3]

Most of New Jersey's bears live in its forested northwest quarter. Since the 1990s, however, bears have visited all twenty-one New Jersey counties, and they now range over some 90 percent of this most urban of US states. New Jersey's bears aren't just numerous and widespread—they're also big. Black bears weighing upwards of five hundred pounds—the average size of a Yellowstone grizzly—are common there, with some stout males growing even larger. New Jersey, more than any other state, is now bear country.

The story of Pedals illustrates some of the conflicts that emerged when large, intelligent, charismatic animals like black bears started appearing in urban areas in greater numbers. As with coyotes, too many of these close encounters didn't end well. New Jerseyans are still wrestling with this new reality: what it means to coexist both with these creatures and with one another. If people in mountain towns, in suburbs, and along urban-wildland interfaces can manage to live peacefully with the occasional black bear, one of more challenging species in modern America's urban wildlife menagerie, then it should be relatively easy to accommodate many others. But this is a very big "if."

.   .   .   .   .

American black bears are one of this continent's most widely distributed types of mammal, found in diverse habitats from the Atlantic to the Pacific Coast and from central Mexico to the Arctic Circle. A medium-sized bear species with a gentle disposition, black bears survived for millions of years in part by avoiding larger, bolder beasts like saber-toothed cats, dire wolves, giant short-faced bears, and, of course, grizzlies. Omnivorous by nature but mostly herbivorous in practice, lumbering on the ground but nimble in the trees, black bears became shy denizens of North America's temperate forests.

Black bears vary in color from bleach blond to jet black. They have better vision and hearing than humans, and their sense of smell is roughly seven times stronger than that of a dog. Adults mate in the summer and give birth in the winter in their dens, where they may hibernate for as many as five months. Cubs remain with their mothers for up to a year and a half. Black bears sometimes gather around food sources, but they usually live alone, communicating with their neighbors by marking trees, which they climb easily. Most black bears are crepuscular, forging at dawn and dusk, but they may be active at any time of day. They will eat almost anything, but most of them subsist on a diet of plants, insects, rodents, and carrion. Black bears may live for more than twenty years in the wild and more than twice as long in captivity.[4]

Black bears' slow decline probably began by the eighteenth century, along the Eastern Seaboard and in the Southeast. Hunting, trapping, and habitat loss, a consequence of cutting forests to harvest timber and clear farmland, took major tolls. So did state and local laws, which labeled black bears pests and offered bounties for their scalps. The population of American black bears, like those of so many other woodland critters, bottomed out by the beginning of the twentieth century.

The story of the black bear's comeback usually begins in November 1902, in the piney woods of Mississippi. President Theodore Roosevelt had traveled there to meet with local officials and do some hunting. He failed to find a bear, but his guide—a colorful character named Holt Collier, who had been both a slave and a Confederate soldier—captured one, tied it to a tree, and ushered the president over to take his trophy. Considering this unsportsmanlike, Roosevelt refused to fire. Two days later, the illustrator Clifford Berryman satirized this episode in a *Washington Post* cartoon. Within months, a Brooklyn candy shop owner named Morris Michtom launched a line of plush stuffed animals bearing the president's name. "Teddy's bear" became one of the most popular toys ever produced and inspired a raft of lovable cartoon characters, including Winnie-the-Pooh (who first appeared in 1924) and Yogi Bear (who debuted in 1958).[5]

Roosevelt's reputation as an ethical sportsman was, at least by the standards of the time, secure. It would take a couple more decades, however, for the black bear's reputation as a pest to begin to change. Studies conducted in the 1920s and 1930s showed that several mammals in the order Carnivora, including black bears, were omnivorous foragers and scavengers, not the bloodthirsty predators that farmers and ranchers imagined. Some black bears had learned to hunt, targeting newborn or sick animals or ambushing or cornering other prey, but catching wild game is difficult and dangerous, and most were so bad at it that they didn't really try.[6]

Around this time, state agencies started changing black bears' official status from a "pest" to a "game" species. Instead of controlling or eliminating black bears, these agencies would seek to maintain healthy populations of them—a "sustained yield" in bureaucratic lingo—for hunters to harvest like deer or trout. This was a crucial turning point, enabling black bear populations in some states to stabilize or even increase for the first time in decades.[7]

In the national parks, meanwhile, bears played a different role: they were performers. At parks such as Yellowstone and Yosemite, tourists gathered on summer evenings, filling the bleachers at dumps and feeding stations, to watch bears eat garbage. It was an ugly scene for anyone who truly loves wildlife. But park officials were under orders to attract more visitors, and people loved seeing bears. Few anticipated how much harm this would do.[8]

In 1944, the US Forest Service adopted Smokey Bear as the face of its fire prevention campaign. The Forest Service had been fighting fires for four decades, but its efforts expanded with Depression-era stimulus funding and then again during World War II, when battling blazes became a matter of national security. On thousands of signs and posters, Smokey cut the unmistakable figure of an ursine Uncle Sam. Looking straight ahead, with a finger pointing directly at the viewer, he warned Americans that "only YOU can prevent forest fires." In 1950, Smokey the symbol became an actual bear. Firefighters working in New Mexico saved an orphaned and injured black bear cub. The service named him Smokey and sent him to the National Zoo in Washington, DC, where he greeted visitors until his death in 1976.

Unfortunately, the Forest Service's campaign had the opposite of its intended effect. By suppressing fires, the service allowed its lands to become overgrown, creating the conditions for more-dangerous burns. But it did help transform the public's view of black bears. No longer just pests or resources or clowns or toys, black bears were now wise stewards of America's precious natural resources.

In the 1970s, some biologists began to wonder if black bears might be set for a rebound. Reforestation in New England and the

Midwest had created more bear habitat. Poisoning and trapping were declining in many areas. Black bears seemed to thrive around mountain towns and in leafy suburbs along the urban-wildland interface, where people appeared more willing than in the past to live with bears in their midst. As late as 1980, biologists believed that black bears had among the lowest birthrates of any land mammal. Within a decade, however, it was clear that black bears could reproduce quickly under the right conditions. And increasingly, the conditions seemed to be right.[9]

From 1970 to 2020, black bear populations in the Lower 48 US states boomed. In both Massachusetts and Florida they grew tenfold, from around four hundred to more than four thousand. Pennsylvania's bear population increased from four thousand to eighteen thousand, and California's jumped from ten thousand to as many as forty thousand. In the Midwest, bears multiplied in forested habitats, then started showing up in agricultural areas where they had not been seen in decades. In 2016, the US Fish and Wildlife Service declared the Louisiana black bear, one of sixteen American black bear subspecies, to be recovered, after a quarter century on the endangered species list. Black bears now live in at least forty of the fifty US states, and their populations appear to be stable or increasing in most regions. Today, there are around nine hundred thousand black bears—around half in Canada and half in the United States, plus a small endangered population in Mexico—making this the most numerous of the world's eight bear species.[10]

·   ·   ·   ·   ·

Most of America's black bears still live in forests. But with so many now wandering around in a country full of cities, bears and people were bound to cross paths more frequently. Before black bears started showing up in cities, few people believed they could succeed there. They seemed to be classic urban avoiders. Even fewer people anticipated that city life would change so many aspects of what it means to be a bear.

If you are what you eat, then the main thing that makes urban bears different from their wildland cousins is access to human foods. Black bears that eat human foods grow bigger and bolder than bears in more natural environments. Whereas forest-dwelling adult black bears often weigh between two hundred and three hundred pounds, well-fed city bears may reach more than four hundred pounds. Bears that eat human foods may also lose their fear of people and then teach their cubs to do the same, creating a toxic, multigenerational culture that mixes dependency with chutzpah. But who can blame them? It's hard to go back to grubs and leaves once you've tried peanut butter.[11]

Urban black bears spend less time hibernating than bears in wildland habitats. Hibernating is a way of coping with seasonally scarce resources. Black bears are remarkable hibernators, using the fats and fluids they store up each fall so efficiently that biologists often call them "the world's best recycling cans." The length of time they spend hibernating varies according to the local climate and ecosystem and the bear's own physical condition. Females with cubs usually remain in their dens for several months regardless of where they live. Overall, however, urban black bears with access to human foods stay active for more of the year compared to bears living in more-natural areas. And this brings them into contact with more people, more often.[12]

Black bears in urban areas also adjust their daily schedules. To avoid people, they shift to a more nocturnal lifestyle, like coyotes. They are active for fewer hours each day because the abundance of food means they require less time foraging to satisfy their voracious appetites.[13]

The size of a black bear's range depends, in part, on the food available in its habitat. Because cities concentrate resources, urban black bears tend to have small ranges and high population densities. According to a study conducted in western Nevada, bears living in developed areas around Lake Tahoe had home ranges 70 to 90 percent smaller than bears living in undeveloped areas nearby. Amazingly, urban areas supported *up to forty times as many bears* as wildland areas of the same size.[14]

Urban black bears reproduce fast and die young. They also skew male. Females reach maturity earlier in life than sows in wildland habitats, and they may have three times as many cubs. Cubs born in urban areas die at twice the rate of those in more natural areas, mainly because of automobile accidents, but their sheer numbers more than make up for these losses.[15]

All together, this adds up to two key insights. Black bear populations may thrive in urban areas even as individual bears die there in large numbers. And black bears have demonstrated an amazing ability, especially for such large animals, to adjust to urban life. But this has turned out to be the easy part. Black bears have adjusted to cities, but most cities have not yet adjusted to them.

．　　．　　．　　．　　．

Black bears are intelligent, powerful, mischievous, and surprisingly athletic creatures that learn quickly and pass on their knowledge. Living with black bears, especially those with histories of accessing human food, can be challenging, and close encounters don't always end well. But effective strategies for managing the relations between our two species in and around urban areas do exist. For the most part, these strategies were developed in America's national parks and their nearby communities, where modern "conflicts" involving people and black bears began more than a century ago.

The feeding of bears at national parks, intentionally or not, started almost as soon as the parks were founded. In 1891, just nineteen years after the establishment of Yellowstone National Park, its acting superintendent complained that bears were causing problems in developed areas. By 1910, black bears in Yellowstone had learned to beg for food in campgrounds, near hotels, and along roadsides. A park created in part to protect wildlife was unintentionally domesticating the wild animals that lived within it.[16]

During the 1920s and 1930s, a group of young biologists based at UC Berkeley and Yosemite conducted the Park Service's first systematic wildlife surveys and wrote its first science-based conservation plans. In the years that followed, partly due to the Berkeley group's urging, several parks ended practices that were common at the time but today would seem utterly out of place. They closed their zoos, banned trapping, outlawed feeding wildlife, and ended their predator control programs. Yet the national parks' treatment of bears was slow to change. Yosemite operated bear-feeding stations from 1923 to 1940, allowed bears to fish for trout at the Happy Isles hatchery until 1956, and did not secure its garbage dumps until 1971. Generations of bears got hooked on human food, visitors traveled hundreds of miles to see them up close, and park officials couldn't kick their own addictive habit of serving their bears to gawking tourists.[17]

Why was anyone surprised when these creatures bit the hands that fed them?

In Yellowstone, from 1931 to 1959, bears injured an average of forty-eight people per year. About 98 percent of these injuries involved black bears—thankfully, not grizzlies. In 1960, park officials launched an initiative that included educating visitors about wildlife, moving "nuisance" animals away from developed areas, and managing garbage better. They also purged large numbers of bears. From 1960 to 1969, rangers in Yellowstone killed 39 grizzlies and 332 black bears. Yet the number of human injuries per year barely budged.[18]

In 1970, Yellowstone officials started pushing more aggressively to wean the park's bears off human food. They installed bear-resistant trash cans, enforced park rules against feeding bears, and moved greater numbers of bears to more-remote areas. They also ignored the advice of the legendary biologists John and Frank Craighead, abruptly shuttering the last dumps on which many grizzlies had come to depend.

The number of human injuries dropped, but Yellowstone's stressed-out bears reeled. The average autumn weight of an adult male grizzly in the park fell from around 740 to less than 400 pounds, and dozens died of starvation or of injuries sustained when they were hit by cars as they searched for food or were shot by rangers or local residents who feared that these animals had become dangerous. In 1975, in part as a consequence of this debacle, the US Fish and Wildlife Service listed grizzly bears in the contiguous forty-eight states as threatened under the Endangered Species Act.[19]

Finding human foods became more difficult when people stopped serving them. But bears that had been reared on hot dogs and Pop-Tarts clearly considered the rewards worth the risks. When the dumps closed, bears started raiding ice chests and garbage cans. When rangers required visitors to secure their food and waste, bears started ripping the doors off Buicks and shattering cabin windows.

This situation metastasized into a crisis at Yosemite, Sequoia, and Kings Canyon National Parks. On the eve of the gold rush in 1848, more grizzlies lived in California than in any other state except Alaska, but by the mid-1920s, California's grizzlies had disappeared, leaving behind a wide-open niche in a diverse and productive landscape. Black bear populations then started to grow in the state's national parks and forests. Problems started to mount, but when these bears misbehaved, rangers often responded by using sloppy or inhumane methods to dispatch them while doing little to address the institutional failures and careless human behaviors at the root of the problem.

In the 1960s, local activists and anonymous Park Service employees started complaining about the parks' bear management practices. It was not until 1974, however, that the photographer Galen Rowell shone light on a dark chapter in the service's history. Acting on a tip, he rappelled off a cliff near Yosemite's Big Oak Flat entrance to find hundreds of black bear bodies that rangers had been dumping there for decades. Rowell's gruesome images and graphic description of rangers accidentally killing a cub while attempting to tranquilize it, in full view of its frantic mother and terrified sibling, ignited a firestorm of public outcry.[20]

Change came slowly at first. Beginning in the 1970s, a series of studies helped managers better understand black bear biology and behavior. New bear-proof food storage lockers and bear-resistant backpacking canisters showed promise but failed to catch on widely, due to a lack of political support and funding. As late as 1998, Yosemite logged more than 1,500 annual bear-related incidents, costing more than $650,000 in damages. These episodes resulted in seven injured humans and three dead bears.[21]

Beginning in 1999, Congress allocated an annual budget of $500,000 to address California's national park bear emergency. The introduction to the *2001 Annual Bear Management Report for Sequoia and Kings Canyon National Parks* illustrates the scope of the effort. In those parks, in a single year, the Park Service installed 378 food storage lockers, contacted more than 45,000 visitors, held over 50 training courses, issued more than 1,600 warnings or citations, and collected 268 bags of trash. When federal funds ran low, officials like the biologist Rachel Mazur—who led much of this work and whose 2015 book recounts this saga in detail—raised money however they could.[22]

It was exhausting work, but well worth the trouble. Over a decade, the Park Service and its partners reduced the number of bear-related incidents in California's national parks by more than 90 percent. A later study would show that Yosemite's bears had reverted to a mostly natural diet. With thousands of visitors passing through these parks every day, the work of keeping apart bears and people— or at least bears and people's lunches—is never done. Yet this qualifies as one of the great successes in American wildlife management. The bears in these national parks are tougher to see now, but they are, for the most part, wild again.[23]

.   .   .   .   .

The same cannot be said of the thousands of black bears living in and around American cities, where challenges first confronted in the national parks have played out over and over.

Black bears have been skulking around mountain towns for decades. Yosemite Valley is a kind of mountain town, but as citylike as it can seem on a sweaty summer day—with its traffic jams, dusty parking lots, overpriced hotels, and fast-food joints—being in a national park makes it different. The Park Service's mission is to preserve and enable people to enjoy the places it oversees. To achieve these goals, it has full control, or "exclusive jurisdiction," over these areas. When things go wrong, as they did with bears in Yellowstone in the 1970s, the Park Service gets the blame. When things go right, as they did in Yosemite in the early 2000s, it can take credit.

Most actual cities face the opposite predicament. Cities don't have a mission. Instead, they have numerous agencies, each with its own mission, and residents with diverse ideas and interests. They contain a patchwork of private and public lands subject to different rules and regulations. New policies are often controversial. Getting them enacted and then getting people to comply with them can be a delicate and drawn-out dance.

The bears don't care. Around 1980, reports of black bears started adding up in urban areas around the country. Some cities that had always had bears in their vicinities—like Anchorage, Boulder, and Missoula—saw more bears, more incidents, and more controversies. In these places, experience sometimes enabled thoughtful and effective approaches. But for most cities, where this was a new phenomenon, the most common response, as with coyotes, was to overreact.

Consider the case of greater Los Angeles, where black bears have a long, strange history. After living there for at least a million years, black bears mysteriously vanished from what is now Southern California around twenty thousand years ago. (Some paleobiologists suspect that a cooler, drier climate at the height of the last ice age reduced this region's forest cover, causing the bears to move farther north.) In the 1930s, Yosemite officials shipped twenty-eight "problem" black bears to Southern California to entertain campers in the Angeles and San Bernardino National Forests. Fifty years later, the descendants of these Yosemite bears were spotted in L.A.'s foothill suburbs.[24]

Officials who lacked experience dealing with large wild animals in urban areas often bungled their response. On June 21, 1982, for example, police and game wardens spent three predawn hours chasing a black bear through the tony L.A. suburb of Granada Hills. Speaking with the *Los Angeles Times* later that day, the animal control officer Michael Fowble said that they had attempted to capture the bear alive "after it was cornered in a backyard." When they finally closed in, the panicked, exhausted animal did what panicked, exhausted animals often do. It charged, and officers shot it. Seeking to reassure worried residents, Vic Sampson, from the California Department of Fish and Game, said that he doubted anyone would see another bear in urban L.A. County anytime soon.[25]

From the perspective of officers who had reason to believe that the people they served would would criticize them regardless of what they did, shooting a bear in a suburb was a regrettable but straightforward decision. It came with no penalties—but if they had let the bear go and a kid had gotten hurt, then they would have taken the blame. The result was that dozens of black bears, many of which posed little danger to people, died on the streets of American cities.

Two insights changed this equation, causing experts and officials to rethink the way they dealt with black bears and other large wildlife in urban areas. Beginning in the 1980s, surveys showed that Americans—having grown up with Teddy, Smokey, Winnie, and Yogi—thought of bears as intelligent, attractive, similar to people, and worthy of protection. Most suburbanites knew little about wildlife, but they valued the lives of animals like bears and supported efforts to protect them. Residents criticized officials who killed these animals before exhausting other options, and they demanded more-humane tactics. The capture-or-kill approach took another hit when scientists and wildlife managers started questioning its safety and effectiveness. By failing to secure their garbage, cities were attracting bears, and by responding with disproportionate force to bear sightings, they were increasing the risks associated with having bears around. The old way wasn't working.[26]

Some new ideas came from unlikely sources. In the High Sierra ski town of Mammoth Lakes, California, not far from the eastern boundary of Yosemite National Park, it took an inexperienced oddball and a self-proclaimed "uneducated redneck" to diagnose the problem and develop a solution. Known as "the bear whisperer" for his starring role in a 2011–12 cable television series of the same name, Steve Searles has said that he preferred the title "bear yeller." In 1996, the Mammoth Lakes Police Department hired him to rid the town of sixteen problem bears. His main qualifications appear to have been that he grew up hunting and fishing and was six feet four inches tall. Searles had no ethical problem shooting bears, but he soon realized that, from a practical perspective, he was fueling a vicious cycle. "Dead bears learn nothing," he told the *Los Angeles Times*. "If you kill one, another will come in from the mountains to replace it."[27]

That's when he started yelling. Instead of shooting Mammoth's black bears, Searles launched a hazing campaign aimed at intimidating the town's furry bandits. He also pushed the city to secure its trash and educate its residents and visitors. A series of slapstick episodes, including several aired on reality TV, led some to conclude that Searles was doing more harm than good, but the results spoke for themselves. The bears that remained learned a few hard lessons from this baseball-bat-wielding madman, but they lived and they learned. The town's bear population stabilized, and the number of incidents plummeted.

When he began his work, Searles liked to provoke crowds by making snide-sounding comments like "A bear is basically a stomach with four feet." But in the years leading up to his abrupt retirement in 2020, Searles grew fond of comparing the town's laid-back bears to one of his favorite bands. Mammoth's bears, he said, were like the Grateful Dead. But the opposite was equally true. Thanks to Searles, Mammoth's bears should have felt grateful to be alive.[28]

·   ·   ·   ·   ·

Back in New Jersey, the black bear story has taken a different turn. In 2003, the state launched its first legal bear hunt in thirty-three years. In 2006, Governor John Corzine temporarily reversed course, issuing a ban on bear hunting that lasted for three years. In 2018, Governor Phil Murphy signed an executive order prohibiting bear hunting on state-owned lands. Neither of these policies made a dent in the harvest. Between 2003 and 2020, New Jersey hunters took a whopping total of 4,082 bears. In fall 2019, a hunter in suburban Morris County bagged a seven-hundred-pound behemoth believed to be the largest black bear ever killed with a bow and arrow. It was New Jersey's first hunting world record of any kind for any species.[29]

From the perspective of state managers, whose goal is to cultivate healthy wildlife populations that support sustainable yields, New Jersey's bear hunt is a success story. Most sportspeople agree. Opponents of this approach, however, argue that you don't have to kill bears to manage them and that the hunt each fall amounts to little more than a slaughter. Media reports tend to focus on the extreme fringes and loudest voices, but research suggests that most of the state's residents fall somewhere in the middle. They agree that bears are important and valuable, bears should be treated humanely, a well-regulated hunt is probably necessary, and people who feed bears should be punished. Seen in this context, the story of Pedals shows how Americans are not only developing a new science and set of policies for urban wildlife—they are actively trying to work out a new ethic for living with animals like black bears in densely populated, mostly urbanized regions.[30]

During the two years that he wandered suburban New Jersey, Pedals became the subject of an emotional debate. With a missing right front paw and damaged left leg, he either was deformed or had been badly injured. Two of Pedals's biggest fans, Sabrina Pugsley and Lisa Rose-Rublack, raised almost $25,000 and collected 300,000 signatures on a petition calling for him to be captured, given veterinary care, and moved to a sanctuary upstate. Officials refused, saying that Pedals was a wild animal that, despite his appearance, seemed healthy. What they really meant was that bears are not individuals to be shown empathy but rather members of populations to be managed as resources. At least one hunter announced online that, if the tree huggers were right and Pedals was suffering, he would be happy to put the bear out of its misery.[31]

On October 10, 2016, Pedals ran out of luck. A hunter stalked him on social media, baited him, and shot him with an arrow near the Greenpond Golf Course in Rockaway, targeting New Jersey's most famous bear on the first day of its annual hunt. A week later, the state released a series of grisly photographs showing a bear with a missing right front paw, hanging upside down from chains, at a state-run check station. It weighed in at a stout 334 pounds. Officials claimed that it was impossible to identify an individual bear without genetic tests, but Pedals's admirers knew him when they saw him— and they didn't see him again. By the end of the season, New Jersey's hunters would take a record 636 bears.[32]

In December, the author Jon Mooallem published an obituary for Pedals—alongside tributes by other writers to David Bowie, Muhammad Ali, Gwen Ifill, Antonin Scalia, and Prince—in the *New York Times*'s annual feature "The Lives They Lived." It was the first *Times* obituary dedicated to a bear. After pondering his appeal, his journey, his followers, his enemies, and the debates that swirled around him, Mooallem concluded that "Pedals stood for something. We may never agree what it was."[33]

One thing Pedals stood for was the challenge of coexisting with wildlife at a time when more people and more animals are huddling into the same crowded habitats. His humanlike appearance blurred the lines between us and them, and by doing so, it brought these issues into sharper focus. Pedals is gone, but the bears, and the humans, keep coming.

8 Home to Roost

With its iconic white head, yellow talons, and hooked beak, the bald eagle is North America's most recognizable bird. A fully grown bald eagle can weigh as much as fourteen pounds (females are around 25 percent bigger than males) and have a wingspan of up to seven feet. In 1782, when the Continental Congress chose the bald eagle as the United States' mascot, it was common throughout the thirteen colonies and across North America from the Gulf of Mexico to the Bering Sea. Yet this bird's fame and regal appearance did not protect it. Like other raptors, bald eagles suffered from habitat loss, shooting, poisoning, and egg collecting. Water pollution, including from DDT, a potent insecticide developed during World War II, further reduced their numbers. By the mid-twentieth century, it seemed as though America's mascot might disappear from everywhere in the country, except Alaska.

Balds were first protected under the Migratory Bird Treaty Act of 1918. Safeguards increased with the Bald Eagle Protection Act of 1940, the Clean Water Act of 1972, and the Endangered Species Act of 1973. Together, these and other state and local efforts made a difference. By the 2000s, bald eagles were gracing the skies in parts of the United States where they had not been seen in decades.[1]

Pittsburgh was one of these places. By the 1970s, bald eagles were all but extinct in Pennsylvania. In 1983, the state set out to bring them back when it imported eighty-eight of the birds from Saskatchewan to jump-start a recovery program. They slowly gained a foothold, and in 2010, a pair of balds established the species's first nest near Pittsburgh in at least 150—and maybe as many as 200—years. By 2013, two new pairs had built nests within the city limits, including one on a hillside overlooking the Keystone Iron and Metal scrapyard, in the Hays neighborhood, along the Monongahela River and less than five miles from downtown.[2]

By spring of that year, the Hays pair had become "avian rock stars," according to the *Pittsburgh Post-Gazette*, and crowds were gathering daily to glimpse the eagles from nearby viewing points. Eagle mania gripped the city. To understand why so many Pittsburghers felt so passionately about the city's eagles, it helps to know why, in the eyes of so many locals, these were more than just birds.[3]

A hearth of American industry, Pittsburgh grew rich on metal processing and manufacturing, but these industries devastated its environment. Gazing north across the Allegheny River from a Cliff Street overlook in 1866, the author James Parton famously described a frightful, yet hauntingly beautiful, landscape. "The entire space lying between the hills was filled with blackest smoke," he wrote, "out of which the hidden chimneys sent forth tongues of flame, while from the depths of the abyss came up the noise of hundreds of steam-hammers. There would be moments when no flames were visible; but soon the wind would force the smoky curtains aside, and the whole black expanse would be dimly lighted with dull wreaths of fire." For Parton, it was "a spectacle as striking as Niagara . . . hell with the lid taken off."[4]

By the mid-twentieth century, Parton's hell had become a haven for diverse immigrant and ethnic communities that prospered in a city with tens of thousands of stable, well-paying blue-collar jobs. The foundations of this economy began to crumble in the 1970s, and when the steel industry collapsed a decade later, Pittsburgh found itself at the epicenter of the new American Rust Belt. Thousands of people slipped into poverty, while tens of thousands more left for the Sunbelt and the West.

Beginning in the 1990s, Pittsburgh, shrunken and humbled, once again reinvented itself, launching an improbable comeback based on health care, education, and tourism. With blue collars giving way to white, inequality grew, and many residents failed to reap the benefits of this transition. The local environment, however, began to recover from 150 years of abuse. Forests, which had started regrowing decades earlier, blanketed the hillsides, and water quality, which had long ranked among the worst in the nation, began to improve. Some fish even returned to the rivers.

To many Pittsburghers, the Hays eagles represented not only Pittsburgh's revival but also the resilience of nature and the potential for people and wildlife to coexist in cleaner, greener, twenty-first-century cities. Conservationists and animal lovers could barely contain their glee. "Did you ever think you'd live long enough to see three bald eagle nests in Allegheny County?" asked Tom Fazi of the Pennsylvania Game Commission.[5]

Yet protecting the birds while engaging the public required tact and patience. Officials and experts could educate Pittsburghers about "eagle etiquette"—for example, urging fans to stay at least one thousand feet from nests—but they still fretted that, in the words of the local Audubon Society director Jim Bonner, "some yahoo will do something that might scare [the eagles]."[6]

One way to achieve both goals was to install a video camera. At the time, nest cams, collar cams, motion-sensing camera traps, and other digital-image-capturing devices were exploding in popularity as their prices dropped, battery lives increased, and solar-powered chargers improved, and as high-speed internet enabled websites to host streaming video. The Game Commission partnered with local firms to install a camera over the Hays nest, which would broadcast around the clock.

What had been a thrilling, if partial, glimpse into the lives of wild animals soon turned into something more like a reality TV show. A slapstick moment came early, in the winter of 2014, when a white-tailed deer briefly disabled the camera's power source in the forest below. Comedy turned to drama on the evening of February 26, when a raccoon raided the nest. The mother eagle, who had been resting atop her eggs, spread her wings to form an imposing posture and lunged at the would-be thief with her razor-sharp can opener of a beak, sending the raccoon fleeing.[7]

No animals were harmed in the making of that film, but wildlife experts predicted that viewers would see more harrowing images. "God sets the wheels in motion," said Henry Kacprzyk of the Pittsburgh Zoo, appearing to forget that Pennsylvania's eagles had been imported from Canada. "Things happen—animals live, animals die. You can't, and you shouldn't, attempt to manage every individual animal." (In the neighboring state of New Jersey, officials were using almost exactly the same words, at almost exactly the same time, to talk about Pedals the bear.)[8]

Pittsburghers watched throughout that spring and summer as the Hays pair had their best year yet, fledging all three chicks in their clutch (see figure 7). The next spring, after both of the pair's eggs broke in the nest, mourners left roses and sympathy cards on a nearby fence, along with handwritten notes like "Next year, Mom and Dad. We love you!" These birds had become symbols not only of a renewed city but also, like Bambi, of monogamous heterosexual relationships, dedicated parenting, and nuclear family values.[9]

It was time for a reality check. At 4:24 P.M. on April 26, 2016, with one of the adults and two chicks in the nest, the other adult returned with dinner. The city of Pittsburgh watched in shock as the family of eagles mangled, dismembered, and ate a kitten on live video. For a moment, it seemed like these heroes might become pariahs. Decades earlier they might have, but times had changed. In the

comments on the video's YouTube page, some viewers expressed horror at the sight of this model family eating another family's pet, but several blamed cat owners for allowing their animals to wander unattended. Others noted that the eagles had been eating squirrels, rats, and other small game on camera for years without much human sympathy for those creatures. A few said that, with cats killing hundreds of thousands of birds each year, the eagles' snack didn't come close to settling the score. One commenter wrote that he was considering putting seasoning on his girlfriend's Chihuahua.[10]

The Hays eagle cam episode offers two important lessons. First, nest cams and other wildlife surveillance devices tell us as much about the people watching them as they do about the animals being recorded. Second, wild animals in cities are not just parasites or freeloaders living off human waste—they are members of complex ecosystems. Creatures like bald eagles can live in urban areas because these places provide the resources they need, including sites to nest and food to eat. It took some scientists decades to recognize these basic facts; it took eagle fans in Pittsburgh, who happened to be watching the Hays pair on that fateful spring afternoon, just a few enlightening seconds.

.   .   .   .   .

One of the great shortcomings of modern ecological science is that for so long it could tell us so little about the places where most people live. Ecologists are finally starting to meet this need, but it took them a long time to recognize it. One reason for this is that ecological science emerged in Western societies with a long tradition of drawing sharp lines between nature and culture. This way of thinking dates back to ancient Greece. In the *Republic,* Plato defined the ideal city, or polis, as the place where a just and virtuous society uplifted its citizens. In Aristotle's *Politics,* the city is an association of people who have come together in pursuit of the good life. Cities were the province of culture, art, and learning. Outside cities lay the realm of wild beasts, uncivilized people, and unrealized potential. To live in a city was to become a *citi*zen in the fullest sense of the word.[11]

In the centuries since, great thinkers have aligned themselves on one side or the other of this rural-urban, nature-culture divide. During the Enlightenment, for example, Voltaire, who was banished, twice, from his beloved Paris, the intellectual center of the Western world, celebrated the benefits of urban life. For Jean-Jacques Rousseau, Voltaire's rival and an early romantic, it was the country-side, not the city, that fostered strength, virtue, independence, and wisdom.[12]

The roots of this divide run deep in Western culture, but the field of ecology, which grew from them, did not germinate until the late nineteenth and early twentieth centuries. By the 1910s, progressive intellectuals and reformers in Europe and North America had founded several applied scientific professions, including forestry and range management. Ecology always had a more theoretical bent, but like any upstart, it too had to find a niche. In North America, this usually meant focusing on protected areas such as national parks, where researchers could study nature as far away as possible from human influence.

Beginning in 1916, the new Ecological Society of America lobbied to create nature preserves for research and teaching. According to its first president, Victor Shelford, "A branch of biological science which obtains its inspiration in the natural order in original habitats must depend upon the preservation of natural areas for the solution of many problems." Shelford knew that most nature reserves had long histories of human use and that *natural* was a relative term. He and his colleagues performed experiments in labs, and some even worked in cities or on farms. Yet their focus on natural areas cast a long shadow. Generations of ecologists who followed them assumed that urban areas were unworthy of study and that only the most pristine sites could teach scientists anything important about nature.[13]

In the 1930s, seeking to shore up their field's reputation as a serious science, the Ecological Society of America's leaders decided that preserving nature was for conservation organizations, not scholarly societies. Shelford and his followers responded by forming a new group, the Ecologists Union, to take up the cause. It eventually changed its name to the Nature Conservancy and grew to be the world's largest conservation organization. In 1937, a second contingent broke off, to form a group for wildlife managers known as the Wildlife Society. The managers affiliated with this group continued to use ecological principles and methods, but over time their field drifted from its scientific moorings to become a service industry for hunters, fishers, farmers, and ranchers—almost all of whom lived, worked, or played in rural areas.[14]

A small minority of scientists and naturalists did, however, work in cities. During the nineteenth and early twentieth centuries, scientific and educational institutions employed the first generation of professional naturalists. Many of these zoologists, botanists, paleontologists, and others traveled to remote field sites where they gathered or purchased specimens to build their employers' collections. Back at home—curing skins, designing exhibits, teaching classes, and writing papers—they often found themselves yearning to be outside. So they sought out nearby sites where they could commune with and study nature. In the process, they became the first true urban ecologists.

Most early urban wildlife research focused on birds. Unlike other groups of land animals, which had been driven out decades earlier, native birds remained in cities, but many species were in trouble. Habitat loss and pest control efforts had taken a major toll. It was the Victorian millinery industry, however, which killed some five million birds each year to serve as ornaments on women's hats, that revealed birds' beauty and diversity while alerting people to the threats that faced them.

Frank Chapman, an ornithologist with the American Museum of Natural History, helped lead local Audubon societies in raising awareness about this slaughter. In 1886, he spent two afternoons strolling around New York City's uptown shopping district, during which time he counted 542 hats sporting feathers of some kind. He was able to identify the body parts of at least forty species, including owls, waxwings, warblers, tanagers, grosbeaks, bobolinks, doves, quails, herons, and terns. Public awareness campaigns and boycotts reduced the demand for bird hats, but the avian millinery fad limped along for decades until the Migratory Bird Treaty Act banned the killing of birds for fashion.[15]

In 1900, Chapman proposed a Christmas Bird Census, now called the Christmas Bird Count. He hoped to replace the notorious holiday derbies, or "side hunts," in which people competed to see who could shoot the greatest number of birds in a single day. An organized event would raise public awareness while generating valuable scientific data, but without all of the bloodshed. Over the next several decades, advances in optical technology—including the invention of high-quality, modestly priced binoculars, spotting scopes, and cameras—aided Chapman's cause by making it easier to observe birds without having to kill them first. Chapman's census was not limited to cities, but it started in cities, and urban birders have always been among its most enthusiastic participants. Today, the Christmas Bird Count is one of the world's longest-running and most successful citizen science projects.

Also in the early twentieth century, ecologists in Europe began to explore human-dominated landscapes. European philosophers had helped invent the nature-culture divide, but the geographic realities of their continent partly erased it. Over time, the line between nature and culture had blurred in this densely populated region with few large undeveloped natural areas and a long, well-documented human history. Most of Europe also lacked wilderness myths of the kinds that emerged in places like North America and Australia, where colonists justified their conquests by pretending that they had discovered virgin lands.

Nowhere was this more the case than in Britain, a country in which thinkers from across the political spectrum embraced the idea of a timeless countryside that combined the best of nature and culture. One of the most famous proponents of this view was Arthur Tansley, who in 1913 became the first president of the British Ecological Society. Tansley worked tirelessly to protect the English countryside, earning a knighthood in part for his effort. He viewed humans and livestock as essential participants in a unique cultural landscape that had taken centuries to produce. If humans had helped create and sustain this landscape, then it made sense to include people in the ecological study of it.[16]

After World War II, urban ecology sprouted from the ashes of bombed- and burned-out cities. One of the first serious works of natural history to focus entirely on urban areas was Richard Fitter's *London's Natural History,* first published in 1945. Fitter had been trained as a social scientist at the London School of Economics, and he had conducted research on civilian morale during wartime. For him, London's plants and animals embodied the resilience of British nature and people, from the darkest days of the Blitz to the long period of recovery and rebuilding that followed. Some of the most important work on devastated postwar landscapes took place in Germany, where West Berlin's brachen offered unique field sites for intrepid ecologists. In the 1970s, Herbert Sukopp developed a pioneering research program that documented the changing vegetation on abandoned lots and rubble piles, with an eye to building a new, green future for a city surrounded by guns, checkpoints, guard towers, and walls.[17]

Back in the United States, the first generation of wildlife managers stressed the value of urban fauna. As early as 1933, the field's founding father, Aldo Leopold, wrote that "a pair of wood thrushes . . . is more valuable to a village than a Saturday evening band concert, and costs less." Rudolf Bennitt, the first president of the Wildlife Society, looked forward to "the day when we shall hear men discuss the management of songbirds, wildflowers, and the biota of a city." Yet few took up his call. Most field research in ecology continued to take place in undeveloped areas.[18]

In the 1960s, pleas for scientists to study urban environments grew more urgent. Raymond Dasmann, a critic of growth in his home state of California, advised his colleagues to "get out of the woods and into the cities." He believed that ecologists could help reshape urban areas into places "where each person's everyday life will be enriched to the maximum extent possible by contact with living things and natural beauty." For Dasmann, this was a key element of the "new conservation," which focused not only on the sustainable use of natural resources in rural areas but also on the overall quality of the environment.[19]

Conservation groups and government agencies responded. The US Fish and Wildlife Service organized two conferences, in 1968 and 1986, on the urban environment. In 1985, the National Park Service renamed its Ecological Services Laboratory, based in Washington, DC, the Center for Urban Ecology. The National Wildlife Federation and the Trust for Public Land supported modest urban programs. The Wildlife Society founded a committee on urban wildlife, which issued supportive statements, surveyed ongoing activities, and published guidelines for state and local programs.

Yet many influential ecologists remained unconvinced. Warning against an "uncritical and overenthusiastic" embrace of urban ecology, C. S. Holling and Gordon Orians argued that urban research lacked coherence and rigor and that getting involved in urban issues would plunge scientists into politics. Their views made an impression on young scholars. The behavioral ecologist Andrew Sih, for example, recalled being pulled aside, when he was a graduate student at UC Santa Barbara in the 1970s, and advised by a mentor to "focus on pristine, natural systems. The goal, after all," Sih said, describing the prevailing attitude of the time, "was to understand Nature—with a capital N." This did not include artificial environments like cities.[20]

In 1985, Lowell Adams, then at the Urban Wildlife Research Center outside Baltimore and later at the University of Maryland, found that fewer than one in ten North American universities offered courses on urban wildlife. In 2000, he conducted a second survey, which revealed that the situation had improved little, with "limited preparation by academia and agencies to address urban wildlife management issues now and in the future."[21]

Practical problems also hindered many promising initiatives. Conducting fieldwork in cities can be difficult. Most of the land is private property, and convincing people to allow wildlife research in their backyards isn't always easy. On public land, red tape abounds. According to Mark Weckel, of the American Museum of Natural History and the Gotham Coyote Project, when he and his colleagues first inquired about permits to study coyotes in New York City, its Department of Parks and Recreation, which had not fielded such a request before, had to develop a new policy. New York cooperated with Weckel and the museum, but other cities have been less willing or able to facilitate research.[22]

Funding has been difficult to come by as well. In 1997, the National Science Foundation endorsed the study of urban nature when it added Baltimore and Phoenix to its federally funded Long-Term Ecological Research network. The investigators at these sites pursued different tacks. Whereas the group in Phoenix tended to focus on biological and physical aspects of urban ecosystems, the group in Baltimore focused more on social and economic issues, including environmental justice. Despite the growing body of work emerging from such sites, many of the NSF's reviewers remained skeptical. The ornithologist John Marzluff, for example, told me that in funding proposals, he sometimes frames his studies of American crows in Seattle as providing insights about related but endangered corvid species in other parts of the world. Why should we pay for research on common birds living in cities, Marzluff's reviewers often asked, when we know so little about threatened species in natural habitats? That this question still arises in ornithology, the zoological field with the richest urban tradition, shows just how tough it can be to convince funders to support wildlife research in cities.[23]

As late as 1996, Robert Blair—who coined the terms *urban avoider, urban adapter,* and *urban exploiter*—could still write that "little is known about the effects of urbanization on ecosystems, communities, species, and populations because ecologists have traditionally worked in pristine, or relatively pristine, environments." Five years later, the ecologist Steward Pickett and his colleagues reviewed the state of urban ecological research. They found good news and bad. Ecologists had recognized the extent of human influence on natural systems and published dozens of books and articles on urban ecosystems. Yet it was unclear what these published studies added up to or where they were going. Research on urban wildlife relied on dubious methods and outmoded ecological theory and lacked a core agenda, set of organizing principles, list of key questions, and dedicated community. "Urban habitats," Pickett and his coauthors concluded, "constitute an open frontier for ecological research."[24]

The early 2000s turned out to be an inflection point for work on urban ecology and wildlife. The number of journal articles and books multiplied, professional organizations and conferences proliferated, universities hired new faculty and began training more students, and several cities and states founded or grew their urban wildlife education and management programs.

After a long history of false starts, several factors contributed to the growth of urban ecology in the twenty-first century. In 2007, for the first time, more people around the world lived in cities than in rural areas. Many American cities—having rebounded from decades of deindustrialization, disinvestment, and decay—now had the resources to clean up brown fields and polluted waterways, plant trees, and install, rehabilitate, or expand open space and park systems. The increasing visibility of wildlife in urban areas piqued public interest. New cohorts of young scholars, including a higher proportion of women scientists than in previous generations, turned to cities as places where they could pursue their careers while attending to personal and family obligations.

The old dividing line between nature and culture was also starting to blur in American environmental thought. In 2000, the atmospheric scientist Paul J. Crutzen popularized the term *Anthropocene,* which he and others defined as the current geologic epoch, in which humans have become a major force shaping earth's geology, ecology, chemistry, and climate. The concept of a human epoch had been around for decades, but after 2000 it intersected with related ideas, took on new urgency, and captured the imagination of a diverse public. If one of the Anthropocene's most important drivers was urbanization, then more urban ecology research could help us understand our changing planet.

In 2016, Pickett and his colleagues again reviewed the state of the field. "Ecology as a whole," they wrote, had "seemed to awaken to urban areas as a legitimate habitat for study." Urban ecology had gone from "a marginal interest to a widely pursued and theoretically motivated ecological field." Fifteen years earlier, Pickett had characterized urban ecology as having two major branches: ecology *in cities*, which focused on the interactions among plants and animals there, and ecology *of cities*, which focused on flows of matter and energy through them. In the years since, it had added a third: ecology *for cities*, which aimed to make urban areas more sustainable. Urban ecology had joined a larger movement, helping bring the discipline of ecology full circle by repositioning it as a biological science with practical applications.[25]

·   ·   ·   ·   ·

Almost 4,000 miles from Pittsburgh, Unalaska has an edge-of-the-world feel about it, and with a year-round population of just around 4,500, it barely counts as a city. Yet despite its small size, it has four genuine claims to fame. The town's Dutch Harbor was one of only a few places in the United States attacked during World War II. It is the country's most productive fishing port. In 2005, it became the on-location filming site for the hit reality TV drama *Deadliest Catch*. Its final claim to fame is the one that connects it to Pittsburgh. Dutch Harbor, like Pittsburgh, is home to bald eagles. Lots of them.

When the author Laurel Braitman, who has written about such topics as animal insanity, visited Dutch Harbor, she found a "Hitchcockian nightmare." Around 650 eagles—a ratio of about 1 eagle for every 7 people—had settled there, and the birds were wreaking havoc. "They stare judgily [*sic*] down from light posts," Braitman wrote, "peer intently into people's windows, eat foxes and seagulls while perched in the trees next to the high school, and sit on rooflines like living weather vanes." At the docks, they swarm boats, harass fishermen, and steal bait. They bicker, they screech, and they jostle.[26]

One young man, Coast Guard lieutenant Andres Ayure, recalled that on his third day in the town, he hiked up nearby Mount Ballyhoo. As he was making his way back down, an eagle attacked, dive-bombing him a dozen times and flying off with the phone he had dropped as he ran for cover. Ayure was left, stunned and terrified, on the mountain in his American Eagle hoodie. His fellow Guardsmen later presented him with a figurine of an eagle engraved with the word *Alaska*.

Ayure is not alone. Each year, around ten people arrive at the local clinic seeking medical attention for eagle-related injuries—mostly talon-inflicted head lacerations—more than the total number of people killed by bears in Yellowstone National Park since its founding in 1872.

Unalaskans call the birds "Dutch Harbor pigeons." Braitman called them "dirty birds." But why has this remote outpost become America's angry eagle capital? The answer, according to local officials, is that this windswept island contains an enormous amount of food, courtesy of the haul at Dutch Harbor, but, with no native trees, it has few spots for roosting or nesting. Large numbers of eagles show up for the smorgasbord; when it's time to rest, they turn to buildings, power lines, pilings, and just about any other built structure that rises at least a couple dozen feet above the land or sea. The longer they live with people, the less they fear us and the bolder they get. And since several laws protect bald eagles, local officials have limited options for deterring them.

Will Pennsylvania's eagles ever become "Pittsburgh pigeons"? It's difficult to say. According to an eye-popping report by the US Fish and Wildlife Service, the number of bald eagles in the Lower 48 more than quadrupled between 2009 and 2019.[27] Yet these eagles are behaving differently in different places, and the habitat around Pittsburgh is unlike that of Dutch Harbor. Food is more thinly distributed across the landscape, and perches for roosting and nesting are easy to come to by in the woodsy Alleghenies. If current trends continue, Pennsylvania will see more bald eagles in the future, and one can be sure that they will respond to changes in the environment there as they have in Alaska, even if the results look different. Pittsburgh's eagles will continue hunting, foraging, mating, roosting, nesting, and raising chicks along the Monongahela River. Scientists will continue studying them to learn about urban ecosystems and wildlife. And occasionally, a momma eagle will return home to her chicks with a kitten for dinner.

9 Hide and Seek

Early on the morning of March 3, 2016, a fourteen-year-old koala named Killarney disappeared from her enclosure at the Los Angeles Zoo. Nobody knows exactly what happened, but circumstantial evidence pointed to an unlikely culprit who had arrived on the scene through an even unlikelier series of events.[1]

Listed as "vulnerable" by the International Union for the Conservation of Nature, koalas are both famously charismatic and increasingly threatened because of habitat loss and climate change. At the L.A. Zoo, Killarney was one of the stars of a popular exhibit drawing tens of thousands of visitors annually. Approaching the end of her life, she had developed a habit, unwise in retrospect, of descending from her roost each night to amble around the floor of her pen.

In the weeks before Killarney disappeared, the dismembered bodies of several animals, including a koala-sized raccoon, had been found on the brushy slopes surrounding the zoo. Security-camera footage from shortly before Killarney disappeared showed the dim figure of a suspect, about 130 pounds and wearing a tan coat, prowling around nearby. The list of suspects was short, but the truth was hard to swallow.

Hours after she vanished, zoo staff discovered Killarney's corpse, bloody and faceless, about four hundred yards from her enclosure. How had this happened? Officials ruled out foul play by a human. But with the rest of the zoo's residents locked in their enclosures, the culprit must have come from outside. The L.A. Zoo had lost animals to wild predators before. In the 1990s, coyotes squeezed through a broken fence and eaten some of its rare birds. One year before Killarney's death, a bobcat raided a different enclosure and dined on two tamarin monkeys. But this time was different. Of all the area's wild animals, only one could have bounded over the eight-foot fence that formed the koalas' enclosure and then clambered back over it carrying a fifteen-pound marsupial.

Pumas—which are also called mountain lions, cougars, catamounts, panthers, and ghost cats—have the largest range of any New World land animal, stretching from the Yukon in Canada to the southern tip of South America. With tawny coats, muscular bodies, long, crooked tails, and small heads, pumas are easy to identify in photos but difficult to see in the wild. Unlike omnivorous bears or coyotes, they are specialized carnivores that hunt hoofed grazers and browsers, including elk, sheep, moose, pronghorn, and especially deer, which may constitute up to 90 percent of their diet. When their favorite prey species are not available, pumas take smaller mammals, reptiles, and even birds. Although they can reach speeds of up to fifty miles per hour in a short sprint, pumas are ambush predators better known for their ability to pounce. They can leap up to fifteen feet vertically and forty feet horizontally, making an eight-foot fence little more than a speed bump.

People have shot, trapped, and poisoned pumas for centuries. By the 1920s, pumas had been driven out of most of the eastern half of North America, with just a few small populations remaining in remote areas like the Florida Everglades. West of the Mississippi, they were persecuted as threats to livestock, but their wariness of people and ability to thrive in diverse habitats enabled them to endure.

In California, pumas have a unique and complicated history. From 1907 to 1963, ranchers, bounty hunters, and state animal control agents—including Jay Bruce, whose best-selling 1953 memoir, *Cougar Killer,* recounts his decades-long killing spree in the name of conservation—destroyed at least 12,462 pumas there, more than in any other state. In 1971, the California Department of Fish and Game held its first recreational puma season, but legislators halted it after just one year, and protests blocked further hunts. In 1990, voters passed Proposition 117, making California's pumas the country's only "specially protected mammals." Hunters attempted to rescind or weaken the ban on killing pumas, but their efforts had the opposite of the intended effect. Today, despite continuing concerns about the risks they pose to public safety and private property, California's pumas are more popular than ever.

Pumas have always prowled the fringes of Los Angeles, a city known for having the longest, sharpest urban-wildland interface in North America. But even as they started to rebound from their decades of persecution, they avoided built-up areas. Sometime around 2011, however, a solitary cat, which officials labeled P-22 (*P* is for "puma"), began making his way east from the Santa Monica Mountains above Malibu to the Hollywood Hills and L.A.'s urban core.

It is unclear exactly how P-22 achieved this feat, but it is easy to understand why he did it. The only mountain range that bisects a major American city, the Santa Monicas are cut off from other open spaces by shorelines and freeways. At most, this small range of brushy mountains can support only around twenty pumas. As a young male in a crowded neighborhood, P-22 must have set out in search of a new territory.

Most such quests do not end well. Adolescent pumas die with disturbing regularity on roads bordering the Santa Monicas. But a stroke of luck may have aided P-22. From July 15 to 17, 2011, the California Department of Transportation closed a ten-mile stretch of the 405 Freeway, which divides the Santa Monica Mountains from the Hollywood Hills, to rebuild the Mulholland Drive Bridge at Sepulveda Pass. For fifty-three hours, this closure, known to frantic L.A. motorists as Carmageddon, left the United States' busiest ribbon of road quiet and empty.[2]

Although he had crossed the 405, P-22's journey was far from over. During the next few months, he made his way, silent and unseen, through brushy ravines and gated communities, past homeless encampments and under glass houses perched on canyon walls. He probably crossed the 101 Freeway, another formidable barrier, early one morning through an underpass. By 2012, he was in Griffith Park, at the eastern end of the Hollywood Hills, overlooking downtown Los Angeles and surrounded by a sea of humanity.

At 4,310 acres, Griffith Park—home to playgrounds, ball fields, hiking trails, museums, an observatory, the Hollywood sign, and the L.A. Zoo—is one of the nation's largest urban green spaces. It is a small fraction of the typical mountain lion's range, which can be fifty times larger, but P-22 found a cozy home there. The park's mule deer, along with an occasional raccoon, coyote, or house cat, kept him well fed, and its thick woodlands offered cover just steps from busy trails. The biologists who discovered him with a camera trap soon captured him, examined him, and fixed him with a GPS collar. Their data showed that, though often within earshot of cheering sports teams and howling toddlers, P-22 had become an expert at avoiding people, living a life of solitude among the masses.[3]

During his first four years in the city, P-22 got into trouble only twice.

The first time, he had to be captured and treated when he acquired a case of mange. A potentially lethal skin infection caused by parasitic mites, mange often results when wild carnivores ingest toxic doses of rat poisons known as anticoagulant rodenticides, which weaken their immune systems. P-22 tested positive for rodenticide, but a vitamin K injection helped him recover.

The second time P-22 got into trouble, it was because he wandered beyond Griffith Park's boundaries. At daybreak, he found himself marooned in a crawl space under what the *Los Angeles Times* described as a "sleek, multi-level white contemporary" home in the fashionable Los Feliz neighborhood. Nestled in his daytime hideaway, the cat never gave biologists, with their tranquilizer darts, a clear shot. They attempted to force him out—pelting him with beanbags and tennis balls and poking him with a stick—but he held his ground. Declaring defeat, officials dispersed the crowd that had gathered and then left the site themselves. By the following morning, P-22 had disappeared back into the park. Instead of fretting about their safety, local residents expressed relief that the cat was unharmed. In the words of one bystander, the Swiss actress Yangzom Brauen, "We live here in a natural park so we live with the animals. We are in their territory."[4]

In 2013, P-22 went from a local curiosity to a regional mascot and global celebrity: the world's most famous, most important puma. In its December issue, *National Geographic* published an article featuring an instantly iconic photograph of P-22 by Steve Winter, who had traveled to remote sites around the world to capture pictures of rare and elusive felines. Winter's image shows a large tan cat, with a graceful tail and heavy haunches, wearing a bulky collar and striding along a ridge as the Hollywood sign glows in the background. Here was the lion of Los Angeles.[5]

P-22's popularity helps explain local reactions to Killarney's demise. In the days after the koala's death, L.A. City Council member Mitch O'Farrell said that "this tragedy just emphasizes the need to contemplate relocating P-22 to a safer, more remote wild area where he has adequate space to roam without the possibility of human interaction. . . . As much as we love P-22," O'Farrell continued, "we know the park is not ultimately suitable for him." O'Farrell's colleague David Ryu, whose district included the park, took a different position. Killarney's death was unfortunate, Ryu said, but moving P-22 "would not be in the best interest of protecting our wildlife species. Mountain lions are a part of the natural habitat of Griffith Park." Ryu was not much of an ecologist, but he was a savvy politician who knew his district. Three weeks after the incident, it was O'Farrell, not Ryu, who had to walk back his statement when outraged constituents rose up against him. "I'm rooting for his survival," O'Farrell said, of a creature that clearly had a larger constituency than his.[6]

The zoo, for its part, apologized to the people of Los Angeles, promising to better protect the creatures in its care. "It is [our] hope that P-22 remains in Griffith Park," zoo spokeswoman April Spurlock told reporters. "This is a natural park and home to many species of wildlife. We will continue to adapt to P-22 as he has adapted to us."[7]

P-22's improbable journey led to a long life in the heart of the nation's second-largest city, but it also left him in a lonely place. He would never leave the Hollywood Hills, and he would almost certainly never sire a cub. His story illustrates, and this chapter highlights, the challenges wild animals face in navigating urban environments. For every P-22, dozens of pumas have died searching for new territories, mates, and food. And for every species, like the eastern gray squirrel or the coyote, that has mastered the urban environment, dozens of others, including most pumas, have withdrawn from populated areas or disappeared altogether. Mobility can be a blessing or a curse. Moving safely through and around cities is a feat most creatures cannot achieve. But for those that do, the rewards—new frontiers of habitat with plentiful resources and few competitors—can be enormous. A few may even find fame in Hollywood (see figure 8).[8]

.   .   .   .   .

To appreciate the challenges that animals like P-22 face while moving through and around cities, a good way to start is by gazing down

at these landscapes from above. Most natural areas contain patches of habitat in many shapes and sizes, some with sharp edges and others with fuzzy boundaries. Viewed from the sky, they create a crazy-quilt pattern known as a mosaic. Urban areas, by contrast, have fewer kinds of habitats, which tend to come in geometric blocks with sharp edges, stark contrasts, and sometimes barriers between them. As one moves outward from the city center, the balance shifts from gray built-up spaces to green leafy spaces. In some cities, like Los Angeles, the boundary between green and gray is abrupt, with dense urban areas bordering rugged mountains. In other cities, like Boston, the boundary is broad and blurry, as tree-lined suburbs fade into fields and forests. Overall, however, in its arrangement of habitats, a protected natural area may differ from a core urban area as much as an impressionistic oil painting differs from a minimalist stone sculpture.

The most striking feature of any urban landscape, as viewed from above and experienced by wildlife on the ground, is that it is fragmented. In natural areas, resources tend to be distributed across the landscape, blurring the distinctions between neighboring habitat patches. In cities, sharp lines, stark discontinuities, and blocks of mostly unusable space (think roofs and parking lots) create more isolated patches. Since cities tend to clump resources into small areas (think gardens and dumpsters), some patches grow rich with life, while others become inhospitable wastelands.

This makes city life a gamble for many species. In urban areas that contain only small patches of suitable habitat, wildlife populations within those patches remain small and are thus more likely to be eliminated by chance events like storms and disease outbreaks. Isolated populations that cannot easily interbreed with others may, over time, develop unique and useful traits. It is far more likely, however, that they will be robbed of the health and welfare benefits that come with a larger and more diverse gene pool. Individuals that attempt to cross the barriers that surround them may die in transit. Such a fragile situation cannot last forever. If usable pathways, known as corridors, fail to open, then populations will decline, and some will eventually disappear.[9]

In the 1980s, conservationists started referring to isolated patches of habitat as islands. It's an imperfect but easy-to-visualize metaphor, which emerged from studies of real islands beginning in the 1960s. Islands that are larger and closer to the mainland are easier to reach, which means that they tend to have more stable and diverse animal communities. If one creature dies, another from the mainland is likely to take its place. Populations living on smaller or more remote islands—like those living in small urban habitat patches—are more isolated and thus more vulnerable to extinction.[10]

The island metaphor is imperfect because land animals experience patches of urban habitat surrounded by seas of humanity differently than they do islands surrounded by actual water. Green spaces in and around cities tend to be easier for people to access and disturb—for example by harassing animals or setting fires—than genuine islands with similar levels of protection. In Southern California, for example, millions of people visit recreational areas in the Santa Monica Mountains each year, whereas far fewer make the bumpy voyage out to the Channel Islands, which are actually just peaks in the same partly submerged mountain range. The same thing goes for many animals. Isolated landlocked habitat patches, like Griffith Park, may be within reach for the occasional Malibu puma, but no self-respecting lion would ever attempt to swim an equal distance to get to Santa Cruz Island.

By far the greatest barriers to animal movements are roads. Less than 20 percent of US land area is more than half a mile from the nearest road. At least one million vertebrate animals die on American roads each day, and vehicle collisions are the most common cause of death for many kinds of creatures living in and around urban areas. A 2008 report to Congress estimated that wildlife collisions cost $8 billion and harmed at least 21 endangered species. Smaller roads—those that are narrower, have less traffic, and have lower speed limits—harm fewer animals than larger ones, but even the smallest roads can prove surprisingly lethal.[11]

Different species experience road hazards in different ways and thus have different degrees of vulnerability. A few species—such as moose that give birth along roadsides to deter predators from attacking their wobbly newborn calves—may even benefit, but they are in the minority. Small carnivores, like skunks, often end up as roadkill, but their high birthrates usually make up for these losses. Coyotes have been observed waiting for traffic to pass before crossing busy intersections, whereas deer, whose dilated eyes may render them temporarily blind when confronted with bright beams, "freeze in the headlights." If one were to invent, from scratch, a creature worst suited to traversing urban landscapes, it might be a lumbering, target-shaped disk like a tortoise. Or it might be long and thin, with a tiny brain and a penchant for resting on warm surfaces, like a snake. Some behaviors and body plans that worked well for hundreds of millions of years seem suddenly out of date in the face of oncoming traffic.[12]

Birds are among the most familiar urban wildlife in part because they can avoid some of the hazards that more earthbound creatures face, but even birds die in great numbers in cities. Hawks, crows, ravens, vultures, and other scavengers perish on roads to which they are lured by the tasty carcasses of other recently departed animals. Far more birds succumb because of collisions with buildings and power lines. As early as 1990, the ornithologist Daniel Klem calculated that 100,000,000 to 1,000,000,000 birds die annually from collisions with buildings. In New York City alone, such collisions kill an estimated 250,000 birds each year, or almost 700 per day. Reflective glass coatings, reduced lighting during spring and fall migrations, and a focus on high-risk areas could prevent many of these deaths, but to date little has been done to combat this carnage.[13]

In California, several projects are attempting to reduce the threats that species face from roads and other built structures. In the

Berkeley Hills, the East Bay Regional Park District closes a stretch of South Park Drive each year to allow California newts to migrate from their woodsy summertime haunts to their wintertime spawning ponds. As part of its habitat conservation plan, Stanford University installed a network of barriers and culverts along a busy stretch of Junipero Serra Boulevard in the hope that amorous tiger salamanders would use these safe passages when searching for mates. It is unclear whether these "love tunnels" have helped the salamanders or just aided the university by attracting good press.[14]

Larger wildlife highway crossings, however, can be extremely effective and are growing in popularity. In North America, the best examples are in Alberta's Banff National Park, which as of 2014 had installed thirty-eight crossings along the Trans-Canada Highway, reducing wildlife collisions by more than 80 percent. If constructed, the biggest such project in the United States would be the proposed Liberty Canyon overpass, crossing the 101 Freeway on the northern fringe of the Santa Monica Mountains. When completed, the Liberty Canyon crossing would be a California landmark and a milestone in American conservation, benefiting deer, coyotes, bobcats, black bears, and of course pumas. As of 2018, local groups had purchased the necessary land adjacent to the freeway, but they had raised just $3.7 million of the project's estimated $60 million price tag. They are now in a race against time. The longer the Santa Monica Mountains' pumas remain isolated, the more likely it is they will disappear.[15]

. . . . .

Animals like P-22 sometimes end up in cities because they are seeking safety and mates, but most of the time they do so because they're hungry. To understand what drives wild animals to move through or into cities and what determines where they go once there, we need to combine our knowledge of urban geography with an understanding of urban food webs.

A food web is network of organisms that exchange energy and nutrients. Most food webs are dizzyingly complex, but one way to picture them is to imagine a pyramid made up of stacked layers called trophic levels. At the bottom are the producers, including green plants and algae, which use energy from the sun to convert inorganic material into the organic matter that fuels the system. Primary consumers, like herbivorous white-tailed deer, eat these producers. Secondary consumers, which include omnivores from gray squirrels to black bears, eat both producers and primary consumers. At the top of the heap are the tertiary consumers, some of which, like pumas, eat a strictly carnivorous diet of primary and secondary consumers. And, of course, there are myriad variations, exceptions, and additions, from rare carnivorous plants to the ubiquitous decomposers that will eventually devour us all. Because some energy is lost at each level of the pyramid, in most ecosystems there is enough available at the top to sustain only a few apex predators like P-22.

When people provide a wild animal with a resource that would not otherwise be available in its ecosystem, ecologists call this a subsidy. One of the qualities that makes urban food webs so unusual is that subsidies seem to be everywhere. Sometimes, for instance, people intentionally provide food for wildlife. One of the most common ways is through bird feeders. This may seem like a harmless hobby, but the numbers are astonishing and the effects, though only partly understood, are growing. In the United States, eighty-two million people feed wild birds at least once each year, and around fifty-two million do so frequently. Americans purchase more than 50,000 tons of birdseed and $750 million in related gear annually, supporting a $3.5 billion industry.[16]

Bird feeding appeals to diverse people. Studies show that those who regularly feed birds tend to be older than the average age for their communities. Some do it because they enjoy seeing birds, but others think of bird feeding as a kind of atonement, making up for other human impacts on the natural world. Well-respected groups, including the National Audubon Society and the Cornell Laboratory of Ornithology, endorse feeding as a way to help individual birds, conserve species, and educate people. Yet even advocates admit that this grand experiment in crowdsourced wildlife management comes with risks in addition to benefits.[17]

Supplementary feeding does not seem to increase the diversity of birds in an area, but it can increase their total number, by raising the carrying capacity of the urban ecosystem, attracting birds from other areas, allowing birds to live outside their normal ranges, and enabling them to lay more eggs earlier in the spring. Feeding favors larger, more aggressive, less picky birds. But it can also help other birds make it through tough times, such as cold snaps or droughts, when they might otherwise perish. There is little evidence that any native species as a whole has come to depend on bird feeders, but some individual birds may. This can help these animals for a time, but it can harm them if the person who owns the feeder fails to fill it.[18]

Bird feeding comes with other hazards. If placed near windows, feeders may increase the likelihood of collisions. When animals congregate at feeders, their risk of transmitting diseases, like salmonella, grows. Commercial birdseeds have improved in quality, but questions remain about their health effects. Bird feeders also attract uninvited guests. Rats, squirrels, and even black bears are as attracted as birds to feeders. And predators, like hawks and raccoons, may be more interested in eating birds than in eating birdseed.

A bird feeder is an obvious example of a subsidy, but in cities it is often impossible to draw a line between what counts as a subsidy coming in from the outside versus a resource produced by the urban ecosystem itself. Are fruit trees in people's yards resources or subsidies? Roadside ditches filled with irrigation water subsidize thirsty animals, but they are also weird wetlands that attract elegant wading birds, like great blue herons and snowy egrets. Are earthworms, which robins pluck by the thousands from manicured lawns, subsidies? Nobody intended to subsidize P-22 with a koala, but we know what happened there. The point here is that some of the resources that ecologists call subsidies are probably better thought of as basic features of urban ecosystems. And yet in the United States, one subsidy—food waste—exists in a class by itself.[19]

When most people think of urban wildlife, food-waste scavenging—by crows, gulls, raccoons, or the "pizza rat" that briefly gained internet stardom in 2015 after being filmed dragging an extra-large slice of thin-crust pie down a flight of New York subway stairs—is probably the first image that comes to mind. This is not a pleasant thought. To most people, the idea of wild animals rummaging through our waste seems just plain gross. Urbanites have probably become more sensitive to this over the past century as cities have become cleaner, with fewer foraging animals. But this revulsion is at least partly natural, since humans seem biologically predisposed to feel sickened at the sight or smell of unsanitary conditions. It's not fair to criticize animals for taking advantage of a situation we created, but seeing them consuming our waste does something that nobody likes: it reminds us of our own filth.

This sense of revulsion is both actual and metaphorical. In her classic 1984 book *Purity and Danger*, the anthropologist Mary Douglas wrote that societies seek to achieve order by classifying things into neat categories. When we encounter facts, objects, or beings that don't fit, we feel discomfort or disgust. We may deny the existence of these rule-breaking things, punish them, force them to comply, or even try to eliminate them. When people use words like *pollution* and *dirt*—Douglas could have added *pest* to her list—what we really mean is "matter out of place."

This isn't how many wild animals see it. To them, our waste is just food, and just where it should be. A heaping portion of our leftovers leaks into urban ecosystems, and from there into the bellies of urban wildlife. Seagulls, which are among the world's most famous dumpster divers, often travel long distances from their nests to landfills on the outskirts of cities. They choke down as much food as they can while still being able to fly, and then return home, where they regurgitate their bounty, feeding it to their chicks as a nutritious paste. Some gulls nesting on the Channel Islands commute up to twenty miles each way to mainland dumps, suggesting that the effort required to make this trip is worth the energy it requires. This all may seem a little unsavory, but focus on the parenting piece instead of the gross factor. The gulls' approach is not all that different from that of the bald eagles bringing dinner back to their nest on the Monongahela River, or even the epic journey celebrated in the 2005 hit film *March of the Penguins*. Just substitute tacos and Pop Tarts for kittens and squid.

Some city-dwelling animals make scavenging for discarded human food seem almost natural. Raccoons get a bad rap, but there is a lot to admire about them. They are intelligent, flexible, and hardy: they have been known to survive in the wild long after losing a limb or even going blind! Raccoons are devoted parents and fastidious groomers that work together to achieve common goals. They are superb climbers and are deft at manipulating artificial objects like knobs, latches, locks, and zippers. Raccoons' ability to scavenge food waste gives them a huge advantage over other animals. Urban raccoons have more offspring, grow fatter, and often live longer than their rural cousins. In northern temperate regions, like the American Midwest and Northeast, rural raccoons may lose as much as 50 percent of their body mass during the winter, compared with just 10 to 25 percent for raccoons in nearby urban areas. For a raccoon, these few extra pounds can be the difference between life and death.[20]

Looking at urban wildlife from the perspective of food, it becomes clear why some species can live in cities while others cannot. Picky specialists that have trouble moving from place to place tend to do poorly, whereas opportunistic omnivores that can get around easily tend to do well. Many of these opportunists are urban adapters, and a few even qualify as urban exploiters.[21]

If we want to reduce the populations of some of these uber-successful urban creatures, an obvious solution is to reduce food waste. Often called the world's dumbest problem, food waste has many causes, from increases in portion sizes and calorie densities of foods to bigger shopping carts, dinner plates, and refrigerators to grocery store marketing and pricing schemes, misleading sell-by labels, and absurd beauty standards for fresh produce. But these are all symptoms of a larger disease. Deeper economic and political forces—cheap oil, agricultural subsidies, immigration policies, low farm-labor wages, industrial food-processing systems, and the political power of multinational agribusiness firms—drive our bloated food system.

A 2012 report by the Natural Resources Defense Council found that Americans waste about 40 percent of their food. Of the thirty-nine million tons of food waste produced in the United States in 2015, 94.7 percent went to dumps or incinerators. Food waste makes up 21 percent of US landfill content. If food waste were a country, it would have the world's third-highest greenhouse gas emissions, after China and the United States. These emissions come from both the energy required to grow the food and the methane it produces while rotting. Americans' food waste has risen by 50 percent since 1990, even as more than forty million, or around one in eight, of us suffer from food insecurity. The amount of food wasted in the United States alone could feed all of the world's hungry people. Instead, we are gobbling up vast quantities of precious land, soil, and water to grow garbage.[22]

Just because human foods are available does not mean that all wild animals will eat them. Scavenging has clear rewards, but it does not necessarily make life easier or safer. It can expose animals to dangers such as diseases, poisoning, toxic chemicals, vengeful humans, aggressive competitors, and predators that use discarded human food as bait.[23]

Some successful urban species, like coyotes, avoid eating human food waste but still benefit from it. Coyotes are more hunters and foragers than scavengers, and many will stick to this strategy even in the most urban environments imaginable. Coyotes living in the hearts of cities like Chicago and Denver subsist on diets of live prey and plants. They don't draw much directly from the waste stream, but they indirectly profit from it because food waste supports some of their favorite prey species.[24]

After food subsidies, the second-most-unusual characteristic of urban food webs is their outlandish abundance of predators. Cities contain way more raccoons, foxes, coyotes, and other toothy little beasts than most other kinds of habitats. With so many of these creatures afoot, one would think that there would be a lot of killing going on. And yet, surprisingly few animals end up as prey in cities. Known as the predator paradox, this explains why tasty morsels like pigeons often seem so nonchalant in cities despite being surrounded by so many potential pigeon killers. Part of the answer to this riddle is that some would-be predators in cities shift from hunting to scavenging, but there's more to the story.[25]

One of the most famous studies of urban predators was conducted in the 1980s, just as biologists were beginning to show interest in urban ecosystems. Between 1860 and 1980, San Diego's human population grew a thousandfold, from fewer than eight hundred to more than eight hundred thousand. Sprawling across a coastal landscape of flat-topped mesas cut by steep-sided ravines, San Diego developed an unusual urban geography of distinct neighborhoods separated by thin green ribbons. As the city sprawled and property values ballooned, developers turned their attention to its urban canyons.

Concerned about the plight of the city's native birds, Michael Soulé and his colleagues from the University of California, San Diego, launched a groundbreaking study. Most large carnivores, like pumas, had disappeared from these canyons decades earlier. In their place, midsize carnivores—including a familiar cast of foxes, raccoons, possums, skunks, coyotes, and house cats—had taken over. But these creatures had different effects on their prey. Good climbers, like raccoons, house cats, and possums, hunted native birds and stole their eggs. Coyotes killed or outcompeted these smaller mammals, but they were poor climbers and thus rarely preyed on birds or eggs. It soon became clear that in canyons where coyotes remained, there were fewer climbing predators, which gave the birds that nested in these patches a fighting chance.[26]

Soulé was a Zen Buddhist and cat lover, but he expressed contempt for free-roaming house cats and their careless owners. "Cats are usually 'subsidized' predators," he and his colleagues wrote, and killing birds "is a leisure time activity for many of them. Consequently, there is virtually no limit to the number of cats that can occur in an urban canyon. Domestic cats can continue to take wildlife in a canyon long after the density of prey is too low to sustain a native predator that must rely on wildlife for most of its food." In the years since this study, its results have been widely debated, with some researchers cautioning that we should not draw too many general conclusions from them. And yet, many ecologists, including those working in cities, still agree with Soulé's central point. Having even a few big, fearsome predators around can benefit an entire ecosystem.[27]

·   ·   ·   ·   ·

On April 16, 2020, with the world on pandemic lockdown, Southern California's pumas once again made news, with two bombshell stories published just hours apart.

That afternoon, the CBS News affiliate in San Diego reported that the city's world-famous Zoo Safari Park, known for its open-range paddocks, had lost two gazelles to a puma. Like Killarney's death, the episode was shocking, but the refrain was familiar. "We respect the mountain lions, they deserve to be here . . . but we also need to protect our wildlife," said the mammal curator Steve Metzler. "This is a fairly new occurrence for us because typically the mountain lions would stay in peripheral areas," he added, "but they've been coming closer."[28]

Later that evening, the *Los Angeles Times* reported that the California Fish and Game Commission had voted unanimously to issue temporary state-level endangered status to six puma populations spanning from San Diego to San Francisco, including those in the Santa Monica Mountains. The state's Department of Fish and Wildlife would have one year to submit a report to the commission recommending longer-term status and conservation measures.[29]

The commission based its decision in part on a study that showed puma populations in Southern and central California declining in genetic diversity. Unlike some other large cats, like cheetahs, which seem to remain relatively healthy despite their populations having little genetic variation, pumas are susceptible to diseases and deformities when inbreeding occurs in small isolated populations. Florida panthers almost succumbed to such ailments before biologists revived their population by introducing healthier cats from Texas. The study cited by the commission found that Southern and central California's pumas were on the brink of a similar extinction vortex. Pumas in the Santa Monica Mountains were in an especially dire predicament, with a 99.7 percent probability of disappearing in the next fifty years. What these cats really needed to refresh their gene pool was a safe way to get into and out of the mountains.[30]

Seen from this perspective, P-22's saga takes on a new meaning. The lion of Los Angeles is a survivor, but his story is also a warning. Cities are fertile ground for creatures that find ways to navigate their hazards while harvesting their resources. Yet for the largest and most wide-ranging animals—apex predators, such as pumas, which are among the most important members in any ecosystem— fragmented cityscapes that lack safe habitats connected by corridors are little more than dead ends.

10 Creature Discomforts

There are hundreds of places to enjoy a balmy summer evening in Austin, Texas. But one of the city's biggest attractions, drawing more than one hundred thousand visitors annually, is not some rowdy bar, glittering theater, or A-list restaurant. It is the concrete underbelly of the Ann W. Richards Congress Avenue Bridge. Every night, spectators line up along the bridge's sidewalk, set up lawn chairs on a grassy hill nearby, sit in rented kayaks, and board tour boats on Lady Bird Lake on which they can sip drinks and watch the twilight spectacle.

In 1980, Austin rebuilt the old Congress Avenue Bridge, a main north-south thoroughfare about ten blocks from the state capitol, replacing it with a six-lane arched structure. This new bridge includes a series of concrete beams that rest atop the arches and support the roadway. Between these beams, the architects left narrow gaps, sixteen inches deep but just one inch wide, enabling the structure to sway, flex, and expand. These warm, dark, and protected crevices turned out to be ideal roosts for Mexican free-tailed bats.

The bats had long lived in the Austin area, part of a population that summers in Texas and other nearby states but winters mostly south of the border. Between 1937 and 1970, Texas built a series of dams and reservoirs, creating Lady Bird Lake and flooding dozens of natural caves. Bats soon showed up in buildings like the University of Texas's football stadium, where they nestled themselves into gaps on the underside of a deck. Officials responded by sealing the cracks and killing thousands of bats with cyanide.

The new Congress Avenue Bridge, according to one city public health officer, "could not have been designed better as a bat cave." Within a few years of its completion, the number of bats that used it ballooned, eventually reaching 1.5 million annually. Some frightened locals, alarmed by the shadowy swarms that flowed out in great waves from under the bridge each summer evening, called for the bats to be eradicated. Others proposed draping the bottom of the bridge with nets to seal off the crevices. Newspapers from as far away as Chicago warned that Austin was besieged by a plague.[1]

All of this fuss may seem silly today, with Austin now hosting a cheerful bat-themed festival each August, but it reflected a larger truth: Americans were not exactly wild about bats. In Stephen Kellert's 1984 national survey ranking the popularity of thirty-three common animals, bats ranked twenty-eighth, behind even coyotes and ahead of only rattlesnakes, wasps, rats, mosquitoes, and cock-roaches. Some people thought bats—long associated with darkness, devilry, and witchcraft—were too creepy to be trusted. Others believed that, like Bram Stocker's Dracula, bats feasted on blood. (For the record, of the world's 1,100 bat species, only 3 drink blood, but none of them regularly prey on humans or live in the United States.) Mostly, however, Austinites and others worried that bats carried diseases.[2]

Bats are the most unusual of the world's twenty-six mammal orders. They are also among the most paradoxical. Bats are as close to cold blooded as warm-blooded animals get. Many are small and have fast metabolisms, but they reproduce slowly and live long lives. They are the only land mammals that navigate by echolocation and the only mammals capable of true flight. And although bats carry dozens of diseases, most stay healthy in the wild. At least until recently.[3]

Bats evolved early in the Age of Mammals. The oldest bat fossils date to around fifty-two million years ago, during a time of global warming known as the Paleocene-Eocene Thermal Maximum, when several mammal groups, including the primates, diversified into new forms. Today, bats are both the second-most-diverse and the second-most-widespread order of mammals, after rodents. They account for more than 20 percent of the world's mammal species and inhabit every continent except Antarctica. Thanks to their ability to fly, on many remote islands bats are the only native mammals.

Bats vary immensely in appearance and play vital ecological and economic roles. The tiniest microbats top out at less than two inches long, around the size of a large bumblebee, and weigh only about as much as a dime, whereas the largest "flying foxes" have six-foot wingspans. Some bats stalk small vertebrate animals, but most eat fruits or insects. Around five hundred plant species—including mangoes, bananas, guavas, and agaves, which are used to make tequila—rely on bat pollinators. Insectivores like little brown bats may consume the equivalent of their body weight in bugs each night, including thousands of disease-carrying mosquitoes and agricultural pests. Bat droppings sustain entire cave ecosystems and have been harvested for centuries for use as fertilizer and in other industrial and commercial products.

To understand a bat's life—as well as its role in disease ecology—a good place to start is with its core body temperature. Warm-blooded animals internally regulate their body temperature. Some stretch this definition by allowing their temperature to fall during hibernation, but most maintain a stable internal climate. Healthy humans, for example, have core body temperatures that vary by just three degrees, from 97°F to 100°F (36°C to 38°C).

Bats challenge this definition of warm-bloodedness. When awake but at rest, most maintain a moderate body temperature. Doing so requires calories, and in temperate climates like that of Austin, bat foods tend to become available in seasonal cycles. To cope with these annual booms and busts, most bats, including 97 percent of smaller species, undergo extended periods of inactivity. While they are in this state, known as torpor, their temperature may drop to as low as 43°F (6°C). When the fruits ripen and insects hatch, bats wake up and flutter out into the world to forage. But now they encounter the opposite problem. Flying consumes a lot of energy and produces a lot of heat. While a bat is in flight, its metabolic rate can spike to as much as thirty-four times the resting level, and its core body temperature may exceed 104°F (40°C).[4]

Bats temper these extremes in several ways. Their wings are filled with blood vessels, which can cool them down by radiating heat into the surrounding air or warm them up by acting like solar panels. Bats also thermoregulate by using their wings as blankets, huddling together to share warmth, licking their fur to simulate sweat, and panting like dogs. They gather in cozy spaces like caves that maintain relatively constant temperatures. They forage by night to avoid overheating. And some migrate seasonally to harvest food in mild weather.

These qualities that have made bats so successful have also made them well suited to sharing diseases. Because fruit bats can't consume heavy meals and still fly, they suck the nutrients from their foods and leave the fleshy parts behind, often seasoned with germs. Bats also pass on germs to other bats by gathering in colonies, lathering themselves in spit, and breathing heavily on their neighbors whenever the mercury rises. Because they get around so much, bats can easily carry their diseases to other creatures in new areas.

So how do bats survive in the petri dishes they create? The best current theory is the "flight as fever" hypothesis. When bats fly, their core temperature rises so high as to simulate fevers, roasting the germs in their bodies and boosting their immune systems. This amazing adaptation has a downside. The rapid heart rates that bats experience while flying and the inflammation triggered by these "flight fevers" cause oxidation that can damage cells. But bats have a secret weapon. They have evolved a set of complex physiological processes that reduce inflammation, minimize oxidation, repair compromised cells, and enable them to avoid the stress that these fevers would cause in most other creatures. The result is that, on average, bats live three and a half times longer than other mammals of similar size—with individuals from some species enduring in the wild for more than forty years.[5]

But just because bats survive doesn't mean their pathogens go away. Quite the opposite. Some bats harbor multiple disease-causing germs without showing any symptoms. Because they live so long, they have many chances to infect other bats. And because they defend themselves so well, their bodies select for superbugs that can devastate other animals unlucky enough to become infected.

It should be no surprise, then, that bats carry several nasty viruses. Viruses are tiny packets of genetic information wrapped in blankets of protein. They are living organisms in the sense that they pass on hereditary information. But because they lack the ability to perform basic biological functions, like metabolizing food to produce energy (they rely on their hosts to do this), many biologists consider them only partly alive. Viruses are the zombies of the microscopic world.

Viruses come in three forms—DNA, RNA, and RNA-RT—each with its own composition, structure, and method of replication. Bats are especially prone to RNA viruses, which have simple genomes but among the highest mutation rates in nature. This shape-shifting quality enables RNA viruses to outmaneuver immune systems in all but the strongest hosts. It also enables them to leap to new hosts, making some RNA viruses both unusually contagious and especially virulent. With the ability to travel so easily from host to host, they are freed from the inconvenience of having to keep their habitats alive.

Epidemiologists have associated bats with diseases since 1911, when healthy-looking vampire bats were first diagnosed with a form of walking rabies. Researchers later showed that rabies, which is a lethal disease in most other mammals, was caused by an RNA virus. Since then, scientists have studied bats carrying around two hundred mostly RNA viruses. These include some truly dreadful bugs, like Hendra, Nipah, Marburg, various forms of hepatitis, and probably Ebola, as well as several that cause respiratory diseases, like influenza, Middle East respiratory syndrome (MERS), severe acute respiratory syndrome (SARS), and of course SARS-CoV-2, the infamous source of COVID-19.[6]

This is pretty scary stuff. But does it mean that bats are dangerous? Were those terrified Austinites, back in the 1980s, right to be creeped out and concerned? The answer to these questions is a little bit of yes and whole lot of no.

Of the world's 1,100 or so bat species, only around 108, or 9.8 percent, share diseases with people. On average, these 108 carry a greater number of human diseases per species than do members of other mammalian orders, and the diseases they carry tend to be pretty awful. But this is only part of the story. Of the approximately 1,415 pathogens known to afflict humans, fewer than 2 percent have bats as hosts. Around 59 percent have other nonhuman animal hosts. The final 39 percent did not come from animals or are unique to our species.[7]

Among mammals, the rodents include the greatest number of species that share diseases with humans. Of the 2,220 rodent species, about 10.7 percent host diseases that afflict people. This may seem like a lot, but three other orders of mammals that are less diverse have higher proportions of human-disease-carrying species. Around 20 percent of the world's 365 primate species, 32 percent of its 247 ungulate species, and a whopping 49 percent of its 285 carnivore species carry human diseases.[8]

Another reason not to worry too much about bats is that they don't often transmit their diseases directly to people. They are rarely aggressive, and unprovoked bites are uncommon. Bats can sometimes transmit diseases indirectly, by passing them on to other animals that then pass them on to us. They may also give diseases to people who eat from the same fruit trees, hunt bats for food, collect their guano, or raise crops or livestock in close proximity to their colonies. We increase these risks when we bring them into more frequent contact with us by destroying their habitats or building structures that attract them into ours.

Despite their ability to infect us with diseases, bats help people far more than they hurt us. They consume billions of insects annually, including mosquitoes that carry human diseases like malaria, dengue, and Zika. They can serve as early warning systems, altering us to the presence of emerging pathogens. And current research, made more urgent by the COVID-19 pandemic, aims to gain a better understanding of how bat immune systems function, with potential applications for human health. This includes work on a "signaling protein" molecule known as interferon alpha, which enables nearby cells to respond to viral infections, and on how bats avoid cell damage despite consuming so much oxygen during flight.

Bats are amazing creatures, but they are increasingly in trouble. According to the International Union for the Conservation of Nature, at least 24 bat species are "critically endangered" and 104 are "vulnerable" to extinction. There are at least 224 additional bat species for which we lack the data to know their status. Overharvesting, persecution, and especially habitat loss are the greatest threats facing bats.[9]

Like humans, bats also suffer from their own novel diseases. Since it was first documented in upstate New York in 2007, the fungal pathogen *Pseudogymnoascus destructans* (*Pd*), which causes white-nose syndrome, has infected thirteen North American bat species, including two listed as endangered. Nobody knows where *Pd* came from, but several bat species seem never to have encountered it before—suggesting that people introduced it. This fungus thrives in cool, damp places like caves. It grows on bats while they're hibernating, causing such irritation that they become restless, wasting precious energy during seasons when little food is available. White nose has killed millions of bats, including more than 90 percent of the individuals in some populations.[10]

.   .   .   .   .

A disease that circulates between humans and animals is called a zoonotic disease or zoonosis. Most often, this term describes a disease caused by a pathogen that is carried in animals and can be passed on to humans. Of the 868 known zoonotic diseases in humans, 19 percent are caused by viruses or prions (twisted proteins), 31 percent by bacteria, 13 percent by fungi, 5 percent by protozoa, and 32 percent by wormlike parasites. Of these 868, around two-thirds can pass indirectly from animal to human, whereas about one-third require direct contact. Approximately one-quarter of these diseases use a third species as a stepping stone to travel between an animal host and a person. Around one in twenty has a transmission pathway that is not yet understood.[11]

Most of the diseases that afflict people, including those that kill the greatest number of us, like heart disease and cancer, don't pass between us and other animals. Even among the world's infectious diseases, most of the worst are not zoonotic. Yet zoonotic diseases get a disproportionate amount of attention. This may be because they include a whole host of "emerging diseases," which are either new in humans or pose increasing threats to us, and about which we often know very little. Of the world's 175 or so emerging diseases, we share 132, or 75 percent, with other animals. Zoonotic diseases are twice as likely as nonzoonotic diseases to be "emerging." Because zoonotic diseases may lurk in complex ecosystems and diverse animal hosts, they are nearly impossible to eradicate.[12]

To understand how these diseases circulate, we need to define a few terms. We also have to change how we picture disease itself. When most of us think about diseases, we probably imagine individual people suffering from faceless maladies. In fact, infectious diseases are ecological relationships involving two or more organisms, each of which plays an essential role.

Pathogens and their *hosts* often evolve together, forming relationships that benefit the pathogens by providing them with habitats while leaving the hosts unaffected or able to recover. But not all hosts are equal. Some are dead ends, unable to transmit the disease any further. Others can contract and transmit pathogens but, for some biochemical or behavioral reason, only inefficiently. On the opposite end of the spectrum are hosts that act as amplifiers, contracting pathogens and then concentrating them in great numbers. For an organism to serve as a competent host, it must be able to acquire the pathogen easily, withstand the pathogen in its body, and pass the pathogen on to a third party.

Vectors transmit pathogens to other organisms. These may be nonliving objects, like dust, but often they are small living organisms such as microbes or arthropods. Mosquitoes, fleas, and ticks are among the best-known disease vectors. Pathogens often have multiple hosts and vectors, and there is no clear line separating the two. Some hosts can act as vectors some of the time, and some vectors transmit diseases only under special conditions or during certain phases in their life cycle.

Modern medicine focuses on individual organisms, but populations, communities, and ecosystems are crucial in determining how diseases circulate. The *densities* of host and vector populations are key, because their members must live close enough together for germs to pass from one creature to the next. The *diversity* of an ecosystem is vital, because in communities with different kinds of hosts, germs tend to circulate less efficiently, a phenomenon known as the dilution effect. Finally, the *stability* of an ecosystem is critical, because disturbances often stir up germs, making transmission more likely. Because the mathematics of disease ecology are often nonlinear, small changes in any of these variables can make big differences.[13]

It is not surprising that, given the complexity of disease ecology, it can be difficult to understand. Perhaps the most famous case of such a misunderstanding involves Lyme disease. First diagnosed in Connecticut in 1975, Lyme is a bacterial infection that can cause symptoms from rashes and joint pain to heart palpitations, headaches, exhaustion, and damage to the nervous system or cardiac tissue. In rare cases, complications of the infection can be fatal. Humans can acquire Lyme when bitten by a black-legged tick infected by bacteria in the genus *Borrelia*. The Centers for Disease Control and Prevention receives around thirty thousand reports of new Lyme cases annually, but the true number could be ten times higher. In New England, where Lyme is most common, residents confront a dilemma: contracting the disease can make one sick, but trying to avoid it by staying inside lowers one's quality of life.

For years, many experts believed that white-tailed deer were Lyme's main reservoir. Since more deer meant more Lyme, cities and states set out to cull their deer herds. In 2011, however, Rick Ostfeld, of the Cary Institute of Ecosystem Studies, published *Lyme Disease: The Ecology of a Complex System*, summarizing more than two decades of research. He found that even in deer-rich areas, 90 percent of Lyme-positive ticks had taken their infected blood from mice, chipmunks, or shrews. The math, based on extensive fieldwork and modeling, showed that once a few deer were present in an area, adding more didn't worsen the problem and culling them wouldn't fix it. Ostfeld concluded that although deer played a role, theirs was only a bit part in the Lyme saga.

There are more layers to this story. In the nineteenth and twentieth centuries, many forests in New England regrew as farmers abandoned the region in favor of greener pastures in the Midwest and along the West Coast, but in the twenty-first century, developers have once again carved them up, this time to make way for suburbs. Even in this region's most forested areas, woodlots are often small and isolated, and they lack many of their native animal species, including large predators driven out centuries ago like pumas, wolves, and lynx. Deer, small rodents, and shrews that host Lyme disease are often the only mammals around, and they have the run of the place. It is this lack of predation, competition, and diversity that enables black-legged ticks, and by extension Lyme disease, to thrive. In New England, where suburbs continue to reach farther into the countryside, the best way to protect people from Lyme may be to protect ecosystems from people.[14]

·   ·   ·   ·   ·

Cities have long been associated with pestilence. Before people settled in cities, infectious diseases were not very common in our species. Our populations were too small, too thinly distributed, and too disconnected for many pathogens to evolve with us and circulate widely. And although we humans have been modifying our habitats for tens of thousands of years, throughout almost all of our species's history we did not do so on a scale that altered the basic equations of disease ecology.

This changed as people began to gather in cities and travel between them. The most infamous of the ancient and medieval diseases that swept through Europe and Asia was the bubonic plague. Caused by a bacterium in the genus *Yersinia*, the plague infects rat hosts and uses fleas as vectors. Some rat populations are immune to the plague, but others are not. When immune rats entered a new area, as stowaways on ships or in caravans, their fleas spread to non-immune populations, infecting local rats and eventually people.

There are still many mysteries surrounding ancient epidemics, such as the one that may have swept through the Roman Empire around 165 C.E. and another that ravaged the Mediterranean beginning in 541. For years, scholars debated whether bubonic plague caused the Black Death, which crested in Europe from 1347 to 1351, killing 30 to 60 percent of the continent's human population. In 2010, researchers examined DNA from skeletons buried in fourteenth-century mass graves scattered across Europe. Finding two forms of *Yersinia,* they concluded that the plague was indeed responsible for these deaths, likely arriving in at least two waves, each with its own novel strain of this devastating disease.[15]

Epidemics have also shaped American history. During the nineteenth century, outbreaks of malaria, yellow fever, rabies, cholera, and other diseases pushed officials throughout the United States to take aggressive measures, including installing sewer lines, collecting garbage, banning livestock, imposing leash laws, and building public parks. Replacing horses—which share more than two hundred diseases with people and dropped massive quantities of dung in the streets, boosting the populations of houseflies and other potential vectors—with electric railways and later automobiles also helped.

American cities are still hospitable places for zoonotic pathogens. Our cities lack the species diversity in many taxonomic groups, including the apex predators that once controlled populations of disease-carrying smaller animals, that has been shown to slow disease transmission. Cities disturb green spaces on their outskirts, keeping germs circulating at high rates. They concentrate resources in small areas, enticing large numbers of animals from the same species to gather in close quarters. Their relatively mild climates, standing water, and food waste can serve as breeding grounds for vectors and thus diseases. Their environmental stressors, such as air and water pollution, reduce immunity among humans and nonhumans alike. When a pathogen does jump to people, cities' high population densities mean the resulting disease can spread more quickly and more widely.[16]

Despite centuries of efforts to protect city dwellers from infectious diseases, the scientific study of urban zoonoses is still a young field. As cities are attracting increasing numbers of wild animals, however, new research is getting under way and more species are receiving attention. Raccoons, skunks, foxes, and squirrels are known to carry parvovirus, roundworms, tapeworms, and the pathogens that cause rabies, distemper, and leptospirosis. Deer host chronic wasting disease, while robins and house finches may serve as amplifiers for West Nile virus.[17]

When the COVID-19 pandemic arrived in 2020, the world briefly turned its attention to the disease risks posed by wildlife like bats, but domesticated animals may pose a greater long-term threat. Among common pets, cats are the biggest concern. Cats carry salmonella, *Pasteurella multocida,* which can cause blood infections in humans, and *Bartonella henselae,* the source of cat scratch disease. They also carry parasites and fungal infections including fleas, scabies, roundworm, hookworm, and ringworm. And they can transmit protozoa like Cryptosporidium, Giardia, and *Toxoplasma gondii,* which reproduces only in cats, is spread through their feces, and causes the disease toxoplasmosis. Hundreds of mammal species have tested positive for toxoplasmosis, and around one-third of all humans are believed to have been infected. It is usually benign in people, but it can produce severe symptoms in pregnant women, and some studies have connected it with neurological and mental health disorders. In mice, it has the diabolical effect of reducing their fear of predators, which leaves them more exposed to cats. Toxoplasmosis has also caused potentially fatal brain infections in Pacific sea otters off the California coast.[18]

One could not have created a better system for cooking up zoonotic diseases than industrial animal agriculture, which packs large numbers of animals, of only a few species, with low genetic diversity, together into dense groups. Industrial livestock operations manage the resulting risks by monitoring their herds, reducing the number of human workers required, and pumping their animals full of antibiotics. Still, studies have shown that industrial livestock workers carry more diseases than nonworkers, and these facilities have been ground zeroes for several disease outbreaks.[19]

Overall, zoonotic diseases endanger wildlife more than us. Because wild animals live outside—getting their food, water, and air from unfiltered sources—they are more exposed than most people to environmental threats. Pollution is the third-greatest cause of endangerment among wildlife species in the United States. When exotic species arrive, they often bring new diseases with them, and such interlopers may disrupt ecosystems or stress native species, which thus become more susceptible to disease. Some species are particularly vulnerable. Social animals like foxes and raccoons can live in dense populations in cities, but doing so exposes them to contagious diseases. Predators like bobcats, which hunt small mammals, are often poisoned by rodenticides intended to kill mice, rats, and gophers. Creatures like bats, which have adapted to carrying outsize disease loads, may be susceptible to new pathogens that can infect them through the same pathways as the old germs but against which these animals have few defenses. Living in cities may also increase wild animals' risk of noninfectious ailments, including heart disease and even cancer, that are associated with stress, inactivity, or poor diet.[20]

And then there is climate change. As humans alter the climate, ticks, mosquitoes, and some types of parasitic fungi multiply in areas where cold winters once kept them out or under control. Climate change also threatens traditional food sources, forcing animals to wander more widely, contracting and spreading germs along the way, and causing stress that lowers their immunity.

In the wake of the COVID-19 pandemic, many people around the world, like the residents of Austin in the 1980s, probably feel under siege from a planet full of disease-ridden animals. The truth is more complicated, but the message remains simple. Zoonotic diseases are bad news for both people and wildlife. In destroying and simplifying natural ecosystems, we are amplifying the risks that all of us face. The best way to prevent the next COVID-19-style pandemic is to treat animals, both wild and domestic, better.

·　　·　　·　　·　　·

In a famous 1974 essay, the philosopher Thomas Nagel argued that humans will never be able to fully perceive reality, because our senses give us only partial access to it. He called this "the subjective character of experience." To illustrate his argument, Nagel asked his readers to imagine what it is like to be a bat, grasping the world in part through echolocation, a type of perception profoundly different from human senses. "Bats," Nagel wrote, "present a range of activity and a sensory apparatus so different from ours" that they can be said to experience a foreign reality. "Even without the benefit of philosophical reflection," he concluded, "anyone who has spent some time in an enclosed space with an excited bat knows what it is to encounter a fundamentally alien form of life."[21]

Nagel's point is probably obvious to the cheering tourists who gather each summer to watch Austin's bats emerge en masse from their roosts under the Congress Avenue Bridge. Witnessing such a marvel can expand our minds and cultivate our compassion by reminding us that different beings experience the world very differently. Human perception is not objective reality; it is just what humans evolved to see, smell, touch, taste, and feel so that we might survive. Nagel's point is also relevant in another way. If, as many virologists and immunologists believe, studying bats can help us better understand our own bodies, leading to treatments that benefit human health and perhaps even help prevent the next pandemic, then science may allow bats and people to become just a little more alike. Humans may—at long last and to our great benefit—get a bit more of a sense of the bizarre, alien, magical experience of what it must be like to be a bat.

11 Catch and Release

To meet Ron Magill is to meet Miami personified. At six feet six inches tall, with a mane of graying, slicked-back hair, a crescent-shaped moustache, a gold chain, and a vanity license plate reading "ZOO GUY" bolted to the rear end of his Cadillac Escalade, Magill cuts a flamboyant figure. The son of a Cuban-immigrant father, he moved from Queens to Miami at the age of twelve and started working at the Miami MetroZoo (now called Zoo Miami) when it opened eight years later. His ascent to B-list stardom began in the 1980s, when he served as an alligator handler on *Miami Vice*. Since then, he has won five Emmys for his work on nature documentaries, received the Nikon Ambassador award for his wildlife photographs, hosted a Spanish-language television program, and appeared as a regular guest for twenty-five years on Univision's smash hit variety show *Sábado Gigante*. Magill met his wife, a physical therapist, while being treated for a crocodile bite.

Magill, who now serves as the zoo's director of communications and goodwill ambassador, is an unforgettable character. But *his* most memorable moment, the one that helped vault him to fame, occurred on a sultry summer morning in 1992. It was a day that illustrates, probably more than any other in recent history, the continuing role of exotic animals in urban ecosystems like that of Miami. It also shows that the categories we use to divide up groups of animals, such as "captive" and "wild," are fluid, flexible, and far from permanent.

Shortly before dawn on August 24, Hurricane Andrew made landfall twenty-five miles south of Miami. Andrew had begun as an ordinary tropical depression off the coast of west Africa, but as it passed over the Gulf Stream's warm waters, it metastasized into a coiled monster. It raked the Bahamas on August 23, then barreled onto the US mainland hours later as a category 5 storm with 175-mile-per-hour winds. With an estimated $27.3 billion in property losses, South Florida took the brunt of what was, at that time, the costliest disaster in American history. Among the hardest-hit places was the suburb of Kendall, home to the Miami MetroZoo.

The day before the storm, Magill noticed something strange. On normal days, dozens of wild native birds—herons, egrets, spoonbills, ibises, and others—flocked to the zoo, wading in its pools and feeding in its exhibits alongside exotic captive species. On the morning of August 23, the wild ones abruptly disappeared.[1]

Zoo staff followed detailed procedures to prepare for the storm, and then hurried to their homes to wait it out. After a harrowing eighteen hours, Andrew moved on toward Louisiana, and Magill set out for the zoo to assist in the recovery. It was an awful and disorienting scene. Debris covered the streets, landmarks had vanished, and a drive that usually took ten minutes lasted more than an hour. "It was like God had come through with a twenty-five-mile-wide weed whacker," he later recalled.[2]

On Coral Reef Drive, Magill had the first of several bizarre encounters. A troop of at least ten rhesus macaque monkeys was loping down the road, as boisterous and carefree as a band of rowdy teenagers on their way to a Friday-night football game. What surprised him most was not the sight of these creatures on a Florida road but that "they weren't even [the zoo's] monkeys!"[3]

At the zoo, Magill found "a war zone." Andrew had tossed vehicles hundreds of yards, toppled concrete walls, felled five thousand trees, wrecked a monorail, and leveled or compromised several buildings. The zoo's state-of-the-art new aviary looked like a smashed snow globe.[4]

By the time Magill arrived, zookeepers were searching the site, armed with guns to protect them from any dangerous animals that might have escaped. Following the zoo's disaster plan, they had locked some animals in restrooms and herded others into concrete barns before the hurricane hit. Other creatures had waited out the storm by hiding in bunkers built in their enclosures. These preparations paid off. Only around 30 of the zoo's 1,600 animals died. Some 300 escaped, but most of these were birds that staff rounded up over the next few weeks. The MetroZoo was in shambles, but the creatures that lived there were, for the most part, okay.[5]

Yet the zoo was only one of many sites in the area holding captive wildlife. Andrew thrashed research labs, breeding facilities, roadside attractions, and neighborhoods that, behind their sleepy façades, contained one of this continent's largest populations of exotic pets.[6]

In the chaotic days after the storm, as MetroZoo staff regrouped and zoos around the country offered their support, locals reported unfamiliar animals wandering the Miami suburbs: exotic birds, rare deer, an African lion, and those raucous macaques on Coral Reef Drive. An undisclosed number of baboons that had escaped from the nearby University of Miami Primate Center swung from trees, bared their teeth, jumped on cars, and broke into at least one home. They even visited the zoo. But these charismatic fugitives, though photogenic and newsworthy, were only a tiny fraction of the estimated five thousand captive animals that Andrew unleashed. And Andrew, which the state wildlife inspector Tom Quinn called "an ecological disaster," was just a blip in the centuries-long history of exotic species in Florida.[7]

Growing up in Florida in the 1980s, I often heard my father, a displaced New Yorker, declare, "If it lives, it lives in Florida!" I think he was referring to the giant palmetto bugs that occasionally breached my mother's air-conditioned fortress of a house and the alligators that listlessly sunned themselves on the opposite bank of the canal behind our suburban backyard. The truth is rather different. Throughout its short history, the Florida peninsula—much of which emerged from the sea less than seven thousand years ago—has been a virtual island: remote, isolated, and, although a haven for migratory birds, home to relatively few terrestrial or aquatic species compared to other regions with similar climates and land areas.

This began to change in 1538, when Hernando de Soto embarked on a three-year fever-dream journey across the American Southeast. De Soto's odyssey ended with his death on the muddy banks of the Mississippi, but he and his followers left behind domesticated European pigs that would give rise to today's wild razorback hogs. Since then, observers have documented around five hundred exotic animal species roaming free in Florida. A 2007 study found that at least 123 of these—including 12 bird, 18 mammal, and 22 freshwater fish species—had become established there, meaning that they had bred in the wild for at least five years and were unlikely to go away without a concerted effort by humans. Many were clearly there to stay.[8]

Florida's list of exotic reptiles and amphibians is astonishing. Since 1863, when the first greenhouse frog arrived as a stowaway from the Caribbean, reports have documented at least 137 nonnative reptiles and amphibians in the state. The list reads like a high school geography quiz: African slender-snouted crocodile, Argentine tegu, Burmese python, Hispaniolan anole, Javan file snake, Honduran milk snake, Madagascar giant day gecko, Malaysian painted frog, Mexican black spiny-tailed iguana, Nile monitor lizard, Texas horned lizard, California king snake. Florida is now the world's undisputed herpetological melting pot, and Miami International Airport is its Ellis Island.[9]

It is impossible to know how many of these animals are in Florida to stay, how many more will arrive, and how many of those that do will create problems. Nobody can predict whether a given species will prosper in a new environment, or explain why certain species hang on for years at low numbers before suddenly booming. Species that move easily, reproduce quickly, tolerate diverse ecological conditions, easily locate and socialize with other members of their species, are comfortable around people, or thrive in disturbed areas may be riskier than others. Of the more than fifty thousand exotic species that have been introduced into the United States, biologists consider fewer than 10 percent "invasive." But once a species becomes invasive, it can wreak havoc. One of the few things we can say for sure is that by the time we find them it is often too late.[10]

·   ·   ·   ·   ·

The trade in live exotic animals dates back millennia. The modern exotic pet trade began in the late eighteenth century, when globalization and economic growth enabled more people—in cities like London, Amsterdam, and New York—to purchase live animals from around the world. Birds have always been among the most popular exotic pets. By the late nineteenth century, North American and European dealers were importing more than one million live birds annually, representing at least seven hundred species. The live bird trade peaked around 1970, when global dealers sold seven and a half million of them. In the years that followed, new regulations, such as those included in the 1973 Convention on International Trade in Endangered Species of Wild Fauna and Flora (CITES), lowered the number of exotic birds sold each year to around three million.[11]

Reptiles and amphibians became popular pets later than other kinds of vertebrate animals. Florida dealers began selling large numbers of live reptiles in the 1920s. With throngs of tourists visiting the state for the first time—attracted by slick marketing campaigns, conveyed by freshly built railroads, and lodged in glittering new resorts—roadside attractions selling baby alligators and other reptiles and amphibians capitalized on this region's tropical allure. At first, the industry grew slowly. As late as 1970, the United States imported around 320,000 lizards and snakes of 176 species. By the 2000s, this had increased to more than 1,000,000 reptiles of 287 species. These figures do not include the millions of animals captured or bred domestically, exported from the United States, or sold on the black market.[12]

Reptiles and amphibians—which don't require exercise, affection, or constant attention—are often marketed as low-maintenance pets compared to cuddly but needy cats and dogs. Sellers like to portray them as the faunal equivalent of easy-to-care-for cacti, compared to fussy ferns. But many people who purchase these animals do so knowing little about the industry that produces them, their ability to escape, their longevity, their fully grown adult size, or the risks they pose.

Today's wildlife trade is mind-bogglingly vast. Illegal wildlife trading alone is now the world's fourth-largest trafficking industry—after the smuggling of drugs, weapons, and people—with annual revenue of up to $23 billion. The entire trade, including both legal and illegal transactions, is many times larger. Nobody knows its exact size in dollars, but we do have a sense of its scope in species. One recent study, which quantified the industry from 2006 to 2012, found trade records for 585 bird, 485 reptile, and 113 mammal species.[13]

The trade in exotic pets reached this point for several reasons. Fast and cheap shipping enabled remote suppliers to tap new markets. Immigrants brought more nonhuman animals from around the world to American cities. Urbanization led potential pet owners to purchase smaller animals that could be kept in apartments. Global tourism introduced more people to exotic creatures. And this exposure increased interest, creating a positive feedback loop fueled by pet stores, television shows, book publishers, and internet influencers. The result of all this is that, in addition to having more wild animals than at any other time in more than a century, American cities now have huge numbers of captive exotic animals. And these two populations often intermingle.

When captive exotic animals escape or are set free, they join a diverse cast of already established nonnative species. Government agencies have introduced alien species to control pests. Pet dealers have released animals to avoid legal penalties, to dump surplus merchandise, or to found wild breeding stocks that they can later harvest. Some religious rituals involve freeing captive animals. Other creatures have escaped or been set loose from commercial wildlife farms, pharmaceutical plants, bait shops, research facilities, and movie sets. Once a population has become established, people may be tempted to release more of the same kind of animal.

After being released, some animals have an uncanny ability to find others of their kind. Since the 1960s, parrots have formed boisterous flocks in hundreds of European and North American cities, including in such unlikely locations as London and Chicago. Exotic parrots in American cities today benefit from milder winters (due to climate change) and the urban heat island effect, fruiting trees planted in parks and gardens, food waste, a lack of predators, and the regular restocking of their populations through continued releases. Of the twenty or so species of exotic parrots that squawk and frolic their way around South Florida, several are considered threatened or even endangered within their native ranges.[14]

The number of pathways by which exotic species can reach the wild continues to grow. These routes are now so many and so diverse that efforts to block them can seem quixotic. Clear, well-enforced policies can help stem the tide, but industry lobbying groups have thwarted them in most states—Hawaii being a notable exception—and they are not a panacea. Even with strong regulations in place, some animals can escape from even the most secure and conservation-minded facilities.

When most of us picture zoos, we think of a handful of marquee institutions—like the San Diego and Bronx Zoos—that feature

roomy, naturalistic enclosures, professional staff, educational programs, research centers, and well-stocked snack bars and gift shops.
To qualify for accreditation, they must meet strict standards,
imposed by oversight bodies such as the Association of Zoos
and Aquariums (AZA) and the European Association of Zoos and
Aquaria (EAZA), for animal welfare, public safety, biosecurity, and
disaster planning. Some zoos, including Ron Magill's employer in
Miami, even house secure facilities for holding illegally imported
exotic species.

Yet these modern flagship institutions are in the minority.
Worldwide, thousands of nonaccredited facilities house and exhibit
exotic animals. Many of these zoos and circuses are poorly constructed, funded, maintained, and regulated. Exotic animals escape
from their makeshift cages in these operations at much higher rates
than they do from accredited zoos. Some of these places are downright dangerous.[15]

According to Born Free, a Maryland-based nonprofit organization that maintains a database of reported incidents involving exotic
species in the United States, over the 28-year period from 1990 to
2018, 1,286 animals escaped from zoos, circuses, and other exotic
animal facilities. Only 128 of these incidents occurred at sites accredited by the AZA. Yet even some of the best-known zoos have struggled to control their animals. In the early 2000s, for example, the US
Department of Agriculture fined the Los Angeles Zoo $25,000 after
a series of brief escapes there by zebras, a chimpanzee, a kangaroo,
and other animals.[16]

As Killarney and P-22 remind us, facilities that keep captive animals tend to attract wild ones. Located in cities that now contain
abundant wildlife, many American zoos are becoming more integrated into their urban ecological surroundings. Zoos produce
sounds and smells that waft across cities, beckoning curious creatures. Spacious open-air enclosures and regular feedings tempt wild
visitors. Parklike zoo campuses offer lush habitats, and many are
close to urban green spaces. All five of Southern California's major

zoos—one each in Los Angeles, Palm Desert, and Santa Barbara, and two in San Diego—are near city parks, wildlife refuges, or national forests. On the north side of the Bronx Zoo sits the New York Botanical Garden, while on its east side flows the once gritty Bronx River, which today tumbles down a series of cascades as wild and scenic as if it were a headwater stream high in the Adirondacks.

Chicago's Lincoln Park Zoo has become an unlikely case study in the relations between wild and captive animals. From the sky above, Chicago looks like a neat half circle made up of concentric rings. With its parks and forest preserves running mostly parallel to these rings, there are few green corridors by which land animals may reach the city center. Yet reach it they do. Coyotes, like number 748, keep a low profile but are never far away. Local rabbits and squirrels are sometimes killed by captive predators in the zoo's enclosures, providing visitors with priceless, if occasionally gruesome, learning moments. Beavers showed up shortly after the zoo redesigned its South Pond in 2010, raising concerns about how these legendary engineers might attempt to improve this carefully planned site. Black-crowned night herons, which the state of Illinois lists as endangered, also found the pond—with its buffet of small reptiles, amphibians, and insects—to their liking. The herons soon established their only Illinois breeding colony a few hundred yards north of the pond, in trees overhanging the zoo's red wolf enclosure. This may seem like a risky place to settle, but it appears that the herons have recruited the wolves to serve as their personal bodyguards, protecting them from wild nest raiders like raccoons.

Zoo Miami has struggled to manage its relationships with both local wildlife and its powerful human neighbors. Its campus straddles a unique remnant of native habitat known as pine rockland, which is home to at least twenty protected plant and animal species. For decades, the University of Miami owned a parcel of pine rockland next door to the zoo, but in 2014 it sold the land to a developer who planned to build an enormous complex on the site, dubbed Coral Reef Commons, with shops, restaurants, nine hundred apartments, and a Walmart superstore—as if taken directly from a Joni Mitchell song. Fearing retribution from politicians in Dade County, which owns Zoo Miami, zoo officials ordered their staff not to comment on the sale and then diverted attention from their silence by launching, with great fanfare, a modest pine rockland restoration project on unused zoo property. In 2019, despite biologists finding several rare plants and a new species of spider in the forest just outside the zoo, opponents lost a key court case seeking to halt the project. Instead of being surrounded by a diminishing native habitat, the zoo would have as its new neighbor a development the size of a small city.[17]

Zoos have reinvented themselves many times over the years. The caged menageries of the eighteenth century gave way to the seedy theme parks and traveling circuses of the nineteenth century. During the early twentieth century, American zoos declared themselves vessels of scientific knowledge and civic education. After World War II they pivoted again, emphasizing their role in conservation and building enclosures meant to show animals in their natural habitats. By the 1980s, some zoos were shifting their focus from global wildlife to native species. In the twenty-first century, zoos are starting to embrace the idea that, instead of hermetically sealed theme parks, they are porous patches of enriched urban habitat. As the examples from Miami and Chicago show, zoos continually struggle to manage multiple competing forces, often seem a step or two behind the cultures in which they exist, and have never succeeded in sealing themselves off from the ecosystems that surround them.[18]

·   ·   ·   ·   ·

If the top priority of a zoo is to contain its wild animals, then the purpose of a wildlife rehabilitation center is to release them. It turns out that this isn't so easy either.

While not quite as flamboyant as Ron Magill, Jennifer Brent is every bit the force of nature. As the executive director of the

California Wildlife Center, a veterinary clinic perched on a wooded hillside twenty-five miles west of downtown Los Angeles, Brent has her hands full with animals, both human and not. Since the center's founding in 1998, it has worked with residents and other nonprofits, as well as local, state, and federal agencies, to care for sick and injured animals from Los Angeles and Ventura Counties. As of 2015, the center had admitted more than forty-five thousand birds, mammals, reptiles, and other wild creatures. Recently, it has agreed to start accepting seals and sea lions from the thirty-five-mile Malibu shoreline.

The center's goal is to enable people and wildlife to live together. "We aim to rescue, rehabilitate, and release the animals that come our way," Brent told me when I visited the center in January 2017. "Our work is about care, but it is also about coexistence. Caring for animals is the easy part—coexisting with them is tougher." People are often the problem. They report or bring in animals that don't need help, attract wildlife to their homes and then demand a response when something bad happens, and expect too much from a center that serves many needs but has limited resources.

The center relies on more than two hundred volunteers, but it is short on permanent staff. Many of the vets that work there do so temporarily, serving either pro bono or on short-term rotations during their training. With so many kinds of animals having so many potential problems, wildlife care is a complex field. Yet most vets arrive with little experience. Working with wildlife is still considered a niche or even a novelty occupation in many veterinary schools, and it remains decades behind the state of the science for livestock and domestic pets.

Located about halfway between the affluent communities of Calabasas to the north and Malibu to the south, the center has a lot of wealthy, animal-loving neighbors. Over the years, it has claimed a number of famous, deep-pocketed donors and celebrity volunteers, including the beauty products firm Paul Mitchell and the model, actress, and animal welfare advocate Pamela Anderson. But there is far less money in caring for wild than domestic animals. The center generates about one-third of its budget from grants, one-third from donors, and one-third from events. As with most other nonprofits, the fund-raising is never done.

But what exactly is the California Wildlife Center raising funds for?

There is little research on how clinics contribute to conservation. Wildlife populations vary over time, mostly because of ecological factors. These include physical forces like temperature and precipitation, biological forces like interactions with other species and exposure to diseases, and human-caused changes to communities and ecosystems. Wild animals need habitats of adequate size and quality to forage, and they must maintain populations of sufficient density to socialize and find mates.

In most cases, wildlife clinics don't treat enough animals to increase these species' populations over time. Even if they did, most of the animals they admit will never again wander free. Some don't fully recover or are too risky to let out, and many more die while in care. In one of the few published studies on this topic, the British Wildlife Rehabilitation Council found that of the up to forty thousand animals admitted to the United Kingdom's eighty wildlife clinics each year, only around 42 percent will ever be released.[19]

Most of those that make it out do not survive for long. In the United Kingdom, the species most often admitted to wildlife clinics is the European hedgehog, a common and widespread creature that lives for an average of three years in the wild. Somewhere between 25 and 82 percent of hedgehogs survive for at least six to eight weeks after being released from a clinic. The huge range in these numbers shows how little we know about the fates of animals released from clinics. Studies in the United Kingdom have found that only around 50 percent of polecats and 66 percent of raptors survive for at least six weeks after their release.[20]

Clinics avoid freeing animals that are doomed to failure, but releases can go awry for many reasons. Some animals may still be too weak to survive, even though they show outward signs of good health. Some may have become too reliant on people to survive on their own. Some may be disoriented or have lost their flocks, packs, or herds. Some may return to a home range that another member of their species has taken over. And some may repeat the same dangerous behaviors that got them into trouble in the first place.

Wildlife clinics straddle the blurry line between animal welfare groups, which aim to improve the lives of individual animals, and conservation groups, which seek to maintain species and populations. If your goal is to help individual animals, then it makes sense to care for the sick and injured. If your goal is to conserve species and populations, then, with a few notable exceptions, providing veterinary care is one of the most expensive and least effective ways to do it.

The staff with whom I spoke at the California Wildlife Center all care deeply about conservation. They have chosen to work at the clinic for many reasons. For some, the motivating factor is a simple desire to work with animals. For many, though, the commitment goes deeper. Healing, releasing, and in some cases euthanizing wild animals allows these creatures to live and die with dignity, cultivates compassion, and enables people to feel more human. The staff do it because they believe it is the right thing to do.

Many conservationists aren't so sure. They argue that expensive veterinary care involves unavoidable trade-offs. Clinics may help individual animals, but this does not aid species or ecosystems in any meaningful way. These facilities may even harm wildlife outside their walls by drawing scarce resources away from habitat protection and restoration projects that could help far more animals.

The situation is not quite that simple. There are at least two kinds of cases in which veterinary care may aid species conservation. The first involves endangered species like the California condor, which by 1987 had a global population of just twenty-seven birds. Over the previous several decades, dozens of condors had been treated for or died from lead poisoning or collisions with power lines. To save the species, managers rounded up every adult condor to participate in a captive breeding program. The condor shows how both acute and long-term veterinary care can prove vital to an endangered species's recovery. In the second case, clinics serve as sentinels, tracking health threats to wildlife and people. These include biological threats like emerging zoonotic diseases and physical threats such as an increase in animal collisions on a stretch of road that may point to the need for a lower speed limit, better enforcement, or improved infrastructure.

Caring for animals at clinics offers opportunities to educate people and spark difficult conversations about coexisting with wildlife. The many small animals that end up in clinics after being attacked by domestic cats offer vivid examples of the kind of preventable carnage that could be reduced with better education and simple, proactive measures. Charismatic creatures not suited for release may aid these educational efforts by becoming emissaries for local wildlife. In my hometown, a great horned owl named Max has played this role for more than two decades. After falling out of his nest as chick near the town of Ojai, Max landed at a local raptor rescue center, where he quickly warmed to people, making it impossible for him to return to the wild. He later moved to the Santa Barbara Museum of Natural History, where he launched a career as a local celebrity, educator, and yes, fund raiser.

There is no arguing with lovable characters like Max. But how can we sort through these opposing arguments about veterinary care and conservation to make the best decisions about helping wildlife? For an answer, I turned to one of the world's best-known ethicists, Peter Singer.

A utilitarian philosopher of practical ethics, Singer catapulted to fame in 1975 when he published his now classic manifesto *Animal Liberation*. According to Singer, we have responsibilities to all sentient animals, because they all experience suffering. In the 1970s, he found plenty of support for his claim that all animals feel pain, but today the evidence is irrefutable. "If a being suffers," he concluded, "there can be no moral justification for refusing to take that suffering into consideration." To act otherwise is to engage in "speciesism"—a form of bigotry no better than ageism, sexism, or racism.[21]

Singer offered an important caveat. All animals suffer, but they experience their suffering in different ways. Invertebrates may feel less suffering than vertebrates, which possess central nervous systems that make them more aware of their plight. Creatures that are intelligent, retain detailed memories, live long lives, and invest in their communities, their families, and themselves—including most people—are able to feel more suffering than other animals. Our duty to act depends on the amount of suffering involved, but overall, reducing any suffering is the right thing to do.

Singer's work from the 1970s would seem to support the objectives of clinics like the California Wildlife Center, which aim to reduce suffering and treat all animals equally, but his more recent writings raise doubts. In his 2015 book *The Most Good You Can Do,* Singer argued that doing good is not enough. "Effective altruism," as he explained it, is not about distinguishing between what is right and what is wrong; it is about determining which is the most effective course of action given a range of altruistic options. The option that reduces the greatest amount of suffering, for example donating to a charity that shows consistent and tangible results instead of to a similar one that hides its finances and is unable to point to clear accomplishments, is the "most right" thing to do. Seen through this prism, wildlife clinics—with their relatively steep budgets, lack of data about the survival rates of released animals, and fuzzy contributions to larger conservation goals—look like a poor way to reduce suffering.

Sensing a conflict, I set up a video call with Singer at his part-time home in Australia. In his early seventies, he still looked youthful and spoke in the kind of thick Australian accent that sounded, to my American ears, at once crotchety and mildly entertained. He flashed a warm smile over the grainy, pre-COVID video feed and patiently listened as I described my conundrum involving the two books he wrote forty years apart. When I finished, Singer launched into a series of brief digressions. He mused about climate change, noted that most people relate more to individual beings than to groups like species, and reminded me that endangered animals don't feel any more pain than common ones. Then he got to the point. Effective altruists must spend their money wisely for the greatest good. "I don't know the answer," he said, "but these clinics seem like inefficient ways to reduce suffering. Focus on the numbers."[22]

.   .   .   .   .

If the Miami MetroZoo's day of reckoning—when it became obvious how inseparable captive and wild animals are, and how the connections between them shape urban ecosystems—had come with Hurricane Andrew in 1994, then the California Wildlife Center's own day of existential terror and insight came more than a quarter century later, on an equally hot but much drier day.

At 3 P.M. on Thursday, November 8, 2018, staff at the center heard that a small blaze, dubbed the Woolsey Fire, was burning in the hills a dozen miles away. This could not have happened at a worse time. An hour earlier, local firefighting crews had deployed to a different blaze nearby. In Northern California, dozens of others were racing to reach the Camp Fire, which over the next forty-eight hours would incinerate the town of Paradise and become the deadliest conflagration in state history. The Woolsey Fire got off a sluggish start, but hot, dry winds soon fanned the flames. That evening, officials issued evacuation orders for almost three hundred thousand people in its path. By 3 A.M., staff had converged on the center. Over the next ninety minutes, they boxed up an ark's worth of animals that still required care—bobcats, possums, red-tailed hawks, a merlin—and hastily released any birds that had a decent chance of surviving in the wild.[23]

Two hours later, the Woolsey Fire jumped the 101 Freeway at Liberty Canyon, site of the proposed wildlife crossing to save

Southern California's pumas. Once on the freeway's south side, it formed a fourteen-mile-wide wall of flames and began advancing south and west through rugged terrain. It would soon burn all of the way to the beach in Malibu, destroying fifteen hundred homes and damaging hundreds of businesses, government buildings, and historic landmarks. In total, it scorched almost ninety-seven thousand acres, including 88 percent of the Santa Monica Mountains National Recreation Area.[24]

The California Wildlife Center survived the Woolsey Fire—but just barely. Hours after staff evacuated it, a line of flames raced along Malibu Canyon Road, passing a within a couple thousand feet of the center. In the days that followed, it received a handful of animals harmed by the fire, including a bobcat with singed paws. Yet, as with Hurricane Andrew, the area's wildlife fared better than its people. Few carcasses were found, and most of the local pumas emerged unscathed. Wild animals know how to stay safe from storms and fires, which they have faced for millennia, even if they have trouble avoiding newfangled hazards like cars, windows, guns, and people.

Zoos, clinics, and other facilities that hold captive animals are underappreciated features of urban ecosystems. They present risks that can be difficult to justify, and they deliver benefits that can be hard to quantify, but one thing is clear: they are increasingly linked to the lands, waters, and wild creatures that surround them. The challenge that these facilities now face, in twenty-first-century American cities, is to keep the captive animals captive, keep the wild animals wild, and try to make sure no one gets hurt.

12 Damage Control

In the classic 1980 slapstick comedy *Caddyshack*, a dim-witted but heavily armed greenskeeper named Carl, played by Bill Murray, is given the job of ridding Bushwood Country Club, in suburban Chicago, of a pesky intruder. A gopher, driven out of its former home by a construction project next door, has taken up residence on the club's golf course and is tearing up its manicured links. "I want you to kill every gopher on the course," Carl's frantic boss orders him, in a thick Scottish brogue. "We can do that," Carl replies. "We don't even have to have a reason."

Bushwood is a conservative place, but it is ripe for change. The hedonistic trust-funder Ty Webb (Chevy Chase) mocks club traditions and polite manners. The developer Al Czervik (Rodney Dangerfield), whose firm razed the gopher's old habitat, trolls club president Judge Elihu Smails (Ted Knight) with his uncouth behavior and zany antics. An ambitious young caddie named Danny (Michael O'Keefe) vies to upend Bushwood's class hierarchy with his skills on the course. And a crafty rodent threatens to destroy the club's façade of control over nature.

The saga of Carl and the gopher was meant as a subplot: the hapless maintenance man wages war against his white whale of the links. Yet more than forty years later, their epic battle is the part of the movie that most people remember.

Carl begins his campaign with a speech. "I think it's about time that somebody teach these varmints a little lesson about morality," he mutters, "and about what it's like to be a decent, upstanding member of a society." When Carl reaches into a burrow and gets bitten, the gloves come off. He decides that the best way to eliminate his adversary is to pump fifteen thousand gallons of water into its network of tunnels. This turns holes on the nearby practice green into geysers but leaves the gopher unharmed.

Next, Carl takes up sharpshooting, a method that proves ill advised in a suburban country club. Finally, the hapless greenskeeper declares war. We see him in his shed, again talking to himself, but this time while assembling an arsenal of plastic explosives. "To kill, you must know your enemy. In this case, my enemy is a varmint, and a varmint will never quit. Ever. They're like the Vietcong. Varmintcong." Carl must destroy the course in order to save it.

In the film's climactic scene, Carl detonates his explosives—toppling trees, sending golfers running for cover, and wrecking much of Bushwood's course. The ground shakes, causing Danny's final putt, which had paused on the edge of the cup, to drop in. He wins his match over Judge Smails, earning a college scholarship and a ticket to social mobility. *Caddyshack* concludes with Carl's gopher, still alive and well, performing an animatronic victory dance to the unmistakable sound of pop-rock star Kenny Loggins:

I'm alright
Nobody worry 'bout me
Why you got to gimme a fight?
Can't you just let it be?

Caddyshack may seem like an absurd place to start a conversation about cities and pest control, but Carl's misadventures are closer to reality than one might think. Vertebrate animal pest control in the United States has been a long, drawn-out, costly, violent, ineffective, and largely pointless boondoggle. It has focused on symptoms rather than underlying causes, failed to solve actual problems, created new problems where none existed, caused incalculable collateral damage, produced immeasurable suffering, and benefited the few at the expense of the many. The field and the people it serves are slowly waking up to this disaster. Yet even today, pest control remains the principal form of wildlife management in many American cities. How did it come to this?

.   .   .   .   .

There is no universally accepted definition of a pest. The same creature may be a pest to one person in one context and a benign, valuable, or even endangered species to another person in another context. A pest is not a thing; it is an idea, a relationship, and a feeling. Yet many people still use this word as if they know what it means. To paraphrase the late Supreme Court justice Potter Stewart, whose 1964 threshold test for obscenity has become a sort of false proverb of intuition, the word *pest* may be impossible to define, but most people think they know one when they see one.[1]

When I look at an animal that some people label a pest—whether a deer browsing in someone's vegetable garden or a sea gull making off with a careless beachgoer's picnic lunch—what I see is a multibillion-dollar industry known as wildlife damage management (WDM). Living with wildlife is not without its drawbacks. Wild animals directly or indirectly cost Americans several billion dollars each year, in the forms of crop and livestock losses, property and infrastructure damage, medical bills, and other harm to public health and safety. But statistics on the costs imposed by wildlife are difficult to find, and those that are available are riddled with errors, caveats, and assumptions. Nobody knows how much "damage" wildlife causes to human lives, livelihoods, or property, and nobody has yet devised a convincing way to compare it to the benefits that wildlife provides.[2]

According to the Internet Center for Wildlife Damage Management, WDM aims to "balance the needs of humans with the needs of wildlife, to the enhancement of both." The center's stated goal is to advance WDM by providing "science-based" solutions to "human-animal conflict." Practitioners of WDM have worked hard in recent years to adjust to changing social expectations and scientific knowledge, and they work in areas—such as disease ecology, invasive species, and travel safety—for which we all can thank them. But this new face of WDM is a work in progress, and the field still has a lot to answer for.[3]

Pest control has a long, strange history. People have always had complex relationships with other species, but for almost all of human history they lived in small bands or villages, supporting themselves through hunting and gathering. There were few true pests, for the same reasons that there were few contagious diseases. Humans didn't live in large enough populations or stay put long enough to offer reliable and rewarding opportunities to other species—that is, until they settled down to grow crops and build cities.

In ancient societies, pests were seen as signs of divine intervention. This often arrived in the form of punishment, but a powerful god could also aid people through nonhuman animals. In ancient Egyptian mythology, for example, Ptah of Memphis, who was said to have been born before time and to have created the universe, mustered an army of rats to do battle against the Assyrian soldiers who attacked Pelusium.

European folklore and philosophy sought an elusive truce between humans and their animal neighbors. Greek texts advised farmers to draw up contracts with potential pests, setting aside portions of their harvests for insects and rodents. Rome's most famous natural historian, Pliny the Elder, believed that menstrual discharge deterred crop-eating vermin. Pliny died in 79 C.E. of asphyxiation caused by toxic fumes spewing from Mount Vesuvius. This same famous eruption produced pyroclastic flows of superheated gas and debris, entombing thousands of rats under ash in Pompeii and thus providing clear evidence of early infestations. Later myths, such as the German tale of the Pied Piper of Hamelin, penned in the fourteenth century, around the time of the Black Death, addressed the fear of pests that gripped medieval societies in which disease and starvation were never far off.[4]

During the Victorian era, urban growth in Britain and elsewhere produced a new army of pest controllers. Jack Black, the self-appointed queen's official ratcatcher, helped define the modern exterminator as a flamboyant self-promoter, social climber, and snake-oil salesman. He paraded around London like a chatty Christmas tree, wearing a green topcoat, a scarlet vest, white breeches, and a thick leather sash embroidered with cast-iron rats. In addition to killing rodents, Black bred them, producing new varieties that he marketed as pets. He is rumored to have sold his "fancy rats" to such prestigious clients as Beatrix Potter and even Queen Victoria herself.[5]

By the 1840s, professional ratcatchers were offering their services in American cities like New York and Philadelphia. One of New York's best-known early ratcatchers was Walter "Sure Pop" Isaacsen, who set up shop in Brooklyn in 1857. To dispatch his quarry, Isaacsen used a combination of trained ferrets and poison pellets rumored to be strong enough to kill an elephant.[6]

When the modern field of wildlife management began in the United States in 1885, its main focus was on pests. The government's Division of Economic Ornithology and Mammalogy, the first federal agency dedicated to cataloging and managing wildlife, set out to distinguish wild animal species that delivered economic benefits from "injurious" ones that cost American businesses and taxpayers. If their costs and benefits could be quantified, so went the thinking, then officials could manage each species accordingly. Decades later, the division would change its name and expand its mission, becoming the Bureau of Biological Survey in 1905 and the US Fish and Wildlife Service in 1940.

The division's efforts mirrored those in place in dozens of individual states, which focused on the Sisyphean task of controlling modern agricultural pests. During the nineteenth century, farmers in the Midwest and Great Plains created the world's most productive breadbasket. Razing the region's forests and grasslands decimated dozens of species, and some of those that remained—along with new exotic species and pathogens—multiplied in the absence of predators that had long kept their populations in check. Blights, infestations, range wars, and dust bowls were not far behind.[7]

In cities, as in rural areas, controlling pests was tougher than it sounded. Two main barriers stood in the way. The first was that cities provided ideal habitats for some potential pests. Killing off rats or bedbugs was no easy task under the best conditions, but it was nearly impossible in urban areas flush with resources for them. The second barrier was bigotry. Politicians and pundits believed that pests were most numerous in poor neighborhoods populated by immigrants and people of color, and they portrayed such neighborhoods as dirty places filled with dirty people who attracted dirty pests. These ideas themselves have been tough to eradicate. In 2019, President Donald J. Trump used this kind of racist language, describing the Maryland district of Representative Elijah Cummings as "a disgusting, rat and rodent infested mess." It is true that poor communities have often suffered disproportionately from living with unwelcome animals, but they did not bring this situation upon themselves. Government neglect, negligence, and disinvestment marginalized and exposed them, leaving them far more vulnerable than the wealthier, whiter communities whose residents were no tidier but who nonetheless enjoyed the benefits of cleaner, safer environments.[8]

Between 1920 and 1950, a series of developments set the stage for a new era of modern pest management. Quixotic and outlandish projects, such as a 1920s proposal to build a rat-proof barrier along portions of New York City's waterfront, went by the wayside. In their place came a new recognition, by a new generation of professional wildlife managers, that ecological conditions determined the number of wild animals that could live in a given area. According to this logic, the best way to manage wildlife, including pests, was to manage their habitat.[9]

The ecologist David E. Davis applied this grand idea to the humble rat. He received his PhD from Harvard in 1939, then worked at Johns Hopkins, Penn State, and North Carolina State Universities, publishing 3 books and more than 230 papers. He developed methods for studying rats in cities and disproved the myth that New York City contained one rat for every person, placing the ratio at closer to one rat for every thirty people. Davis argued that the only way to control rats was to manage their habitats. His approach had the potential to send pest control on a more humane, sensible, and effective path, but three factors derailed his vision.[10]

In the 1930s, private pest control firms, many of which were run by German or Jewish immigrants, banded together to build the National Pest Control Association into an influential lobbying group. The association fought efforts to regulate pesticides, blocked legislation requiring licenses for exterminators, and found creative ways to skirt Depression-era labor laws. The owners of these firms took pride in the role they played in cleaning up and modernizing American cities, and they were determined to maintain their private, independent status. For the most part, they succeeded.[11]

In 1931, Congress got involved, passing a law authorizing the secretary of the US Department of Agriculture (USDA) to "conduct a program of wildlife services with respect to injurious animal species and take any action the Secretary considers necessary in conducting the program." This new law expanded the scope of the government's "nuisance" wildlife management efforts, leading to the creation of the Division of Predatory Animal and Rodent Control, which in 1985 was renamed Animal Damage Control and in 1997 became the USDA Animal and Plant Health Inspection Service's Wildlife

Services. Today, this organization conducts research and helps other agencies manage invasive species. Its main focus, however, like that of private pest control firms, is helping clients dispose of problem animals, and it does this with minimal regulation, oversight, or scientific evidence and few clear or compelling conservation objectives. In 2019 alone, Wildlife Services killed an estimated 1.2 million animals.[12]

Technology has also played a crucial part in the rise of modern pest control. Some widely used pesticides, like strychnine, have been around since the nineteenth century, but during and after World War II, military, industrial, and agricultural research made potent new chemicals cheap and easy to find. Sodium fluoroacetate, or compound 1080, which hit the market in 1942, prevents cells from metabolizing carbohydrates, thus depriving them of energy. DDT, which became widely available as an insecticide in 1945, opens the sodium ion channels in neurons, causing them to fire spontaneously and repeatedly, resulting in cell death. Warfarin, an anticoagulant first sold commercially as rat poison in 1948, makes its victims bleed to death. In their quest to control other animals, Americans in the postwar era flooded their habitats and bodies with a toxic cocktail of industrial poisons.[13]

Things have changed since then, but only somewhat. In 1972, for example, the Nixon administration banned the use of compound 1080 on federal lands. This prohibition did not, however, apply to state or private lands or recall existing stockpiles. As with other pest control regulations, exceptions and loopholes abounded. Meanwhile, the private pest control industry kept growing and remained largely unregulated in most states. Today, it is a field dominated by state and federal agencies that cater to individual clients, by private firms whose claims of effectiveness have little if any basis in science, and by techniques and mentalities that continue to wreak ecological damage while causing animal suffering on an industrial scale.

One of the harshest indictments of the pest control industry is that it causes so much harm while failing to address actual problems—including in cities, where the number of wildlife-related conflict incidents has risen rapidly. In a single ten-year period, from 1994 through 2003, Wildlife Services reported a tenfold increase, from around $10 million to nearly $100 million, in average annual losses associated with urban wildlife. Although specific numbers are unreliable, evidence suggests that this trend of increasing costs is very real.[14]

The losses come in many forms. Damages to property—including cars, homes, and gardens—are among the most frequently reported. Impacts on the broader environment are also common. These range from inconveniences like offensive sounds and smells to more serious problems, such as damage caused to forests or water bodies by invasive species. Public health and safety risks include exposure to diseases, as well as threatening behaviors by wild animals and even physical altercations, sometimes with harm inflicted on pets and children.

Some of the scariest public safety risks associated with wildlife involve accidents that occur when cars or planes hit animals. From 2008 to 2018, the Federal Aviation Administration's Wildlife Strike Database recorded 244,162 entries, with the creatures involved ranging from bats to kestrels, vultures, and even woodchucks. The most common aircraft strike victims are Canada geese. Not surprisingly, cars hit animals far more often than planes do. According to statistics published by the insurance firm State Farm, during the one-year period ending in June 2018, 1.33 million automobile accidents in the United States involved deer, elk, moose, or caribou, costing an average of $4,341 per incident. Animal-related accident claims were least common in California, where just 1 in 1,125 motorists filed one, and most common in West Virginia, where a whopping 1 in 46 drivers reported such an incident.[15]

Damages to other kinds of property also vary by region and species. Between 1994 and 2003, raccoons were responsible for the largest number of wildlife-related damage complaints in the United States. Coyotes, skunks, beavers, deer, geese, squirrels, opossums, foxes, and blackbirds filled out the top ten. In the West, skunks pulled ahead by bringing up their rears. In the central region, coyotes, blackbirds, and deer got into the most trouble. In the East, beavers and geese led the pack, each causing several thousand headaches.[16]

In the United States, our traditional approach when confronted with inconvenient animals is to shoot, trap, or poison first and ask questions later. This was how state and federal agencies operated throughout most of their histories, and it remains a common mentality among public agencies and private pest control firms today. It would be wrong to say that it is never appropriate or justified to manage wildlife using lethal methods. Sometimes there are emergencies. Sometimes killing a few animals benefits many more. Sometimes it is the best thing for the creatures involved. Sometimes management programs are designed around a carefully regulated hunt. And sometimes there just aren't any other good options. But even a cursory look at the driving forces behind urban wildlife-related problems shows why bloodshed is often ineffective or even counterproductive.

Killing animals can reduce a wildlife population in the short term, but unless it is driven out of an area entirely, the population is likely to bounce back when given the chance. This means that any wildlife management program based on culling must continue indefinitely, consuming scarce time and resources. This is particularly the case for animals that reproduce quickly. In urban areas, this includes the most successful species, which also happen to be the ones that most often bother people. Raccoons, possums, rats, starlings, pigeons, and cottontails are examples of creatures that can quickly respond to culling with increased fertility among the population's surviving members. If you kill one today, you're likely to get two more tomorrow.

For long-lived social animals, killing even a few high-ranking individuals can cause chaos in the population. The individuals that replace them will be younger and less experienced, lack established territories, and have fewer adults to teach them or keep them in line. These are the exact kinds of animals most likely to get into trouble, as "bear yeller" Steve Searles discovered when he started killing mischievous bears in Mammoth Lakes, California, during the 1990s. Culling populations thus not only tends to increase wild creatures' birthrates but also scrambles social structures and territorial boundaries, making the animals less predictable and tougher for people to live with.[17]

Culling is also more difficult in urban than in rural areas. Urban residents are more likely to oppose culling, particularly for large and charismatic animals like deer and bears. Many cities ban the discharge of firearms. Bowhunting is an option in some communities, but it can produce gruesome scenes of wounded, suffering animals desperately bounding through people's backyards as they bleed to death. Cities are filled with rat poisons, but these too are increasingly controversial as residents become aware of the dangers they pose to children and pets.

One of the worst aspects of lethal animal control is its collateral damage. Traps often capture the wrong animals. Rodenticides take time to kill the animals that eat them, which become easier prey as they grow sick and disoriented. Poisons accumulate in the food web, reaching toxic levels in predators like bobcats, coyotes, hawks, owls, and pumas. In one California study, for example, 70 percent of mammals, including 85 percent of bobcats, tested positive for rat poison; in another, in New York, 49 percent of raptors, including 81 percent of great horned owls, had similar results. The sad irony is that the predators that are suffering from these poisons are the very creatures that consume rats and mice. They help us by eating our pests, and we repay them with poison.[18]

On the other side of the equation, many of the target species for these poisons have acquired greater immunity to them. As early as the 1970s, Norway rats began showing resistance to anticoagulants. Second-generation anticoagulants, which appeared soon afterward, are now widely available, but they are also more toxic than the earlier chemicals and remain longer in living tissues and the environment.

Direct nonlethal approaches, which instead of killing animals seek to alter their behavior, are often expensive and impractical.

Aversion therapy may work for a black bear that—after an extended session of exposure to noise, bright lights, and rubber bullets—concludes that people are scary and annoying, perhaps even a little crazy, and should definitely be avoided. But nobody, except maybe a behavioral psychologist practicing retro, 1950s-style science, is likely to experiment with aversion therapy on a rat. Moving wild animals from one place to another rarely ends happily, since most don't fare well in unfamiliar places and this usually just moves the problem to another person's backyard. Sterilization programs are expensive—up to ten times as costly per animal as culling—and inefficient. Yet they have become options of last resort for some species in some places, such as white-tailed deer on Staten Island, but only where residents can't seem to agree on any other course of action.

One of the few cases in which a large-scale culling program may be required is one of most controversial in which to do it. There are an estimated sixty million to one hundred million feral cats in the United States. Cats evolved to eat meat, and many are superb predators. Because, as Michael Soulé noted in San Diego, they have strong hunting instincts that seem to compel them to stalk prey whether they are hungry or not, they kill far more animals than they can possibly consume, and feeding them more kibble doesn't help. Feral and free-ranging pet cats kill billions of wild animals—small amphibians, fish, reptiles, mammals, and especially birds—each year, and injure or infect many more. Large numbers of these victims die slow, painful deaths, and more than a few end up in clinics like the California Wildlife Center, where they consume scarce time and money. Outdoor cats also suffer, living lives that are far shorter and more painful than the lives of indoor pets. Yet despite the clear need to lower the population of feral cats and convince owners to keep their pets indoors, opposition to these measures remains fierce. It's hard to beat a cuddly but ferocious predator with powerful and determined patrons.[19]

.   .   .   .   .

Carl lost his gopher war, but his obsessive fight to eradicate his furry nemesis revealed some important truths. There are no simple solutions for living with pesky wildlife, but a society that imposes the death penalty on millions of animals whose greatest crime is inconveniencing someone seems headed in the wrong direction. Killing is sometimes unavoidable, but the more we avoid it, focusing instead on systemic solutions like restoring habitats and recovering native predators, the better off we all will be. Cities, for the first time in their histories, are in a unique position to take the lead in developing more sensible, humane, and effective approaches to coexisting with wildlife. In the immortal words of Carl the greenskeeper, "We can do that." Except in this case, we do have a reason.

13 Fast-Forward

In the 1990s and early 2000s, bird watchers sounded an alarm that nobody expected to hear. The house sparrow (see figure 9), which had lived in cities around the world for thousands of years, was vanishing. From London to Mumbai to Philadelphia, house sparrow populations had dropped by as much as 95 percent from their twentieth-century highs. Nobody knew exactly why this was happening, but a lot of people had strong feelings about it. Some bird lovers said "good riddance" to an exotic species they believed was harmful to native birds. But the house sparrow's sudden collapse worried many ecologists and epidemiologists, who saw it as an indicator of urban environmental health. If even the house sparrow, one of the world's toughest and most adaptable songbirds, was disappearing, something must have been very, very wrong.[1]

The house sparrow is one of a small number of species—including chimney swifts, barn owls, roof rats, and bedbugs—so closely associated with humans that even its name recalls the built environment. Its relationship with people has altered its destiny and even changed

its nature. Over thousands of years, almost all house sparrows settled on farms or in cities, coming to depend on people and evolving
into creatures ideally suited for life on the street. Their ability to live
among us has enabled house sparrows to spread around the globe,
but by embracing humanity, they placed all of their eggs in the same
basket.[2]

Humans are now one of the most potent drivers of evolution on
our planet. When we transform habitats, we scramble the forces of
natural selection, creating new opportunities and placing new pressures on the plants and animals that live in them. Many species find
it difficult or impossible to adjust, but some are able to adapt through
a process known as human-induced rapid evolution. House sparrows are one example of this, and cities, long ignored by most biologists, are increasingly seen as laboratories for studying evolutionary
change. The idea that some species can quickly adapt may seem like
a reason for hope in an era when many are declining or disappearing. Yet there are reasons to worry that evolution—nature's greatest
mechanism for coping with change—will be unable to keep up with
the changes being wrought by the most restless, inventive, and
destructive species it has ever produced.[3]

·   ·   ·   ·   ·

It is a little odd that one of the world's most common birds is so non-
descript that most people probably can't even identify it. House
sparrows are the plump, calico-colored songbirds that bounce
around, pecking at seeds and food scraps on city streets, sidewalks,
and picnic tables the world over. If you're in a city and you're outside
right now, look around and there's a decent chance you'll see one.

House sparrows are members of the genus *Passer*, which includes
around twenty species of "true sparrows" native to Europe, North
Africa, and Asia. Birds that resemble house sparrows first appear in
the fossil record about four hundred thousand years ago, in a
cave near the present-day city of Bethlehem. They evolved to live in

boisterous flocks, foraging in the grasslands and woodlands that were common in the Middle East around that time.[4]

Around eleven thousand years ago, the house sparrow found itself in an ideal position to tap the growing bounty of grains and seeds that humans were starting to cultivate. Within a millennium, most house sparrows were living in or around human settlements. Like the people with whom they dwelled—but unlike every other species in their genus—they stopped migrating. The few that continued to travel hopscotched from village to village, founding new populations along the way. By three thousand years ago, they were showing up at Bronze Age sites as far north as present-day Sweden.[5]

The house sparrow was one of the first species to receive a scientific name, described, in 1758, by none other than Carl Linnaeus, the Swedish inventor of modern taxonomy. By that time, the species had become a staple and an icon, hunted for food, kept as a pet, and featured as a character or symbol in popular literature, religious texts, and folklore.

It is not clear precisely when house sparrows arrived in North America. In 1850, the Brooklyn Institute, forerunner of today's Brooklyn Museum, imported a shipment of house sparrows from England, releasing them the following year. Additional releases appear to have occurred in New York in 1852 and 1853 and in the Midwest in 1854 and 1881, but the records are fuzzy. As few as sixteen birds from the initial flock may have been enough to give them a foothold in this foreign land. By the 1870s, they had arrived or been introduced in Chicago, Denver, Galveston, and San Francisco. Today, house sparrows live in every major urban area in North America, and they inhabit towns and cities on six continents.[6]

Museums and clubs imported house sparrows because their members thought that the species was beautiful and that it would help control pests in parts of the United States where farming had upended the balance between avian predators and insect prey. Things didn't work out exactly as planned. House sparrows ate insects, but they also devoured crops, sparking a debate about their value. Known as the Sparrow War, this controversy pitted the US Department of Agriculture and the American Ornithologists' Union, both of which viewed house sparrows as a threat, against recreational birders who enjoyed having them around. The sparrow's detractors were relentless. They called it "a tramp," "a marauder," and a "feathered brigand," urging anyone with a gun to "kill him, wherever you find him, in season and out of season." For Frank Chapman, of Christmas Bird Count fame, house sparrows just stank. Having them around, he wrote, was as if "some foul odor had forever defiled the fragrance of our fields and woods."[7]

In 1889, Walter Barrows, of the USDA's Division of Economic Ornithology and Mammalogy, published a study of house sparrow gut contents. He concluded that house sparrows outcompeted seventy species of native birds and consumed far more grains than insect pests. House sparrows were also suspected of carrying infectious diseases. Indeed, later research showed that they served as hosts or vectors for at least twenty-nine pathogens that infect humans or other animals, including West Nile virus, paramyxovirus, aphthovirus, conjunctivitis, Saint Louis encephalitis, the virus that causes avian influenza, and a form of chlamydia that also infects chickens. Its ability to carry these pathogens makes the house sparrow a superb bioindicator, offering early warnings of potential public health threats, but in the nineteenth century, scientists were far from appreciating the beneficial role these birds could play. With the species cast as a villain, the American war *about* house sparrows shifted to a strychnine-laced war *against* house sparrows, with fronts in North America, Europe, and Asia.[8]

As these debates unfolded, the house sparrows themselves were changing. In 1896, Hermon C. Bumpus, an embryologist at Brown University, delivered a lecture in which he argued that the spread of house sparrows in North American was an evolutionary event. He compared 868 sparrow eggs from Great Britain with an equal number from Massachusetts, finding that the North American eggs were shorter and more variable in color and size. Bumpus showed that evolution had occurred, but he remained unclear about the cause.[9]

Two years later, Bumpus seized on a natural experiment. On February 1, 1898, a severe winter storm struck New England. While most of his colleagues sat inside sipping tea by the fire, Bumpus slogged around Providence, collecting 136 sparrows that had become immobilized in the storm. Back in his laboratory, sixty-four died. The remining seventy-two birds on average were shorter, weighed less, and had thicker skulls but longer wing bones, leg bones, and sternums. Bumpus concluded that the storm was a selection event, killing off individuals that were less well adapted to New England's fickle climate. His study was an important scientific contribution, and because he published his data along with his analysis, it became an open-source classic. In the years since, dozens of biologists have reanalyzed Bumpus's data, making the house sparrow a model organism for the study of evolutionary biology.[10]

In 1964, Richard Johnston and Robert Selander, from the University of Kansas, reported that house sparrows showed "conspicuous adaptive differentiation in color and size" since arriving on American shores. Remarkably, these changes matched two principles of evolutionary biology: warm-blooded species tend to grow larger (Bergmann's rule) and paler (Gloger's rule) when placed in relatively colder environments, like that of Bumpus's New England home. At the time, most ornithologists and evolutionary biologists believed that evolution in birds required thousands of years. Johnston and Selander concluded that, in house sparrows, it had taken "no more than 50."[11]

This may seem like no big deal today, in a world where everything, evolution included, seems to proceed at a breakneck pace. But in the 1960s, Johnston and Selander were peddling a radical idea. Charles Darwin believed that evolution was a slow and gradual process—so slow, in fact, that he could never account for how it had produced so much biological diversity on that a planet that he thought was only a few hundred million years old. Earth, of course, turned out to be much older than Darwin imagined. Four and a half billion years was plenty of time to produce spectacularly rich biospheres, then have them annihilated several times over in mass extinctions. Yet, for Johnston and Selander, Darwin's dilemma was beside the point. For certain species, under the right circumstances, evolution doesn't require eons—it requires decades.

Johnston and Selander made the house sparrow a poster child of rapid evolution, but they weren't the first to observe such a transformation in the wild. In the 1860s, naturalists around Manchester, in northwest England, noticed that peppered moths with dark pigmentation were growing more numerous than the lighter-colored variety that had long prevailed in the area. For decades, soot from coal-burning engines and furnaces had been blanketing the landscape, making the lighter-colored moths more visible as they roosted on blackened tree trunks—and thus more liable to be eaten. Albert B. Farn was one of the first to speculate that this was an example of evolution unfolding in front of naturalists' eyes. In 1896, James William Tutt made the peppered moth story a staple of school biology when he labeled it a case of "melanism," now often called "industrial melanism." It was not until 2016, however, that a Liverpool-based team found a genetic explanation for this change. According to this group, sometime around 1819, a twenty-two-thousand-letter sequence of "jumping" DNA had inserted itself into a gene that controls the moths' wing color, then spread throughout the population. One of the most famous cases of evolution in the history of biology was taught as such for more than a century before biologists gained a full understanding of what had caused it.[12]

A year after Tutt published his description of melanism, researchers in Washington State made a related observation. They noticed that lime sulfur was becoming less effective at controlling crop pests such as scale insects, aphids, and mites. In 1914, A. L. Melander identified the culprit as acquired resistance. Synthetic organic insecticides developed in the 1940s, including DDT, promised to fix this problem, but they provided only temporary reprieves. As late as

1954, the scientific literature described only 12 cases of acquired resistance to insecticides, but this number jumped to 137 by 1960 and 428 by 1980. More than five hundred species are now impervious to at least one chemical insecticide, and the remarkable Colorado potato beetle can withstand more than fifty. Today, pest managers focus as much on delaying resistance to pesticides as on managing pests themselves.[13]

These cases hinted that rapid evolution was common, but scientists tend to be skeptical, cautious, and conservative. Many believed that industrial melanism and acquired pesticide resistance were exceptions, and that rapid evolution was rare outside the laboratory. Beginning in the 1980s, however, research started showing real-time evolution in the wild in response to harvesting, pollution, emerging diseases, exotic species, climate changes, and habitat losses. The potential for rapid evolution was a normal part of nature, but people were driving most of the ecological changes that were causing wild populations to evolve.[14]

It was not until the early 2000s that scientists began to see cities as evolutionary laboratories. They found that cliff swallows nesting in roadside culverts had grown shorter wings, enabling them to forage more nimbly while reducing their risk of being hit by cars. Mummichogs, tough little fish common in brackish East Coast bays, used protein receptors to protect their vulnerable embryos from nasty industrial chemicals called polychlorinated biphenyls, or PCBs. Anolis lizards grew longer limbs and stickier toe pads for clinging to smooth surfaces like concrete walls. Catfish started hunting pigeons in southern France, leaping out of the water and briefly beaching themselves before dragging their stunned prey into the murky depths. The London Underground now has its own species of mosquito, which lives only in the Tube, with a vampiric lifestyle that matches its cavelike home.[15]

Birds provide some of the best-studied examples of rapid evolution among vertebrate animals in urban environments. City noise can pose serious problems for many birds, because they rely on sound for communication and the urban din may drown out their songs. Some species avoid cities for this reason, but others have been able to remain by altering the volume, melody, tempo, timing, or pitch of their calls. Most vocal animals, from humans to orcas, unconsciously raise the volume of their voice in loud environments. But a shift in pitch may sound like a different song for a species that has evolved to hear it in another key. In such cases, whole populations must change how they sound and how they listen. Some species, like blackbirds and great tits, have done this in cities by raising the pitch of their voices or by singing at odd times to avoid being drowned out during rush hour. Others, like frogs and some insects, are also along for the evolutionary ride, adjusting in similar ways.[16]

To appreciate what rapid evolution means for wildlife, we should define what it means more generally, beyond a few flashy examples. Most people probably think of evolution as a change in a species's traits—its genetic code and physical appearance—caused by natural selection. These changes occur because they confer some advantage that leads to greater reproductive success and are thus passed to the next generation. When a species evolves in this way, we say it has adapted. This is the textbook version of evolution, but out in the field things get complicated in a hurry.

Some species may undergo an evolutionary process known as hard selection. This happens when a mutation changes a gene's DNA sequence in a way that significantly alters that gene's effects. If the individuals that inherit this new gene produce more offspring than those that don't have it, the gene may spread, causing the population to evolve. This is what happened with Manchester's peppered moths. A second mode of evolution, often called soft selection, takes place when a gene already present in a population becomes more common, often because of natural selection. No new mutations are required. Soft selection happens all the time in many species, because genes typically have alternative forms, called alleles, that exist in different frequencies throughout a population. The greater the variety of alleles in a population, the greater its genetic diversity and its potential for soft selection.

In many cases, evolution is not so much a positive product of natural selection as a negative consequence of genetic drift, which is a loss of diversity that occurs by random chance and is more likely in small populations. In fragmented urban habitats, genetic drift is a threat because wildlife populations there can easily shrink and become more isolated. These populations lose genetic diversity by chance and by attrition, and their members may breed more often with close relatives, increasing the likelihood that they will pass on harmful traits. Some isolated populations, like those of the London Underground mosquito, may branch off to form new species. But most, like the pumas of Southern California, are far more likely to suffer than to succeed.

Some species can adjust to living in urban environments without evolving, at least in the short term. This happens when individuals in a population change their behavior, for example by commuting or by shifting to a more nocturnal lifestyle. Some animals lack the ability to make such changes, whereas other creatures have a wider range of options. This gives them a greater capacity to learn, adjust, and teach their offspring. Behavioral changes may lead to evolution, but the pressure to evolve genetically may not be as great for species that are more behaviorally flexible.[17]

Sometimes, what looks like evolution isn't. Consider a red-tailed hawk, American kestrel, or peregrine falcon that nests on a skyscraper and eats pigeons. These urban raptors may be evolving relative to their kin in the country, but nesting on buildings and hunting in parks probably aren't in themselves examples of evolution. Some buildings mimic, in their height and the features on their façades, the natural cliffs on which many raptors naturally nest, and pigeons offer a perfect substitute for the birds and small rodents found on many prairies. All these raptors had to do was adjust their old techniques to new places. Plants do this too. Some that have evolved to grow in soils with naturally occurring heavy metals, for example, may thrive in urban soils polluted with the same toxic elements. It is tempting to think of these as adaptations to novel ecosystems, but they're really just transferred skills and lucky breaks.

Several of the animals in this book are intelligent, social, long-lived omnivores that can do a lot of different things well. But some of them too may be undergoing human-induced rapid evolution. Black bears in New Jersey may hibernate for shorter periods than their wild relatives. White-tailed deer in the Northeast have changed their diets in urban areas, annoying gardeners by sampling the many kinds of plants available in parks and yards. The big city coyotes living in Chicago are more nocturnal than those in nearby forests. A 2021 study of more than 140,000 records found that a wide range of North American mammal species living in urban habitats have grown larger over time. In all of these cases, it is possible—even likely—that urban wildlife is evolving.[18]

But is evolution the solution to the biodiversity crisis unfolding in so many ecosystems around the world? Perhaps no one has written more about evolution in urban environments than the Dutch biologist Menno Schilthuizen. In his 2018 book *Darwin Comes to Town*, Schilthuizen described human-induced rapid evolution as both a wonder of nature and its potential savior. We should conserve as many wild areas as possible, he wrote, but, "barring global disaster or dictatorial birth control, humans will be smothering the earth with their cities . . . before the century is up." Since the struggle for survival will leave many species behind, those that remain will deserve our respect. We are doing plenty of damage, Schilthuizen and others are quick to point out, but they ask us to take the long view. Nature will adjust, adapt, heal itself. Instead of pining for those we have lost, we should love the ones we're with.[19]

There is nothing wrong with hope, but this sunny account may blind us to a darker truth: evolution, as miraculous as it is, cannot make up for the loss of biological diversity. The simple reason is time. Despite many remarkable cases of rapid evolution, it is far easier for people to drive a species extinct than to help cultivate a newer, better-adapted one. Some believe that genetic engineering will fix the problem of time, propelling us forward into a future in which we take a more active role in guiding evolution to the benefit of all. Yet our ability to create fanciful new life-forms will almost certainly outpace our ability to produce beings well adapted to living in actual ecosystems on our actual planet. For every London Underground mosquito, there are thousands of animal species nearing extinction. As long as humanity continues on its current course, extinction will vastly outpace evolution and our world will grow less diverse.

There is another aspect of evolutionary optimism that should give us pause: the authors who place their faith in evolution tend to confuse ecology with economics. Americans in particular, but many Dutch as well, like stories about achieving great things by working hard and beating the competition. But when we place our faith in evolution, we project a particular set of human ideas onto nonhuman species. Species that can adapt to our modern world are entrepreneurs who deserve to succeed, whereas those that can't adapt are the hapless, the less fit, the less talented, the losers. This logic may be appealing to some, but it isn't grounded in ecology or evolutionary biology: it's social Darwinism in reverse. A better approach, for those who insist on framing these issues in economic terms, would be to think about conservation in a manner similar how the Dutch approach their country's meticulously maintained physical infrastructure and tightly woven social safety net.

As is often the case in capitalist rhetoric, what is sold as being about merit is actually about power. We can flatter ourselves by thinking that we are doing nature a favor by weeding out species unfit for the modern world, but what we're really doing is favoring the haves over the have-nots. Species that fare poorly in urban areas are unlikely to adapt to these novel ecosystems. Species that already do well in cities, on the other hand, will probably change in ways that make them even better suited to living there. Biological diversity will decline while we create an ecological oligopoly dominated by new breeds of superadapted urban exploiters. If you have read this far, then you know that I have nothing against crows, pigeons, and rats. I admire them and believe we have much to learn from them. But I don't think a world in which they are the only wildlife around is the future any of us want.

·　·　·　·　·

The house sparrow's decline remains an unsolved mystery, but several factors have probably contributed to it. The Migratory Bird Treaty Act of 1918 made it illegal to keep most songbirds as pets, a well-intentioned and successful policy with a few unintended consequences. At that time, house finches, colorful little birds with thick beaks and pink heads, native to the American Southwest and the Pacific Coast, were popular house pets. In the 1930s and 1940s, officials in cities like New York began to enforce the act aggressively, and many owners released their birds into nearby parks. House finches aren't quite the urban exploiters that house sparrows are, but, as their name suggests, they usually do well around people.

House finch populations appear to have remained small until the 1960s, when suburban sprawl opened up new frontiers for them. Studies soon found that in areas where the finches were new, they were outcompeting house sparrows. In the 1990s, the sparrows got a brief reprieve when at least one hundred million East Coast house finches died after contracting a bacterial infection that can cause respiratory disease, sinusitis, and conjunctivitis. The finches soon recovered, however, extending their range from coast to coast and reaching an estimated North American population of 1.4 billion.[20]

As early as 1920, the decline of horses as working animals in cities and better grain storage on farms may have slashed house sparrows' access to surplus food, contributing to their woes. Air pollution, limited nesting sites on modern buildings, and predation by cats and raptors may also all have played roles. Since house sparrows eat insects as well as seeds, insect declines, which scientists are only now coming to appreciate, could likewise be a factor.

House sparrows are unlikely to disappear anytime soon. They have lived with people since the end of the last ice age, and they have accompanied us around the world. They have qualities that give them advantages in urban environments, they have shown a remarkable capacity for change, and they remain common in many cities. Their future is not, however, assured. Human-dominated environments change constantly. New threats emerge and old resources disappear. With many bird lovers still regarding the house sparrow as a pest or an invader, the sparrow war continues, though it's more of a cold war than a hot one these days. Yet even the house sparrow's biggest detractors would likely agree that this is a remarkable little bird. It is tough, flexible, and fearless—but it is not invincible.

14 Embracing the Urban Wild

In the early 1980s, a sea lion named Hershel—or rather, a group of adolescent male California sea lions that cheeky locals gave the collective name Hershel—started hanging around the Hiram M. Chittenden Locks on the Lake Washington Ship Canal in the Ballard neighborhood of Seattle (see figure 10). A liberal and famously outdoorsy city, Seattle is the kind of place where one would think a raft of playful sea lions could find safe harbor. Instead, they sparked a decades-long battle that pitted state against state, agency against agency, conservationist against conservationist, and species against species. By the mid-1990s, even their most enthusiastic supporters agreed that Ballard's sea lions had outstayed their welcome.

California sea lions eat squid, fish, and occasionally clams. There probably aren't many squid or clams in the Lake Washington Ship Canal, but salmon migrate through it each year to spawn. When they reach the locks, they funnel into a fish ladder: a staircase comprising twenty-one small pools, or weirs, each about a foot higher than the one below it. Fish leap from pool to pool, as they would up the cascades in a stream, finding fresher water in each weir, until they reach the inland side of the locks. But first they have to enter the ladder itself. At its base, where the current slows, they must orient themselves, prepare for the shock of salt-free water, and wait their turn. It is here that they become easy prey.

It didn't take long for Hershel to figure this out. Sea lions are highly intelligent, a quality that helps them thrive in diverse marine habitats, in captivity where they can learn to leap through hoops and balance beach balls on their noses, and in urban waterways in cities like Seattle. Dominant males may grow to more than 1,100 pounds and preside over harems of females one-quarter to one-third their size. Smaller males often form their own groups, the marine equivalent of bar-hopping stag parties, migrating seasonally from rookeries in California and Mexico to rich feeding grounds like Puget Sound.

When Europeans arrived on the Pacific Coast, California sea lions numbered in the hundreds of thousands. By 1900, hunting had isolated them to a handful of remote sites and slashed their numbers to as few as ten thousand. The Fur Seal Treaty of 1911 reduced some of the pressure on them, and the Marine Mammal Protection Act of 1972 did much more. Around 2012, their population broke 300,000 for the first time in at least 150 years, making them the most numerous of the 14 species of sea lions and fur seals in the family Otariidae. This recovery was well under way by the early 1980s, when Hershel arrived in Seattle (see figure 10).[1]

The Ballard locks were the cornerstone of a forty-year effort to replumb the city. Prior to their completion in 1917, Salmon Bay, an inlet on Seattle's northwest side, lacked a passage to lakes Union and Washington, the city's two big freshwater bodies. Thomas Mercer proposed a link in 1854, but it was not until 1883 that excavators dug the first in a series of west-trending canals, known as "cuts." In 1906, Hiram Chittenden, the US Army Corps of Engineers' district chief, took control of the controversial project, which many locals considered poorly designed, poorly managed, or just too expensive.

Ten years later, when the corps finally completed the locks, Lake Washington's level dropped by nine feet and the ship canal on the inland side of the locks rose by an average of sixteen feet to meet the level of Lake Union. The locks enabled boats to travel through the canal between the sound and the lakes; the ladder alongside the locks did the same for migrating fish.[2]

Steelhead, like California sea lions, are native to Puget Sound. Members of the salmon family, steelhead are the same species as rainbow trout. The difference is that whereas rainbows remain in freshwater throughout their lives, steelhead migrate from fresh to salt water. Steelhead that survive for two to three years in the ocean return to the streams where they were born to spawn with their rainbow kin. History has been far kinder to rainbows than to steelhead. Since the late nineteenth century, rainbows have been bred by the millions in hatcheries and planted in lakes and streams on six continents, making them one of the world's most widespread vertebrate species. Steelhead, blocked from migrating by dams and diversions, have been decimated throughout most of their range, and they are now listed as threatened or endangered all along the West Coast from San Diego to Seattle.[3]

The Army Corps renovated the Ballard Locks fish ladder in 1976, and within a decade as many as three thousand steelhead were making their way up and through it each year to spawn. Tens of thousands of tourists ventured into the structure's bowels to peer through its underwater windows as steelhead and their close relatives, coho and Chinook salmon, swam upstream toward Lake Washington. Scientists, fishers, and conservationists, meanwhile, declared a rare success in native fish conservation. This was not to last. During the 1993–94 season, with Hershel gorging himself at the base of the locks, biologists counted just seventy-six steelhead passing through.[4]

The pitchforks had been sharpened years before, but now the villagers were on the march. Seattle newspapers labeled the Ballard sea lions "freeloaders," and the Pacific Coast Federation of Fishermen's Associations called them "a gang" of marauders. These were vivid accusations in an era when national politics focused on immigration, welfare reform, gang-related violence, and tough-on-crime law enforcement. The word *California* in the sea lions' name also branded them as intruders. The early 1990s was a tough time for the Golden State, which suffered from a deep recession, civil unrest, the Oakland Hills fire, and the Northridge earthquake. Tens of thousands of residents packed up and left, raising fears that they would bring California's problems—traffic, pollution, high housing costs—to nearby states like Washington. The disdain for Californians extended even to wild animals. Calls soon grew to have Ballard's sea lions sent back south "where they belonged." Or worse.[5]

The Marine Mammal Protection Act of 1972 allowed for the "lethal control" of protected species only in special circumstances. When Congress reauthorized the act in 1994, however, it included language inserted by Washington State representatives giving wildlife officials more latitude to cull marine mammals that were threatening other protected species. Ballard's sea lions now had targets on their backs.[6]

Animal welfare and environmental groups weren't going to accept this without a fight. They argued that steelhead were suffering not because of sea lions but rather because of habitat destruction and mismanagement at the hands of a far more dangerous species. The marine mammal advocates Will Anderson and Toni Frohoff pointed out that the scientific literature offered little support for the idea that culling predators helped prey species over the long term, and that the razor-sharp, barnacle-encrusted locks themselves "descaled" hundreds of fish, killing or injuring them as they passed through. "It is time," they wrote, "to face up to and address the real culprits in this fishery decline—ourselves."[7]

Wildlife officials had, in fact, spent years trying to discourage Hershel without destroying him. In 1989, they tranquilized and tagged thirty-nine Ballard sea lions. Two died, but thirty-seven were successfully moved three hundred miles to the south. Within a week, twenty-nine had returned. Underwater explosives and a two-hundred-decibel "acoustic barrier" failed to deter the sea lions, as did baiting them with fish covered in a sour-tasting chemical. Officials received death threats when they suggested using rubber bullets. The California Coastal Commission rejected a proposal to move the sea lions to the Channel Islands near Santa Barbara. A Seattle radio station turned the episode into a publicity stunt, lowering a life-size fiberglass whale, named Fake Willy after the 1993 orca-themed movie *Free Willy*, into Salmon Bay. In 1995, officials captured a nine-hundred-pound male named Hondo, which they deemed the worst of the offenders, with the intent of holding him until the end of the steelhead spawning season. Hondo broke out of his cage and wandered half a mile before the authorities apprehended him.[8]

This was not going well.

In 1996, Washington State and the National Oceanic and Atmospheric Administration struck a deal with SeaWorld to move Hondo and two of his coconspirators, Big Frank and Bob, to Orlando, where they would join the park's Pacific Point Preserve exhibit. Officials captured the animals and sent them to the Point Defiance Zoo and Aquarium in Tacoma, where veterinarians examined them and placed them in quarantine before shipping them, by Federal Express, to Florida. The three sea lions plunged into Pacific Point's two-acre saltwater pool for the first time on July 4, Independence Day. "I would tend to think that they'd be content," said Brad Andrews, SeaWorld's vice-president for zoological operations. "It's better off than being shot."[9]

By September 2, Hondo was dead, having succumbed to a previously undiagnosed infection. Because his checkup in Tacoma had showed no sign of disease, veterinarians concluded that he had probably acquired it in transit or in Florida. With the worst offenders gone from Ballard, some onlookers declared success. The Environmental News Network went so far as to declare that Seattle's sea lion problem was "solved." Yet it was a pyrrhic victory. Thousands of coho, Chinook, and sockeye salmon have continued to migrate through the ship canal, but a quarter century after Hondo's death, only a few dozen steelhead reach Lake Washington each year.[10]

.   .   .   .   .

Wild animals have come to urban areas for many reasons, but now that so many of them are here, the challenge we all face is living together. In crowded cities, it's easy to step on someone else's toes, or in the case of Ballard's sea lions, to eat someone else's fish. Seattle's sea lion conundrum is unique in its particulars, but the difficulties of living together that it—and so many of the other stories in this book—brings up are now practically universal. What do we really want out of urban ecosystems? And what would it take for people and wildlife to coexist in twenty-first-century cities?

Most authors who have written about urban wildlife, beyond the technical scientific literature, fall into one of two camps on these questions. For the writers of books with ominous, melodramatic titles, such as *Nature Wars* and *The Beast in the Garden,* coexistence is a fantasy indulged in by privileged suburbanites who know little about nature and the often bloody work required to keep it in check. For the authors of books with more pleasant, even whimsical titles, such as *Unseen City* and *The Urban Bestiary,* cities are already sites of coexistence; all one need do to see myriad species thriving in shared habitats is open one's eyes.[11]

The truth is that coexisting with wildlife, like any relationship, is hard work. It takes time, money, effort, organization, knowledge, patience, vision, and persistence. But it is no fantasy. Across the United States—in cities big and small, in both liberal and conservative regions—public agencies, private institutions, and civic groups are building on foundations laid and lessons learned. Their goal is to foster diverse, multispecies communities where most wild creatures can live their lives without being harmed by people just for doing what they do. Some of these creatures will cause problems, but more often they will educate, inspire, and, if all goes well, ignore their human neighbors. Even the richest, most ambitious, and most forward-thinking American cities still have a long way to go. But someday we may come to appreciate those now working to create wildlife-friendly cities in the same way that we now appreciate those who have worked to create parks, save species, and pass landmark environmental laws. We may even come to recognize cities as unlikely arks: refuges for biodiversity during an era of mass extinction.[12]

Luring wild animals into urban areas is rarely a good idea. But as we have seen, the ones that live with us provide many benefits. They educate us, spark our imaginations, protect us from and warn us of emerging diseases, force us to confront the forces degrading our habitats, and inspire us to be more flexible, accommodating, and compassionate. To see the good in wildlife and to work to coexist with it, even with creatures that can sometimes be annoying, is also to see the good in humankind and to work toward a more just, humane, and sustainable future. Cities that are more friendly to wildlife also tend to be more friendly to people.

But cities that seek to become more wildlife friendly—on purpose instead of just by accident—face daunting challenges. The first is a basic fact of economic geography: over time, land in and around cities usually becomes scarcer, more expensive, and more attractive for development. In the United States, this has produced two countervailing trends. Since the 1970s, cities have spent billions of dollars purchasing, restoring, or redesigning hundreds of thousands of acres of parks and other open spaces, benefiting humans and wildlife alike. Meanwhile, construction has gobbled up vast swaths of additional green space. Most people probably prefer well-tended parks to scruffy hedgerows and empty lots, but it is not clear that wild creatures feel the same way.

Another challenge that wildlife advocates face is the swarm of laws, institutions, and stakeholders that have a say in local planning decisions. An urban creek restoration project may require the approval of more than a dozen departments, including the city's

Parks and Recreation, county's Flood Control, and state's Fish and Game, as well as the federal government's Army Corps of Engineers. Even within a municipality, different agencies often work at cross purposes, such as when a lineworker is sent to cut down a tree planted by a city arborist. Since most land-use planning takes place at the county level, counties are among the most important venues for advancing wildlife-related goals. Yet their boards, tasked with everything from approving affordable housing to handling hazardous waste and reducing traffic congestion, may balk at allocating scarce resources to wildlife-related projects. In such cases, local grassroots organizing combined with legal mandates and financial incentives from the state and federal governments can prove crucial.

As important as this organizing is, however, grassroots urban wildlife advocates face a structural disadvantage. In rural areas, fees charged for entering public lands and purchasing hunting and fishing licenses help support conservation. In cities—where hunting is usually illegal, fishing for food is often inadvisable, and most parks do not charge for admission—wildlife lacks a clear revenue stream and paying constituency. Gear manufacturers represented by the Outdoor Industry Association, including firms with glossy green reputations like REI, have long resisted efforts to levy a modest "backpack tax" on their sales to support public-sector conservation programs, such as those that would benefit high-use recreational areas in and around the cities where these companies make most of their money. In the future, conserving urban wildlife will require larger and more-predictable revenue streams, as well as taxpaying constituencies that see themselves as investors in the ecological health of their communities.

Despite these challenges, several trends make it possible to envision a bright future for wildlife in American cities. One is that we're still learning so much about urban ecosystems and the creatures with which we share them. Every so often, a scientific discovery about urban wildlife makes the headlines, as when, in 2012, biologists identified a new species of leopard frog less than ten miles from the Statue of Liberty in New York City. Stories like this are astonishing and inspiring, but the truth is that most urban ecology research does not render dramatic discoveries; it produces basic data and small insights that add to our understanding of urban nature. Yet these little insights have an outsize importance, because the more we know about the creatures with which we share our habitats, the better chance we have of coexisting with them.[13]

Along with this boom in research has come a flood of education and outreach efforts. In every major American city and in many smaller ones, there are now agencies, zoos, schools, or museums with programs that educate their communities about local wildlife. In New York City, the Department of Parks and Recreation has taken the lead with field-based interpretive programs and slick advertising campaigns. The Lincoln Park Zoo's Urban Wildlife Institute has made Chicago a model for combining research with outreach in diverse urban neighborhoods. In Southern California, the National Park Service, the Natural History Museums of Los Angeles County, the National Wildlife Federation, and other groups have organized citizen science projects, conferences, publications, festivals, and exhibits reaching hundreds of thousands of people.

Urban planners too are starting to take wildlife more seriously. One of the best reasons for doing so, they have found, is that protecting and restoring habitat often furthers other goals. Setting aside habitat can create open space for people to use and enjoy, benefiting public health and improving quality of life. Planting trees is a way to attract birds, insects, and small mammals while combatting urban-heat-island effects worsened by climate change. Restoring urban streams improves water quality, recharges groundwater, and can create space for new waterfront parkland and reduce flood risk. Nurturing healthy, well-managed forests on the edges of cities helps protect against the fires that are increasingly jumping from wild to urban spaces. Planting native or other climate-appropriate vegetation may aid diverse species that rely on them while enabling dry-climate cities like Las Vegas to save billions of gallons of water. As they do some or all of these things, cities are starting to see wildlife-friendly habitats as more than mere amenities: they are a form of "ecological infrastructure" that, if well designed and tended, often comes with benefits that greatly outweigh its costs.

Other innovative efforts have moved beyond setting aside lands or waters to focus on neglected features of urban habitats that are nevertheless crucial for wildlife. In 2001, for example, Flagstaff, Arizona, became the world's first International Dark Sky Place. Recognized for its commitment to maintaining an unobstructed view of the heavens—for birds, bats, and insects, as well as humans—the city has pioneered design codes and related programs that reduce upward-facing waste light while maintaining public safety and reducing energy consumption. Flagstaff may seem like a unique example, perched as it is at the airy elevation of seven thousand feet, but many other cities have followed suit. In 2021, the decidedly more earthbound city of Philadelphia launched a voluntary program in which skyscrapers pledge to dim their lights after midnight during the spring and fall bird migrations. This measure resulted in part from a horrifying but all-too-common type of episode that took place on the night of October 2, 2020, when an estimated 1,500 birds collided with the city's tallest and brightest buildings. The following morning, Philadelphia's downtown streets were littered with the bodies of dead and injured birds, leading to a public outcry and policy response. Events such as this remind us that urban environments are deeply connected to more-natural habitats via their air, their water, and the creatures that pass through them.[14]

Protecting and restoring urban habitats is clearly worth the investment. It is crucial, however, that diverse people get to share in the benefits and that the costs not fall on those who can least afford them. Whiter and wealthier communities tend to enjoy healthier, cleaner, and more verdant neighborhoods, a pattern known in urban ecology as "the luxury effect." They also endure fewer environmental hardships, like industrial pollution. One might assume that disadvantaged communities would want the same. Yet this is not always so. The term *ecological gentrification* refers to the idea that environmental enhancements tend to increase the cost of living, making life harder for and even pushing out longtime residents. With parks and trees sometimes viewed in the same suspicious light as fancy coffee shops and boutique grocery stores, many members of historically disadvantaged communities now say they want a "just green enough" neighborhood: one that neither poisons nor evicts its residents. A challenge for policy makers is keeping down the cost of living while providing safe, healthy, and nurturing environments.[15]

Creating such spaces will require leadership and coordination. Though not a model of affordability, Boulder, Colorado, has pioneered ambitious wildlife, habitat, and open-space programs, helping make it one of this country's most attractive small cities. Nestled between the Rocky Mountains to the west and the Great Plains to the east, Boulder, like many American cities, occupies an ecological crossroads. In the 1970s, it set out to preserve a range of sites with diverse social and ecological values. It also worked to maintain the connections among these sites, ensuring, for example, that raptors had both places to roost in mountain forests and places to hunt in nearby prairies. Because Boulder Creek, which flows through town, is prone to flash flooding, city planners worked to keep businesses and infrastructure back from its banks while creating a ribbon of downtown parks perfect for a cool plunge on hot summer days, which are growing more numerous. Boulder achieved these goals over decades of sustained political leadership and with efforts coordinated across its many agencies—approaches that should not be out of reach for cities with fewer resources.[16]

Even in well-resourced and well-governed cities, change is difficult when it involves people's livelihoods. Yet cities, counties, and states must focus on the greater good and take more of a lead in developing goals and standards for urban wildlife management, including better regulating the pest control industry. Many cities have animal control units, and some contract with state or federal agencies for animal-related services. Yet throughout their histories,

American cities have outsourced many of their responsibilities for wildlife to private firms. With little regulation, these firms have turned wildlife management into a business. Pest control firms do have a role to play, but their work should be better regulated, driven by science, and brought into line with community environmental standards and goals. Killing healthy animals that pose little risk should always be a last resort and should never be the basis of a business plan or service industry.

.   .   .   .   .

I first visited the Ballard Locks on a sticky Saturday afternoon in July 2017, during the facility's centennial celebration. To get there, I strolled past a street festival blaring reggae music, hipster neighborhoods filled with old brick buildings, and a seemingly endless stream of yoga studios, coffee shops, cannabis dispensaries, and craft breweries. The trip took longer than expected because I made a few stops along the way. It was midafternoon when I arrived at the Carl S. English Jr. Botanical Garden, next door to the locks. English, a botanist and horticulturalist credited with describing three new plant species, designed the site for the Army Corps and managed it from 1931 to 1974. Today, the shady, 7-acre garden contains some 500 species and 1,500 varieties of plants from around the world. Who knew that palm trees could survive in Seattle?

Despite its exotic plants, the garden's most popular attraction is the corps's engineering masterpiece, which lies just to the south. On the day I visited, the area around the locks was packed with tourists who had come to see them fill and drain and fill again—a process as mesmerizing as the tumbling of water down Niagara Falls—and gawk at sunbathers sipping mojitos on the decks of the yachts queuing to pass.

People also come here to see fish. A series of metal walkways provide access from the garden to the south side of the locks, where visitors can read about the virtues of bold engineering, gaze at the weirs below, and enter the structure itself, where thick windows turn the fish ladder into a gurgling aquarium. Sure enough, the weirs were filled with fish, but they weren't steelhead. Most were probably sockeye salmon, born around five years earlier at the Cedar River Hatchery sixty miles upstream. They were products of a vast artificial system, as much industrial as ecological. But they were still fish, and you had to admire their single-minded grit.

As I emerged from the locks' cavelike innards into the blazing afternoon sun, an interpretive sign caught what remained of my eyesight. It described the difference between sea lions and harbor seals. A text box at the bottom asked, "Have you heard of Hershel?" The sign explained that Hershel was an eight-hundred-pound sea lion who, in the 1980s, learned to time his annual migration to the ship canal's steelhead run. Despite the Washington Department of Fish and Wildlife's "distraction attempts," other sea lions had followed. "Hershel and his friends are controversially blamed," the sign dryly noted, "for the dramatic decrease in the steelhead run within this watershed."

In telling this story, the Army Corps had left out almost all of the interesting parts, got others wrong—the Lake Washington Ship Canal is not even technically a watershed—and then arrived at a misleading conclusion. It was a great story poorly told. Maybe, I thought, the time had come for newer and better stories.

We're not there yet.

Since the 1970s, salmon stocks in the Pacific Northwest have collapsed. Dams, pollution, farming, logging, fishing, and climate change have taken tolls that individually might not have been enough to demolish the system but together have caused a crisis. The damage extends beyond big cities to small coastal communities, First Nations groups, diverse species, and distant ecosystems. With so few salmon reaching the ocean, marine predators like Puget Sound's unique tribe of southern resident orcas are being starved of one of their traditional foods. And with so few salmon reaching their headwater spawning grounds, ecosystems deep in the interior of the continent are being robbed of vital nutrients from the sea.

Federal agencies have often responded to these problems by focusing on their symptoms rather than their causes. One solution has been to kill thousands of wild birds and marine mammals to protect mostly hatchery-bred fish. From 2015 to 2017, the Army Corps culled the world's largest gathering of double-crested cormorants, destroying at least 6,181 nests and killing a reported 5,576 of the seabirds, which had been accused of feasting on salmon in the Columbia River west of Portland. This accidentally wiped out the colony. In 2020, the National Oceanic and Atmospheric Administration approved a plan to kill as many as 716 sea lions in the same river basin for the same crime. At the Ballard Locks, meanwhile, officials were testing a new generation of high-tech noisemakers in their umpteenth attempt to scare off hungry predators. This time, harbor seals were the villains.[17]

Almost four decades into this saga, it still was not going well.

There is no simple solution for this complex situation, but it's tough not to see our collective response as an example of what not to do. Engineers laid a trap by creating conditions that attracted animals like sea lions and then punishing them when they arrived. Activists and journalists demonized some species while celebrating others. Bureaucrats complied with the letter of some laws, like the Endangered Species Act, while violating the spirit of others, like the Marine Mammal Protection and Migratory Bird Treaty Acts. Legislators have decided to leave these creaky old laws just as they are, not because changing them is wrong but because it is hard. Politicians have been mostly absent, leaving difficult decisions to powerless expert panels, exasperated judges, and demoralized managers put in the awful position of having to kill some animals to protect others. In this leadership and ethical vacuum, agencies pursued limited, self-interested policies rather than working together toward broader goals. And throughout all of this, we've failed to address the driving forces that are making these problems worse by the day. None of this looks like coexistence. It looks like a mess.

Karl Marx famously observed that people make their own history, but they do not do so entirely as they please. Marx was referring to the influence of history on current events, but something similar can be said of urban ecosystems, and even the current era of global ecological disruption we now call the Anthropocene. Though humans may transform nature, we lack the power to fully control it. This does not, however, mean that we cannot be more intentional in how we interact with it, nurture it, and plan for our common future. We will never achieve anything like coexistence between people and wildlife, in cities or anywhere else, if we cling to the old approaches of attempting to dominate, manufacture, and micromanage nature, or if we continue trying to solve systemic problems with piecemeal solutions. Coexistence is about care, not control. It is about reciprocity, not retribution. It is about creating a context for mutual thriving while having the humility to understand that things will not always go as planned.[18]

We must start by asking what we actually want from urban ecosystems and the creatures with which we share them. Despite the long history recounted in this book, this most important of questions has rarely been asked. Yet only by answering it can we move from an accidental to a more intentional era in the history of urban wildlife. This story is not over. Just because wildlife has returned to American cities doesn't mean it's here to stay. We've come a long way, but we still have a long way to go.

Coda

If you took the city . . . and turned it upside down and
shook it, you would be amazed at the animals that
would fall out. It would pour more than cats and
dogs, I tell you. Boa constrictors, Komodo dragons,
crocodiles, piranhas, ostriches, wolves, lynx,
wallabies, manatees, porcupines, orangutans, wild
boar—that's the sort of rainfall you could expect on
your umbrella.

Yann Martel, *Life of Pi*

In March 2020, public health orders to combat the exploding
COVID-19 pandemic forced hundreds of millions of people around
the world to shelter in their homes. Most of us who lived through
those harrowing days will probably remember them for the rest of
our lives. When the lockdown came, I was working on the final chapters of this book. One of the things I will never forget about that time
is that for one brief, bewildering moment, the world turned its attention to urban wildlife.

With streets quiet and empty, huddled city dwellers watched from
their windows as wild beasts wandered free. Pictures and videos
posted on social media showed flamingos, boars, pumas, coyotes,
mountain goats, and hordes of frantic macaques roving desolate
neighborhoods that had bustled with cars and pedestrians just a

week or two earlier. Newsrooms on six continents declared that wild animals were "reclaiming" cities. It was as if, in the words of Yann Martel, cities around the world had been turned upside down and shaken. Within days, it started raining animals.[1]

Some of these stories and images, such as an instantly famous picture of bottlenose dolphins frolicking in a crystal-clear Venice canal, turned out to be fakes. For decades, best-selling books like *The World without Us* (2007) and Hollywood blockbusters like *Twelve Monkeys* (1995) and *I Am Legend* (2007) had primed people to believe that nature would waste no time replacing humans in a postapocalyptic world. With so many people under so much stress, it was no wonder that so many of us were so easy to deceive.[2]

Yet many more of these reports and images were authentic. Wild creatures—sensing that people had vanished and that, in many cases, the resources that people normally provided had vanished with them—really did venture out with uncharacteristic abandon. Biologists are still trying to make sense of what this grand, unplanned experiment tells us about animal behavior and urban ecosystems. What we can say for sure is that the brief flush of wildlife that appeared in many cities during the spring of 2020 resulted less from the pandemic than from the century of growth in urban wildlife populations that preceded it.

A few weeks later, I received a text from a friend. "Come down to Shoreline Park," she wrote. "I found something you need to see." I was at home feeling a little sorry for myself. My first outing since the lockdown began, a hike in the Los Padres National Forest, had ended with a hurt back and a sore ego. My friend assured me that what she'd found would raise my spirits. "I'm near the picnic tables by the beach," she said. "Get over here."

An hour later, we were standing on a patch of brown grass next to a clump of scruffy bushes at the base of a palm tree a few feet from the sand. It was muggy outside, and through my surgical mask, I could smell the restroom on the far side of the parking lot. My spirits were not yet raised.

"Look in the bushes," my friend said. I bent over with a groan. Nothing. "Look again," she said. Nothing. "Look again." Then it came into view. I reached down and gently scooped up the most beautiful thing I had ever seen. I had read many accounts of objects just like it. But now that I was holding one in my hand, I realized that I hadn't really understood what I'd read. What it meant. How it felt.

I was holding a common cup nest of the kind built each spring by robins, warblers, and hummingbirds. It appeared to have fallen out of that palm tree. But this was different than the nests I'd seen in my field guides or up in the Los Padres. And the scientific literature I'd studied that described urban nests didn't come close to doing justice to this dazzling piece of contemporary architecture.

The next day, I sat down at my kitchen table to catalog the materials the nest contained. There were needles from Italian stone pines, fibers from the trunks of Canary Island date palms, and twigs from Australian eucalyptus trees, as well as lichens, feathers, and grasses from species native to Europe and Asia. The nest also contained brown wool, blue string, and yarn in purple, orange, yellow, white, and black. I found scraps of napkins and paper towels, along with several cigarette butts, which have antimicrobial properties that may deter some nest parasites. There was aluminum foil and a swatch of gray stitched nylon that looked like it had once been part of a tent. There were half a dozen straw sleeves, both paper and plastic, and the kind of synthetic filling used to stuff pillows. The tinsel was a nice touch.

When it finally dawned on me, I was glad to be sitting down. This gorgeous nest—this postmodern collage in the form of a cradle—said more about urban ecosystems and wildlife than the book I'd been writing for the previous five years. Yes, this book.

Judging by the nest's size, shape, and location, its most likely architect was an American robin. Robins are North America's fourth-most-common bird, after redwing blackbirds, European starlings, and house finches. Because robins subsist on a diverse omnivorous diet, can live in almost any region with woods and fields, and seem at home around people, they are well suited for city life. Since robins consume large numbers of ground-dwelling inverte-brates like earthworms, some scientists also consider them useful indicators of soil and water quality.

Yet despite these admirable traits and the nursery rhyme that helped make them famous—

> Little Robin Redbreast
> Sat upon a rail;
> Niddle noble went his head,
> Widdle waggle went his tail

—robins don't get much respect. Even their Latin name, *Turdus migratorius,* seems a little passive-aggressive. Yet to behold an urban robin's nest—its design, its structure, its function, its whimsy— is to be reminded that in nature nothing goes to waste. It is also to be reminded that some human-made waste may never completely dis-appear. Robins may be building nests with our garbage long after *Homo sapiens* have gone the way of the dodo.

·   ·   ·   ·   ·

In this book, I set out to explain how, over the course of several dec-ades, cities unexpectedly filled with wildlife, and what this means for the people and other creatures who now share these urban habitats. If the outpouring of wildlife that appeared during the pandemic lock-downs of 2020 illustrates the extent of this ecological transformation, then the robin's nest suggests how living together may influence and inspire us all. Other beings experience other realities, but when we share our homes we share our lives, and we are never the same. We change, we adjust, we compromise, we improvise, we evolve.

The more than 80 percent of Americans who now live in cities have been given a rare opportunity. One of the greatest victories in the history of conservation happened mostly by accident. Wild spe-cies decimated during the eighteenth and nineteenth centuries returned to urban areas, along with a host of newcomers, in the twentieth and twenty-first centuries, largely because of decisions people made decades earlier and for other reasons. Most Americans now live in cities that are more populous, in both people and wildlife, than they have ever been before. In a sense, these cities have "rewilded" themselves. Living with wildlife comes with challenges, but it provides even greater benefits. It is time that we embrace this for the gift it is, following pioneers in ecology, conservation, environmental science, city planning, and other fields to begin integrating a concern for wildlife into every aspect of urban life. Doing so won't be easy. But if we adopt measures based on science, implement them with community input and support, maintain them with reliable public investments, and design them with care for the neediest and most vulnerable among us, then someday we may all live in cleaner, greener, healthier, more just, and more sustainable communities defined by diversity and coexistence.

Notes

INTRODUCTION

1. Sharon M. Meagher, ed., *Philosophy and the City: Classic to Contemporary Writings* (Albany: State University of New York Press, 2008).

2. M. Grooten and R. E. A. Almond, eds., *Living Planet Report—2018: Aiming Higher* (Gland, Switzerland: World Wildlife Fund, 2018); Kenneth V. Rosenberg et al., "Decline of the North American Avifauna," *Science* 366, no. 6461 (October 4, 2019), 120–24; E. S. Brondizio et al., eds., *Global Assessment Report on Biodiversity and Ecosystem Services of the Intergovernmental Science-Policy Platform on Biodiversity and Ecosystem Services* (Bonn, Germany: IPBES, 2019).

3. See, e.g., Michael L. McKinney, "Urbanization as a Major Cause of Biological Homogenization," *Biological Conservation* 127 (2006): 247–60; Jim Sterba, *Nature Wars: The Incredible Story of How Wildlife Comebacks Turned Backyards into Battlegrounds* (New York: Broadway, 2013).

4. For examples, see Emma Marris, *Rambunctious Garden: Saving Nature in a Post-wild World* (New York: Bloomsbury, 2011); Menno Schilthuizen, *Darwin Comes to Town: How the Urban Jungle Drives Evolution* (New York: Picador, 2018); Chris D. Thomas, *Inheritors of the*

Earth: How Nature Is Thriving in an Age of Extinction (New York: Penguin, 2018).

5. U.S. Census Bureau, *Geographic Areas Reference Manual* (Washington, DC: U.S. Department of Commerce, Economics and Statistics Administration, and Bureau of the Census, 1994), ch. 12; N. E. McIntyre, K. Knowles-Yánez, and D. Hope, "Urban Ecology as an Interdisciplinary Field: Differences in the Use of 'Urban' between the Social and Natural Sciences," *Urban Ecosystems* 4 (2000): 5–24; Karen C. Seto et al., "A Meta-analysis of Global Urban Land Expansion," *PLOS One* 6, no. 8 (2011): 1–9.

6. Peter Coates, *American Perceptions of Immigrant and Invasive Species: Strangers on the Land* (Berkeley: University of California Press, 2007).

CHAPTER 1. HOT SPOTS

1. Eric W. Sanderson, *Mannahatta: A Natural History of New York City* (New York: Abrams, 2009), 138.

2. Sanderson, *Mannahatta,* 36–39.

3. Jelena Vukomanovic and Joshua Randall, "Research Trends in U.S. National Parks, the World's 'Living Laboratories.'" *Conservation Science and Practice* 3, no. 6 (2021): e414.

4. William J. Broad, "How the Ice Age Shaped New York," *New York Times,* June 5, 2018.

5. Sanderson, *Mannahatta.*

6. William Cronon, *Nature's Metropolis: Chicago and the Great West* (New York: W. W. Norton, 2009).

7. Ethan H. Decker et al., "Energy and Material Flow through the Urban Ecosystem," *Annual Review of Energy and the Environment* 25 (2000): 685–740.

8. Thomas Edwin Farish, *History of Arizona,* vol. 6 (San Francisco: Filmer Brothers Electrotype, 1918), 70; Charles L. Camp, "The Chronicles of George C. Yount: California Pioneer of 1826," *California Historical Society Quarterly* 2, no. 1 (April 1923): 3–66.

9. Karin Bruilliard, "Harvey Is Also Displacing Snakes, Fire Ants and Gators," *Washington Post,* August 28, 2017.

10. Clark County Multiple Species Habitat Conservation Plan (2000), available at https://www.clarkcountynv.gov/government/departments

/environment_and_sustainability/desert_conservation_program/current_
mshcp.php.

11. Urban areas with "very high" biodiversity were mapped by the author
using publicly available spatial data from The Nature Conservancy. See also
Erica N. Spotswood et al., "The Biological Deserts Fallacy: Cities in Their
Landscapes Contribute More Than We Think to Regional Biodiversity,"
BioScience 71, no. 2 (February 2021): 148–60; Mark W. Schwartz, Nicole L.
Jurjavcic, and Joshua M. O'Brien, "Conservation's Disenfranchised Urban
Poor," *BioScience* 52, no. 7 (2002): 601–6; Sanderson, *Mannahatta*, 142.

12. Norbert Müller and Peter Werner, "Urban Biodiversity and the Case
for Implementing the Convention on Biological Diversity in Towns and Cities," in *Urban Biodiversity and Design*, ed. Norbert Müller, Peter Werner,
and John G. Kelcey (Chichester, UK: Wiley-Blackwell, 2010), 3–34; Gary
W. Luck, "A Review of the Relationships between Human Population Density and Biodiversity," *Biological Reviews* 82, no. 4 (2007): 607–45.

13. W. Jeffrey Bolster, *The Mortal Sea* (Cambridge, MA: Harvard University Press, 2012).

14. David R. Foster et al., "Wildlife Dynamics in the Changing New
England Landscape," *Journal of Biogeography* 29, nos. 10–11 (October
2002): 1337–57.

CHAPTER 2. THE URBAN BARNYARD

1. Ashley Soley-Cerro, "Runaway Cow Captured in Brooklyn after
Hours-Long Chase," PIX 11, October 17, 2017, https://pix11.com/news
/watch-cow-on-the-loose-in-brooklyn/.

2. Alex Silverman, "Child Injured after Bull Runs Loose in Prospect
Park, Brooklyn," WLNY–CBS New York, October 17, 2017, https://newyork
.cbslocal.com/2017/10/17/cow-on-the-loose-in-brooklyn/.

3. Ellen McCarthy, "Jon Stewart Just Saved a Runaway Bull in Queens.
Here's the Backstory," *Washington Post*, April 2, 2016.

4. Peter J. Atkins, *Animal Cities: Beastly Urban Histories* (Farnham,
Surrey: Ashgate, 2012).

5. Thomas Jefferson, *Notes on the State of Virginia*, "Query XIX" (1787),
available at https://teachingamericanhistory.org/library/document/notes-
on-the-state-of-virginia-query-xix-manufactures/; Jefferson to Uriah For-
rest, with Enclosure, December 31, 1787, available at https://founders
.archives.gov/documents/Jefferson/01–12–02–0490.

6. Clay McShane and Joel A. Tarr, *The Horse in the City: Living Machines in the Nineteenth Century* (Baltimore: Johns Hopkins University Press, 2007).

7. Catherine McNeur, *Taming Manhattan: Environmental Battles in the Antebellum City* (Cambridge, MA: Harvard University Press, 2014), 161–72.

8. Frederick L. Brown, *The City Is More Than Human: An Animal History of Seattle* (Seattle: University of Washington Press, 2016), 82.

9. Jessica Wang, "Dogs and the Making of the American State: Voluntary Association, State Power, and the Politics of Animal Control in New York City, 1850–1920," *Journal of American History* 98, no. 4 (2012): 998–1024.

10. McShane and Tarr, *Horse in the City,* 105.

11. McNeur, *Taming Manhattan,* 101–20; McShane and Tarr, *Horse in the City,* 26.

12. McNeur, *Taming Manhattan,* 136–39; Atkins, *Animal Cities,* 95–103.

13. Melanie A. Kiechle, *Smell Detectives: An Olfactory History of Nineteenth-Century Urban America* (Seattle: University of Washington Press, 2017), 5.

14. "The Water Question Again," *Chicago Tribune,* March 5, 1862, quoted in Kiechle, *Smell Detectives,* 143–55.

15. Dawn Day Biehler, *Pests in the City: Flies, Bedbugs, Cockroaches, and Rats* (Seattle: University of Washington Press, 2013).

16. McShane and Tarr, *Horse in the City,* 103, 128–29, 169; Horse Association of America, "Grain Surplus due to Decline in Horses" leaflet (1930), National Agricultural Library.

17. McNeur, *Taming Manhattan,* 170.

18. McNeur, *Taming Manhattan,* 19–20.

19. Katherine C. Grier, *Pets in America: A History* (Chapel Hill: University of North Carolina Press, 2010).

20. Andrew A. Robichaud, *Animal City: The Domestication of America* (Cambridge, MA: Harvard University Press, 2019), 170.

21. Kiechle, *Smell Detectives.*

CHAPTER 3. NURTURING NATURE

1. "New-York City: An Unusual Visitor," *New-York Daily Times,* July 4, 1856, p. 6; Etienne Benson, "The Urbanization of the Eastern Gray Squir-

rel in the United States," *Journal of American History* 100, no. 3 (2013): 691–710.

2. Benjamin Franklin to Georgiana Shipley, September 26, 1772, in *The Two-Hundredth Anniversary of the Birth of Benjamin Franklin: Celebration by the Commonwealth of Massachusetts and the City of Boston in Symphony Hall, Boston, January 17, 1906* ([Boston]: Printed by order of the Massachusetts General Court and the Boston City Council, 1906), 106.

3. Benson, "Urbanization of the Eastern Gray Squirrel," 694.

4. Vernon Bailey, "Animals Worth Knowing around the Capitol" (1934), unpublished manuscript, p. 1, folder 5, box 7, record unit 7267, Vernon Orlando Bailey Papers 1889–1941 and undated, Smithsonian Institution Archives, Washington, DC, quoted in Benson, "Urbanization of the Eastern Gray Squirrel," 691.

5. Peter Hall, *Cities of Tomorrow: An Intellectual History of Urban Planning and Design in the Twentieth Century*, 3rd ed. (Oxford: Blackwell, 2002).

6. Benjamin Heber Johnson, *Escaping the Dark, Gray City: Fear and Hope in Progressive-Era Conservation* (New Haven: Yale University Press, 2017).

7. Justin Martin, *Genius of Place: The Life of Frederick Law Olmsted* (New York: Hachette Books, 2011).

8. Simon Parker, *Urban Theory and the Urban Experience: Encountering the City* (New York: Routledge, 2015).

9. Parker, *Urban Theory;* Bill Steigerwald, "City Views: Urban Studies Legend Jane Jacobs on Gentrification, the New Urbanism, and Her Legacy," *Reason,* June 2001.

10. Ian L. McHarg, *Design with Nature* (New York: J. Wiley, 1992); Frederick Steiner, "Healing the Earth: The Relevance of Ian McHarg's Work for the Future," *Philosophy and Geography* 23, no. 2 (February 2004): 75–86.

11. "Central Park's Creator Tells of Its Beginning," *New York Times,* August 11, 1912; Roy Rosenzweig and Elizabeth Blackmar, *The Park and the People: A History of Central Park* (Ithaca, NY: Cornell University Press, 1992).

12. Paul H. Gobster, "Urban Park Restoration and the 'Museumification' of Nature," *Nature and Culture* 2, no. 2 (Autumn 2007): 95–114; Matthew Klingle, *Emerald City: An Environmental History of Seattle* (New Haven: Yale University Press, 2007).

13. Henry W. Lawrence, *City Trees: A Historical Geography from the Renaissance through the Nineteenth Century* (Charlottesville: University of Virginia Press, 2008).

14. Cook County Forest Preserve District Act (70 ILCS 810/), sec. 7, available at https://www.ilga.gov/legislation/ilcs/ilcs3.asp?ActID=876&ChapterID=15; Liam Heneghan et al., "Lessons Learned from Chicago Wilderness—Implementing and Sustaining Conservation Management in an Urban Setting," *Diversity* 4 (2012): 74–93.

15. Gerard T. Koeppel, *Water for Gotham: A History* (Princeton: Princeton University Press, 2001).

CHAPTER 4. BAMBI BOOM

1. Ralph H. Lutts, "The Trouble with Bambi: Walt Disney's *Bambi* and the American Vision of Nature," *Forest and Conservation History* 36, no. 4 (October 1992): 160–71.

2. Miles Traer, "The Nature of Disney," interview with Richard White, May 13, 2016, in *Generation Anthropocene,* produced by Leslie Chang, Mike Osborne, and Miles Traer, podcast, 29:45, https://www.genanthro.com/2016/05/13/the-nature-of-disney/.

3. Lutts, "Trouble with Bambi"; Jim Sterba, *Nature Wars: The Incredible Story of How Wildlife Comebacks Turned Backyards into Battlegrounds* (New York: Broadway, 2013).

4. Aldo Leopold, Lyle K. Sowls, and David L. Spencer, "A Survey of Over-populated Deer Ranges in the United States," *Journal of Wildlife Management* 11, no. 2 (April 1947): 162–77.

5. Steeve D. Côté et al., "Ecological Impacts of Deer Overabundance," *Annual Review of Ecology, Evolution, and Systematics* 35, no. 1 (2004): 113–47.

6. Timothy J. Gilfoyle, "White Cities, Linguistic Turns, and Disneylands: The New Paradigms of Urban History," *Reviews in American History* 26, no. 1 (1998): 175–204.

7. Peter Hall, *Cities of Tomorrow: An Intellectual History of Urban Planning and Design in the Twentieth Century,* 3rd ed. (Oxford: Blackwell, 2002), 319.

8. Hall, *Cities of Tomorrow,* 316–28; James F. Peltz, "It Started with Levittown in 1947: Nation's 1st Planned Community Transformed Suburbia," *Los Angeles Times,* June 21, 1988.

9. Adam Rome, *The Bulldozer in the Countryside: Suburban Sprawl and the Rise of American Environmentalism* (Cambridge: Cambridge University Press, 2001); Kenneth T. Jackson, *Crabgrass Frontier: The Suburbanization of the United States* (Oxford: Oxford University Press, 1987).

10. Stephen DeStefano and Richard M. DeGraaf, "Exploring the Ecology of Suburban Wildlife," *Frontiers in Ecology and the Environment* 1, no. 2 (March 2003): 95–101; Hall, *Cities of Tomorrow*, 330–33.

11. Larry R. Brown, M. Brian Gregory, and Jason T. May, "Relation of Urbanization to Stream Fish Assemblages and Species Traits in Nine Metropolitan Areas of the United States," *Urban Ecosystems* 12, no. 4 (2009): 391–416.

12. Rachel Surls and Judith B. Gerber, *From Cows to Concrete: The Rise and Fall of Farming in Los Angeles* (Los Angeles: Angel City Press, 2016).

13. Hall, *Cities of Tomorrow*, 303–8, 350.

14. Eric D. Stein et al., *Wetlands of the Southern California Coast: Historical Extent and Change Over Time,* Southern California Coastal Water Research Project Technical Report 826, San Francisco Estuary Institute Report 720, August 15, 2014.

15. Eric D. Stein et al., *Historical Ecology and Landscape Change of the San Gabriel River and Floodplain,* Southern California Coastal Water Research Project Technical Report 499, February 2007.

16. V. C. Radeloff et al., "Rapid Growth of the U.S. Wildland-Urban Interface Raises Wildfire Risk," *Proceedings of the National Academy of Sciences* 115, no. 13 (March 27, 2018): 3314–19.

17. Louis S. Warren, *The Hunter's Game: Poachers and Conservationists in Twentieth-Century America* (New Haven: Yale University Press, 1999).

18. Thomas Heberlein and Elizabeth Thomson, "Changes in U.S. Hunting Participation, 1980–90," *Human Dimensions of Wildlife* 1, no. 1 (1996): 85–86; U.S. Department of the Interior, U.S. Fish and Wildlife Service, and U.S. Department of Commerce, U.S. Census Bureau, *2016 National Survey of Fishing, Hunting, and Wildlife-Associated Recreation*, available at https://www.census.gov/content/dam/Census/library/publications/2018/demo/fhw16-nat.pdf.

19. Sterba, *Nature Wars*, 89–90.

20. U.S. Department of the Interior, Fish and Wildlife Service, and U.S. Department of Commerce, U.S. Census Bureau, *2006 National Survey of Fishing, Hunting, and Wildlife-Associated Recreation*, available at https://

www.census.gov/content/dam/Census/library/publications/2006/demo
/fhw06-nat_rev_new.pdf.

21. Côté et al., "Ecological Impacts of Deer Overabundance."

CHAPTER 5. ROOM TO ROAM

1. Lee Jones, "Cooperation Is Key," *Los Angeles Times*, August 28, 1991. I use the term *Southern California* here to refer to the region that encompasses Santa Barbara, Ventura, Los Angeles, Riverside, San Bernardino, Orange, Imperial, and San Diego Counties. This area is considerably larger than the gnatcatcher's coastal sage scrub range. For an extended discussion of the gnatcatcher and development in Southern California, see Audrey L. Mayer, *Bird versus Bulldozer: A Quarter-Century Conservation Battle in a Biodiversity Hotspot* (New Haven: Yale University Press, 2021).

2. J. L. Atwood and D. R. Bontrager, "California Gnatcatcher (*Polioptila californica*)," in the Cornell Lab of Ornithology's Birds of the World (database), ed. A. F. Poole and F. B. Gill, https://birdsoftheworld.org/bow /home; Joseph Grinnell, "Birds of the Pacific Slope of Los Angeles County," *Pasadena Academy of Sciences* 11 (1898): 50; Joseph Grinnell and Alden H. Miller, "The Distribution of Birds of California," *Pacific Coast Avifauna* 27, no. 1 (1944): 369–70.

3. J. T. Rotenberry and T. A. Scott, "Biology of the California Gnatcatcher: Filling in the Gaps," *West Birds* 29 (1988): 237–41; J. L. Atwood et al., "Distribution and Population Size of California Gnatcatchers on the Palos Verdes Peninsula, 1993–1997," *West Birds* 29 (1988): 340–50.

4. Department of the Interior, U.S. Fish and Wildlife Service, "Determination of Threatened Status for the Coastal California Gnatcatcher," *Federal Register* 58 (March 20, 1993): 16742–57.

5. Daniel Pollak, *Natural Community Conservation Planning (NCCP): The Origins of an Ambitious Experiment to Protect Ecosystems* (Sacramento: California Research Bureau, March 2001).

6. Pollak, *Natural Community Conservation Planning*.

7. California Department of Fish and Wildlife, *Summary of Natural Community Conservation Plans (NCCPs)*, October 2017.

8. Cristina E. Ramalho and Richard J. Hobbs, "Time for Change: Dynamic Urban Ecology," *Trends in Ecology and Evolution* 27, no. 3 (March 2012): 179–88.

9. Galen Cranz, *The Politics of Park Design: A History of Urban Parks in America* (Cambridge, MA: MIT Press, 1982); Richard A. Walker, *The*

Country in the City: The Greening of the San Francisco Bay Area (Seattle: University of Washington Press, 2013).

10. Walker, *Country in the City.*

11. Matthew Booker, *Down by the Bay: San Francisco's History between the Tides* (Oakland: University of California Press, 2020).

12. Walker, *Country in the City.*

13. Hadley Meares, "A Cast of Characters: The Creation of the Santa Monica Mountains National Recreation Area," KCET (website), June 25, 2015, https://www.kcet.org/shows/california-coastal-trail/a-cast-of-characters-the-creation-of-the-santa-monica-mountains-national-recreation-area.

14. Rebecca Coleen Retzlaff, "Planning for Broad-Based Environmental Protection: A Look Back at the Chicago Wilderness Biodiversity Recovery Plan," *Urban Ecosystems* 11, no. 1 (2008): 45–63.

15. Peter Simek, "Dallas May Now Get Two New Trinity River Parks," *D Magazine,* September 19, 2018, https://www.dmagazine.com/frontburner/2018/09/dallas-may-now-get-two-new-trinity-river-parks/.

16. Joe Trezza, "Where Coyotes, Foxes and Bobolinks Find a New Home: Freshkills Park," *New York Times,* June 9, 2016.

17. Cait Fields, Fresh Kills research director, interview with the author, New York, April 28, 2017; Kate Ascher and Frank O'Connell, "From Garbage to Energy at Fresh Kills," *New York Times,* September 15, 2013.

18. Virginia H. Dale, "Ecological Principles and Guidelines for Managing the Use of Land," *Ecological Applications* 10, no. 3 (June 2000): 639–70.

19. George R. Hess et al., "Integrating Wildlife Conservation into Urban Planning," in *Urban Wildlife Conservation,* ed. Robert A. McCleery, Christopher E. Moorman, and M. Nils Peterson (New York: Springer, 2014), 239–78.

20. Mark Hostetler and Sarah Reed, "Conservation Development: Designing and Managing Residential Landscapes for Wildlife," in McCleery, Moorman, and Peterson, *Urban Wildlife Conservation,* 279–302.

21. Cranz, *Politics of Park Design.*

22. *Natura Urbana: The Brachen of Berlin,* directed by Matthew Gandy (UK and Germany, 2017), 72 min.

23. Ellen Pehek, New York City Parks wildlife biologist, interview with the author, New York, May 1, 2017.

24. Joseph Berger, "Reclaimed Jewel Whose Attraction Can Be Perilous," *New York Times,* July 19, 2010.

CHAPTER 6. OUT OF THE SHADOWS

1. For more about the Kelly Keen case, see Stuart Wolpert, "Killing of Girl Underlines Urban Danger of Coyotes," *Los Angeles Times*, August 28, 1981.

2. Dan Flores, *Coyote America: A Natural and Supernatural History* (New York: Basic Books, 2016); Stephen DeStefano, *Coyote at the Kitchen Door: Living with Wildlife in Suburbia* (Cambridge, MA: Harvard University Press, 2010).

3. D. Gill, "The Coyote and the Sequential Occupants of the Los Angeles Basin," *American Anthropologist* 72 (1970): 821–26; William L. Preston, "Post-Columbian Wildlife Irruptions in California: Implications for Cultural and Environmental Understanding," in *Wilderness and Political Ecology: Aboriginal Influences and the Original State of Nature*, ed. Charles E. Kay and Randy T. Simmons (Salt Lake City: University of Utah Press, 2002), 111–40.

4. Joy Horowitz, "Urban Coyote: Prairie Wolf Has Become Citified," *Los Angeles Times*, August 19, 1980.

5. Sid Bernstein, "County Will Renew War against Coyote," *Los Angeles Times*, July 29, 1982.

6. "County Bans Coyote Feeding," *Los Angeles Times*, November 11, 1981.

7. Jianguo Wu, "Urban Ecology and Sustainability: The State-of-the-Science and Future Directions," *Landscape and Urban Planning* 125 (May 2014): 209–21.

8. Clark E. Adams and Kieran J. Lindsey, *Urban Wildlife Management*, 2nd ed. (Boca Raton, FL: CRC Press, 2010), 68.

9. Ethan H. Decker et al., "Energy and Material Flow through the Urban Ecosystem," *Annual Review of Energy and the Environment* 25 (2000): 685–740.

10. Kirsten Schwarz et al., "Abiotic Drivers of Ecological Structure and Function in Urban Systems," in *Urban Wildlife Conservation*, ed. Robert A. McCleery, Christopher E. Moorman, and M. Nils Peterson (New York: Springer, 2014), 55–74; S. T. A. Pickett et al., "Urban Ecological Systems: Linking Terrestrial Ecological, Physical, and Socioeconomic Components of Metropolitan Areas," *Annual Review of Ecology and Systematics* 32 (2001): 127–57.

11. Christopher J. Walsh et al., "The Urban Stream Syndrome: Current Knowledge and the Search for a Cure," *Journal of the North American*

Benthological Society 24, no. 3 (2005): 706–23; Seth J. Wenger et al., "Twenty-Six Key Research Questions in Urban Stream Ecology: An Assessment of the State of the Science," *Journal of the North American Benthological Society* 28, no. 4 (2009): 1080–98.

12. Matthew Gandy, "Negative Luminescence," *Annals of the American Association of Geographers* 107, no. 5 (2017): 1090–107; Jeremy Zallen, *American Lucifers: The Dark History of Artificial Light* (Chapel Hill: University of North Carolina Press, 2019).

13. Travis Longcore, *Ecological Consequences of Artificial Night Lighting* (Washington, DC: Island Press, 2005).

14. J. L. Dowling, D. A. Luther, and P. P. Marra, "Comparative Effects of Urban Development and Anthropogenic Noise on Bird Songs," *Behavioral Ecology* 23, no. 1 (January–February 2012): 201–9.

15. S. S. Ditchkoff, S. T. Saalfeld, and C. J. Gibson, "Animal Behavior in Urban Ecosystems: Modifications due to Human-Induced Stress," *Urban Ecosystems* 9 (January 2006): 5–12.

16. Robert B. Blair, "Land Use and Avian Species Diversity along an Urban Gradient," *Ecological Applications* 6, no. 2 (1996): 506–19; J. D. Fischer et al., "Categorizing Wildlife Responses to Urbanization and Conservation Implications of Terminology: Terminology and Urban Conservation," *Conservation Biology* 29, no. 4 (August 2015): 1246–48. For examples of the extensive literature building on Blair's study, see Solène Croci, Alain Butet, and Philippe Clergeau, "Does Urbanization Filter Birds on the Basis of Their Biological Traits?," *Condor* 110, no. 2 (2008): 223–40; several chapters in McCleery, Moorman, and Peterson, *Urban Wildlife Conservation.*

17. Joy Horowitz, "Urban Coyote: Prairie Wolf Has Become Citified," *Los Angeles Times,* August 19, 1980; S. R. Kellert, "American Attitudes toward and Knowledge of Animals: An Update," *International Journal for the Study of Animal Problems* 1, no. 2 (1980): 107.

18. Hal Herzog, *Some We Love, Some We Hate, Some We Eat: Why It's So Hard to Think Straight about Animals* (New York: HarperCollins, 2010), 1.

19. Andrew Flowers, "The National Parks Have Never Been More Popular," FiveThirtyEight, May 25, 2016, https://fivethirtyeight.com/features/the-national-parks-have-never-been-more-popular/; Oliver R. W. Pergams and Patricia A. Zaradic, "Evidence for a Fundamental and Pervasive Shift Away from Nature-Based Recreation," *Proceedings of the National Academy of Sciences* 105, no. 7 (2008): 2295–300; Kristopher K. Robison

and Daniel Ridenour, "Whither the Love of Hunting? Explaining the Decline of a Major Form of Rural Recreation as a Consequence of the Rise of Virtual Entertainment and Urbanism," *Human Dimensions of Wildlife* 17, no. 6 (2012): 418–36.

20. Benjamin Mueller and Lisa W. Foderaro, "A Coyote Eludes the Police on the Upper West Side," *New York Times,* April 22, 2015.

21. Heather Wieczorek Hudenko, William F. Siemer, and Daniel J. Decker, *Living with Coyotes in Suburban Areas: Insights from Two New York State Counties*, HDRU Series No. 08–8 (Ithaca, NY: Human Dimensions Research Unit, Department of Natural Resources, Cornell University, 2008), iv, https://ecommons.cornell.edu/bitstream/handle/1813 /40431/HDRUReport08-8.pdf.

22. Christine Dell'Amore, "Downtown Coyotes: Inside the Secret Lives of Chicago's Predator," *National Geographic* (website), November 21, 2014, https://www.nationalgeographic.com/animals/ article/141121-coyotes-animals-science-chicago-cities-urban-nation.

23. Coyote 748's history is detailed in Stan Gehrt and Shane McKenzie, "Human-Coyote Incident Report, Chicago, IL, April 2014," Max McGraw Wildlife Foundation, July 22, 2014, https://urbancoyoteresearch.com /sites/default/files/resources/Bronzeville%20Hazing%20Final%20Public %20Report.pdf.

CHAPTER 7. CLOSE ENCOUNTERS

1. Greg Macgowan, "Oak ridge nj bipedal bear," YouTube, posted July 19, 2014, https://www.youtube.com/watch?v=vuJlsmTG2ik.

2. John McPhee, "Direct Eye Contact: The Most Sophisticated, Most Urban, Most Reproductively Fruitful of Bears," *New Yorker,* February 26, 2018.

3. In North America, brown bears (*Ursus arctos*) include both "grizzlies" and "Kodiak bears," which are part of the same species. For more about New Jersey's black bears, see the New Jersey Division of Fish and Wildlife's "Know the Bear Facts: Black Bears in New Jersey," updated January 21, 2021, https://www.state.nj.us/dep/fgw/bearfacts.htm.

4. Michael R. Pelton et al., "American Black Bear Conservation Action Plan (*Ursus americanus*)," in *Bears: Status Survey and Conservation Action Plan,* compiled by Christopher Servheen, Stephen Herrero, and Bernard Peyton (Gland, Switzerland: IUNC, 1999), 144–56.

5. Jon Mooallem, *Wild Ones: A Sometimes Dismaying, Weirdly Reassuring Story about Looking at People Looking at Animals in America* (New York: Penguin, 2014), 62–71.

6. See, e.g., Joseph Dixon, "Food Predilections of Predatory and Fur-Bearing Mammals," *Journal of Mammalogy* 6, no. 1 (February 1925): 34–46.

7. Sterling D. Miller, "Population Management of Bears in North America," *Bears: Their Biology and Management* 8 (1990): 357–73.

8. Richard West Sellars, *Preserving Nature in the National Parks: A History* (New Haven: Yale University Press, 1999), 78–80.

9. Hank Hristienko and John E. McDonald Jr., "Going into the 21st Century: A Perspective on Trends and Controversies in the Management of the American Black Bear," *Ursus* 18, no. 1 (2007): 72–88.

10. David L. Garshelis and Hank Hristienko, "State and Provincial Estimates of American Black Bear Numbers versus Assessments of Population Trend," *Ursus* 17, no. 1 (2006): 1–7.

11. D. L. Lewis et al., "Foraging Ecology of Black Bears in Urban Environments: Guidance for Human-Bear Conflict Mitigation," *Ecosphere* 6, no. 8 (August 2015): article 141.

12. Jon P. Beckmann and Joel Berger, "Rapid Ecological and Behavioural Changes In Carnivores: The Responses of Black Bears (*Ursus americanus*) to Altered Food," *Journal of Zoology* 261, no. 2 (2003): 207–12; Clark E. Adams and Kieran J. Lindsey, *Urban Wildlife Management*, 2nd ed. (Boca Raton, FL: CRC Press, 2010), 258.

13. Beckmann and Berger, "Rapid Ecological and Behavioural Changes."

14. Jon P. Beckmann and Joel Berger, "Using Black Bears to Test Ideal-Free Distribution Models Experimentally," *Journal of Mammalogy* 84, no. 2 (May 2003): 594–606.

15. Wildlife Conservation Society, "Urban Black Bears 'Live Fast, Die Young,'" *ScienceDaily*, October 1, 2008, https://www.sciencedaily.com/releases/2008/09/080930135301.htm; Beckman and Berger, "Using Black Bears."

16. Kerry A. Gunther, "Bear Management in Yellowstone National Park, 1960–93," *Bears: Their Biology and Management* 9 (1994): 549–60.

17. Sellars, *Preserving Nature;* Joseph S. Madison, "Yosemite National Park: The Continuous Evolution of Human–Black Bear Conflict Management," *Human-Wildlife Conflicts* 2, no. 2 (Fall 2008): 160–67.

18. Gunther, "Bear Management."

19. Mary Meagher, "Bears in Transition, 1959–1970s," *Yellowstone Science* 16, no. 2 (2008): 5–12.

20. Galen A. Rowell, "Killing and Mistreating of National-Park Bears," *New York Times,* March 23, 1974.

21. Rachel Mazur, *Speaking of Bears: The Bear Crisis and a Tale of Rewilding from Yosemite, Sequoia, and Other National Parks* (Guilford, CT: Rowman and Littlefield, 2015), 181.

22. Mazur, *Speaking of Bears,* 193.

23. John B. Hopkins et al., "The Changing Anthropogenic Diets of American Black Bears over the Past Century in Yosemite National Park," *Frontiers in Ecology and the Environment* 12, no. 2 (March 2014): 107–14.

24. Sarah K. Brown, "Black Bear Population Genetics in California: Signatures of Population Structure, Competitive Release, and Historical Translocation," *Journal of Mammalogy* 90, no. 5 (2009): 1066–74.

25. Bill Billiter, "6-Foot Bear Killed in Granada Hills," *Los Angeles Times,* June 22, 1982, C-1.

26. Stephen R. Kellert, "Public Attitudes toward Bears and Their Conservation," *Bears: Their Biology and Management* 9 (1994): 43–50.

27. Chris Erskine, "It's Words, Not Bullets, for the 'Bear Whisperer' of the Eastern Sierra," *Los Angeles Times,* February 12, 2020.

28. Steve Searles, interview with the author, Mammoth Lakes, CA, September 17, 2019.

29. For more data on New Jersey's bear hunt, see "New Jersey's Black Bear Hunting Season," New Jersey Department of Environmental Protection, Division of Fish and Wildlife, updated June 14, 2021, https://www.nj.gov/dep/fgw/bearseason_info.htm; Frank Kummer, "At 700 Pounds, Black Bear Killed in New Jersey Sets World Record, Says National Hunting Group," *Philadelphia Inquirer,* February 14, 2020.

30. Branden B. Johnson and James Sciascia, "Views on Black Bear Management in New Jersey," *Human Dimensions of Wildlife* 18, no. 4 (2013), 249–62.

31. Jon Mooallem, "Pedals the Bear," *New York Times,* December 21, 2016.

32. Daniel Hubbard, "NJ Releases Disturbing Photos Believed to Be 'Pedals,' Bear Feared Dead," Patch (website), October 17, 2016, https://patch.com/new-jersey/mahwah/state-releases-alleged-photos-killed-bipedal-bear-pedals.

33. Mooallem, "Pedals the Bear."

CHAPTER 8. HOME TO ROOST

1. Mark V. Barrow Jr., "Science, Sentiment, and the Specter of Extinction: Reconsidering Birds of Prey during America's Interwar Years," *Environmental History* 7, no. 1 (January 2002): 69–98.

2. John Hayes, "Bald Eagles Thriving in Southwestern Pa.," *Pittsburgh Post-Gazette*, April 24, 2016; Marcus Schneck, "How Bald Eagles Returned to Pennsylvania," *Patriot-News*, August 6, 2013.

3. John Hayes, "Burghers of a Feather," *Pittsburgh Post-Gazette*, March 12, 2013, B1.

4. James Parton, "Pittsburg [*sic*]," *The Atlantic*, January 1868.

5. Hayes, "Burghers of a Feather."

6. Hayes, "Burghers of a Feather."

7. John Hayes, "Bald Eagles Tending Second Egg," *Pittsburgh Post-Gazette*, February 25, 2014, B-2; "Eagle vs. Raccoon," *Pittsburgh Post-Gazette*, March 2, 2014, D-11.

8. John Hayes, "Close-Ups of Eagles Bring Dose of Reality," *Pittsburgh Post-Gazette*, March 9, 2014, A-1.

9. Molly Born, "Mom and Dad Know Best—Experts Trying to Calm Public Fear for Eaglets," *Pittsburgh Post-Gazette*, May 6, 2014, A-9; Mahita Gajanan, "Memorial Springs Up in Hays for Eagle Eggs That Didn't Hatch," *Pittsburgh Post-Gazette*, March 31, 2015, B-1.

10. John Hayes, "Hays Eagles' Feline Meal Disturbing for Some Viewers," *Pittsburgh Post-Gazette*, April 28, 2016, B-1; PixCams, "Hays bald eagles bring cat to nest for eaglets," YouTube, posted April 28, 2016, https://www.youtube.com/watch?v=PWc6aF6aMQ8.

11. Menno Schilthuizen, *Darwin Comes to Town: How the Urban Jungle Drives Evolution* (New York: Picador, 2018), 2; Sharon M. Meagher, ed., *Philosophy and the City: Classic to Contemporary Writings* (Albany: State University of New York Press, 2008), 20–39.

12. Meagher, *Philosophy and the City,* 72–80.

13. Victor E. Shelford, introduction to *Naturalist's Guide to the Americas,* ed. Shelford (Baltimore: Williams and Wilkins, 1926), 3. See also Jianguo Wu, "Urban Ecology and Sustainability: The State-of-the-Science and Future Directions," *Landscape and Urban Planning* 125 (May 2014): 211; Jennifer R. Wolch, Kathleen West, and Thomas E. Gaines, "Transspecies Urban Theory," *Environment and Planning D: Society and Space* 13 (1995): 743.

14. Mark V. Barrow Jr., *Nature's Ghosts: Confronting Extinction from the Age of Jefferson to the Age of Ecology* (University of Chicago Press, 2010), 201–33

15. Frank Chapman, "Birds and Bonnets," *Forest and Stream* 26, no. 6 (1886): 84.

16. Peter G. Ayres, *Shaping Ecology: The Life of Arthur Tansley* (Chichester: John Wiley and Sons, 2012).

17. R. S. R. Fitter, *London's Natural History,* Collins New Naturalist Library, Book 3 (London: HarperCollins, 2011); Ulrike Weiland and Matthias Richter, "Lines of Tradition and Recent Approaches to Urban Ecology, Focussing on Germany and the USA," *Gaia* 18, no. 1 (2009): 49–57.

18. Aldo Leopold, *Game Management* (New York: Charles Scribner's Sons, 1933), 404; R. Bennitt, "Summarization of the Eleventh North American Wildlife Conference," *Transactions of the North American Wildlife Conference* 11 (1946): 517. For a much more recent assessment of field research locations, see Laura J. Martin, B. Blossey, and E. Ellis, "Mapping Where Ecologists Work: Biases in the Global Distribution of Terrestrial Ecological Observations," *Frontiers in Ecology and the Environment* 10 (2012): 195–201.

19. Raymond F. Dasmann, "Wildlife and the New Conservation," *Wildlife Society News* 105 (1966): 48–49.

20. C. S. Holling and Gordon Orians, "Toward an Urban Ecology," *Bulletin of the Ecological Society of America* 52, no. 2 (1971): 2–6; Andrew Sih, Alison M. Bell, and Jacob L. Kerby, "Two Stressors Are Far Deadlier than One," *Trends in Ecology and Evolution* 19, no. 6 (2004): 274–76.

21. Lowell W. Adams, "Urban Wildlife Ecology and Conservation: A Brief History of the Discipline," *Urban Ecosystems* 8 (2005): 139–56.

22. Mark Weckel, interview with the author, New York City, April 27, 2017.

23. John Marzluff, interview with the author, Seattle, July 11, 2017.

24. Robert B. Blair, "Land Use and Avian Species Diversity along an Urban Gradient," *Ecological Applications* 6, no. 2 (1996): 506; S. T. A. Pickett et al., "Urban Ecological Systems: Linking Terrestrial Ecological, Physical, and Socioeconomic Components of Metropolitan Areas," *Annual Review of Ecology and Systematics* 32 (2001): 128.

25. Steward T. A. Pickett et al., "Evolution and Future of Urban Ecological Science: Ecology in, of, and for the City," *Ecosystem Health and Sustainability* 2, no. 7 (2016): e01229; Pickett et al., "Urban Ecological Systems."

26. Laurel Braitman, "Dirty Birds: What It's Like to Live with a National Symbol," *California Sunday Magazine,* March 30, 2017.

27. U.S. Fish and Wildlife Service, *Final Report: Bald Eagle Population Size—2020 Update* (Washington, DC: U.S. Fish and Wildlife Service, Division of Migratory Bird Management, 2020).

CHAPTER 9. HIDE AND SEEK

1. On P-22 and the L.A. Zoo, see Martha Groves and Angel Jennings, "P-22 Vacates Home, Heads Back to Griffith Park, Wildlife Officials Say," *Los Angeles Times,* April 13, 2015; Carla Hall, "Opinion: The Griffith Park Puma, P-22, May Be Guilty of Killing a Koala at the Zoo, but Let's Not Rush to Judge Him," *Los Angeles Times,* March 11, 2016.

2. Joseph Serna, "Mountain Lions Are Being Killed on Freeways and Weakened by Inbreeding. Researchers Have a Solution," *Los Angeles Times,* May 16, 2018.

3. Thomas Curwen, "A Week in the Life of P-22, the Big Cat Who Shares Griffith Park with Millions of People," *Los Angeles Times,* February 8, 2017.

4. Groves and Jennings, "P-22 Vacates Home."

5. Douglas Chadwick, "Ghost Cats," *National Geographic,* December 2013, 1–7.

6. Ian Lovett, "Prime Suspect in Koala's Murder: Los Angeles's Mountain Lion," *New York Times,* March 23, 2016; Joseph Serna and Hailey Branson-Potts, "Is P-22 Mountain Lion Too Dangerous for Griffith Park?," *Los Angeles Times,* March 11, 2016.

7. Louis Sahagún, "L.A. Zoo Wants Mountain Lion to Remain a Neighbor despite Koala Death," *Los Angeles Times,* March 16, 2016.

8. K. L. Evans et al., "What Makes an Urban Bird?," *Global Change Biology* 17, no. 1 (January 2011): 32–44.

9. K. S. Delaney, S. P. D. Riley, and R. N. Fisher, "A Rapid, Strong, and Convergent Genetic Response to Urban Habitat Fragmentation in Four Divergent and Widespread Vertebrates," *PLoS One* 5, no. 9 (2010): e12767.

10. David Quammen, *The Song of the Dodo: Island Biogeography in an Age of Extinctions* (New York: Random House, 2012).

11. Richard T. T. Forman and Lauren E. Alexander, "Roads and Their Major Ecological Effects," *Annual Review of Ecology and Systematics* 29, no. 1 (1998): 207–31; U.S. Department of Transportation, *Wildlife-Vehicle Collision Reduction Study: Report to Congress* (August 2008).

12. Joel Berger, "Fear, Human Shields and the Redistribution of Prey and Predators in Protected Areas," *Biology Letters* 3, no. 6 (2007): 620–23.

13. Daniel Klem Jr., "Collisions between Birds and Windows: Mortality and Prevention," *Journal of Field Ornithology* 61, no. 1 (1990): 120–28; Becca Cudmore, "This Website Collects Obituaries for Birds—Here's Why You Should Use It," *Audubon*, Summer 2016, 1–9.

14. Seth P. D. Riley et al., "Wildlife Friendly Roads: The Impacts of Roads on Wildlife in Urban Areas and Potential Remedies," in *Urban Wildlife Conservation*, ed. Robert McCleery, Christopher E. Moorman, and M. Nils Peterson (New York: Springer, 2014), 323–60; Bill Workman, "Tunnel of Love for Stanford's Salamanders," *SFGate / San Francisco Chronicle*, August 30, 2001.

15. Avishay Artsy, "Here's What You Need to Know about the Liberty Canyon Wildlife Crossing," KCRW (website), February 20, 2018, https://www.kcrw.com/culture/shows/design-and-architecture/heres-what-you-need-to-know-about-the-liberty-canyon-wildlife-crossing.

16. Darryl N. Jones and S. James Reynolds, "Feeding Birds in Our Towns and Cities: A Global Research Opportunity," *Journal of Avian Biology* 39, no. 3 (May 2008): 265–71; Jameson F. Chace and John J. Walsh, "Urban Effects on Native Avifauna: A Review," *Landscape and Urban Planning* 74, no. 1 (2006): 46–69.

17. David N. Clark, Darryl N. Jones and S. James Reynolds, "Exploring the Motivations for Garden Bird Feeding in South-east England," *Ecology and Society* 24, no. 1 (2019): https://www.jstor.org/stable/26796915.

18. Richard A. Fuller, "Garden Bird Feeding Predicts the Structure of Urban Avian Assemblages," *Diversity and Distributions* 14, no. 1 (January 2008): 131–37.

19. Amanda D. Rodewald, Laura J. Kearns, and Daniel P. Shustack, "Anthropogenic Resource Subsidies Decouple Predator–Prey Relationships," *Ecological Applications* 21, no. 3 (2011): 936–43.

20. John Hadidan et al., "Raccoons (*Procyon lotor*)," in *Urban Carnivores: Ecology, Conflict, and Conservation*, ed. Stanley D. Gehrt, Seth P. D. Riley, and Brian L. Cypher (Baltimore: Johns Hopkins University Press, 2010), 35–46; Suzanne Prange, Stanley D. Gehrt, and Ernie P. Wiggers, "Demographic Factors Contributing to High Raccoon Densities in Urban Landscapes," *Journal of Wildlife Management* 67, no. 2 (2003): 324–33; William J. Graser et al., "Variation in Demographic Patterns and Population Structure of Raccoons across an Urban Landscape," *Journal of Wildlife Management* 76, no. 5 (July 2012): 976–86.

21. Chace and Walsh, "Urban Effects on Native Avifauna"; Michael L. McKinney, "Urbanization, Biodiversity, and Conservation," *BioScience* 52, no. 10 (2002): 883–90.

22. Natural Resources Defense Council, *Wasted: How America Is Losing up to 40 Percent of Its Food from Farm to Fork to Landfill*, 2nd ed. (August 2017). This is an update of the 2012 report.

23. Amy M. Ryan and Sarah R. Partan, "Urban Wildlife Behavior," in McCleery, Moorman, and Peterson, *Urban Wildlife Conservation*, 149–73.

24. S. A. Poessel, E. C. Mock, and S. W. Breck, "Coyote (*Canis latrans*) Diet in an Urban Environment: Variation Relative to Pet Conflicts, Housing Density, and Season," *Canadian Journal of Zoology* 95, no. 4 (April 2017): 287–97.

25. Jason D. Fischer et al., "Urbanization and the Predation Paradox: The Role of Trophic Dynamics in Structuring Vertebrate Communities," *BioScience* 62, no. 9 (September 2012): 809–18.

26. Michael E. Soulé et al., "Reconstructed Dynamics of Rapid Extinctions of Chaparral-Requiring Birds in Urban Habitat Islands," *Conservation Biology* 2, no. 1 (March 1988): 75–92.

27. Soulé et al., "Reconstructed Dynamics," 84; Kevin R. Crooks and Michael E. Soulé, "Mesopredator Release and Avifaunal Extinctions in a Fragmented System," *Nature* 400 (August 5, 1999): 563–66.

28. Kelly Hessedal, "San Diego Zoo Safari Park Sees Spike in Mountain Lion Sightings," CBS 8 San Diego (website), April 16, 2020, https://www.cbs8.com/article/life/animals/san-diego-zoo-safari-park-sees-spike-in-mountain-lion-sightings/509-ce458ca5-c6f9-4776-8b10-30479a48fdad.

29. Louis Sahagún, "Southern California Mountain Lions Get Temporary Endangered Species Status," *Los Angeles Times*, April 16, 2020.

30. John F. Benson et al., "Interactions between Demography, Genetics, and Landscape Connectivity Increase Extinction Probability for a Small Population of Large Carnivores in a Major Metropolitan Area," *Proceedings of the Royal Society B* 283, no. 1837 (August 31, 2016): 1–10.

CHAPTER 10. CREATURE DISCOMFORTS

1. W. Gardner Selby, "Austin's I-Beam Bat Haven," *Austin American Journal*, October 13, 1984, A-3; James Coates, "2 Problems Vex LBJ's Town: Rapid Bats, Leprous Armadillos," *Chicago Tribune*, November 7,

1984; "Bats Plaguing City in Texas during Annual Migration," *Chicago Tribune,* October 4, 1984.

2. Stephen R. Kellert, "American Attitudes toward and Knowledge of Animals: An Update," *International Journal for the Study of Animal Problems* 1, no. 2 (1980): 87–119.

3. The figure of twenty-six mammal orders is commonly used in the scientific literature, but there is no universally agreed-upon classification for mammals at this level.

4. Cara E. Brook and Andrew P. Dobson, "Bats as 'Special' Reservoirs for Emerging Zoonotic Pathogens," *Trends in Microbiology* 23, no. 3 (March 2015): 172–80.

5. Brook and Dobson, "Bats as 'Special' Reservoirs."

6. N. Allocati et al., "Bat–Man Disease Transmission: Zoonotic Pathogens from Wildlife Reservoirs to Human Populations," *Cell Death Discovery* 2 (2016): 16048; Andrew P. Dobson, "What Links Bats to Emerging Infectious Diseases?," *Science* 310 (October 28, 2005): 628–29; Charles H. Calisher et al., "Bats: Important Reservoir Hosts of Emerging Viruses," *Clinical Microbiology Reviews* 19, no. 3 (July 2006): 531–45.

7. Louise H. Taylor, Sophia M. Latham, and Mark E. J. Woolhouse, "Risk Factors for Human Disease Emergence," *Philosophical Transactions of the Royal Society B* (2001): 356983–89; Barbara A. Han, Andrew M. Kramer, and John M. Drake, "Global Patterns of Zoonotic Disease in Mammals," *Trends in Parasitology* 32, no. 7 (July 2016): 565–77.

8. Han, Kramer, and Drake, "Global Patterns of Zoonotic Disease."

9. For more on the status of bats and how to help them, visit the website of Bat Conservation International, https://www.batcon.org/.

10. For more information, visit the website of the White-Nose Syndrome Response Team, https://www.whitenosesyndrome.org/.

11. David Quammen, *Spillover: Animal Infections and the Next Human Pandemic* (New York: W. W. Norton, 2012); William B. Karesh et al., "Ecology of Zoonoses: Natural and Unnatural Histories," *Lancet* 380, no. 9857 (2012): 1936–45.

12. Quammen, *Spillover.*

13. Vanessa O. Ezenwa et al., "Avian Diversity and West Nile Virus: Testing Associations between Biodiversity and Infectious Disease Risk," *Proceedings of the Royal Society* 273, no. 1582 (January 7, 2006): 109–17; S. A. Hamer, E. Lehrer, and S. B. Magle, "Wild Birds as Sentinels for Multiple Zoonotic Pathogens along an Urban to Rural Gradient in Greater Chicago, Illinois," *Zoonoses and Public Health* 59, no. 5 (August 2012): 355–64.

14. David R. Foster et al., "Wildlife Dynamics in the Changing New England Landscape," *Journal of Biogeography* 29, nos. 10–11 (October 2002): 1337–57.

15. S. Haensch et al., "Distinct Clones of *Yersinia pestis* Caused the Black Death," *PLoS Pathogens* 6, no. 10 (2010): e1001134.

16. Catherine A. Bradley and Sonia Altizer, "Urbanization and the Ecology of Wildlife Diseases," *Trends in Ecology and Evolution* 22, no. 2 (2007): 95–102.

17. Stanley D. Gehrt, Seth P. D. Riley, and Brian L. Cypher, eds., *Urban Carnivores: Ecology, Conflict, and Conservation* (Baltimore: Johns Hopkins University Press, 2010).

18. Bill Sullivan, "Is the Brain Parasite *Toxoplasma* Manipulating Your Behavior, or Is Your Immune System to Blame?" *The Conversation*, May 4, 2019, https://theconversation.com/is-the-brain-parasite-toxoplasma-manipulating-your-behavior-or-is-your-immune-system-to-blame-116718.

19. Bryony A. Jones et al., "Zoonosis Emergence Linked to Agricultural Intensification and Environmental Change," *Proceedings of the National Academy of Sciences* 110, no. 21 (May 21, 2013): 8399–404; P. A. Conrad et al., "Transmission of Toxoplasma: Clues from the Study of Sea Otters as Sentinels of *Toxoplasma gondii* Flow into the Marine Environment," *International Journal for Parasitology* 35, nos. 11–12 (October 2005): 1155–68.

20. Seth P. D. Riley, Laurel E. K. Serieys, and Joanne G. Moriarty, "Infections Disease and Contaminants in Urban Wildlife: Unseen and Often Overlooked Threats," in *Urban Wildlife Conservation*, ed. Robert McCleery, Christopher E. Moorman, and M. Nils Peterson (New York: Springer, 2014), 175–215; Sepp Tuul et al., "Urban Environment and Cancer in Wildlife: Available Evidence and Future Research Avenues," *Proceedings of the Royal Society B* 286, no. 1894 (January 2, 2019): 20182434.

21. Thomas Nagel, "What Is It Like to Be a Bat?," *Philosophical Review* 83, no. 4 (October 1974): 438.

CHAPTER 11. CATCH AND RELEASE

1. "Zoo Miami's Ron Magill Recounts Hurricane Andrew," NBC 6 South Florida, August 23, 2012, https://www.nbcmiami.com/multimedia/zoo-miamis-ron-magill-recounts-hurricane-andrew/1904328/.

2. Burkhard Bilger, "Swamp Things: Florida's Uninvited Predators," *New Yorker,* April 20, 2009.

3. "Zoo Miami's Ron Magill."

4. Steve Lohr, "After the Storms: Three Reports," *New York Times,* September 27, 1992.

5. John Donnelly, "The Rebuilt MetroZoo Ready to Roar Once More," *Miami Herald,* December 16, 1992.

6. Dan Fesperman, "In Andrew's Wake, a New Wild Kingdom: Monkeys, Cougars Still Running Loose Weeks after Storm," *Baltimore Sun,* September 22, 1992.

7. Abby Goodnough, "Forget the Gators: Exotic Pets Run Wild in Florida," *New York Times,* February 29, 2004; Fesperman, "In Andrew's Wake."

8. Scott Hardin, "Managing Non-native Wildlife in Florida: State Perspective, Policy, and Practice," *Managing Vertebrate Invasive Species* 14 (2007): 43–52.

9. Kenneth L. Krysko et al., "Verified Non-indigenous Amphibians and Reptiles in Florida from 1863 through 2010: Outlining the Invasion Process and Identifying Invasion Pathways and Stages," *Zootaxa* 3028 (2011): 1–64.

10. L. C. Corn et al., *Harmful Non-native Species: Issues for Congress,* Congressional Research Service Issue Brief, RL30123 (November 25, 2002); D. Pimentel, R. Zuniga, and D. Morrison, "Update on the Environmental and Economic Costs Associated with Alien-Invasive Species in the United States," *Ecological Economics* 52, no. 3 (February 15, 2005): 273–88.

11. Vernon N. Kisling, ed., *Zoo and Aquarium History: Ancient Animal Collections to Zoological Gardens* (Boca Raton, FL: CRC Press, 2001).

12. Christina M. Romagosa, "Contribution of the Live Animal Trade to Biological Invasions," in *Biological Invasions in Changing Ecosystems,* ed. João Canning-Clode (Warsaw: De Gruyter, 2015), 116–34; Tracy J. Revels, *Sunshine Paradise: A History of Florida Tourism* (Gainesville: University of Florida Press, 2011); Jack E. Davis, *The Gulf: The Making of an American Sea* (New York: Liveright, 2017).

13. Emma R. Bush, "Global Trade in Exotic Pets, 2006–2012," *Conservation Biology* 28, no. 3 (June 2014): 663–76.

14. Hazel Jackson, "Parakeets Are the New Pigeons—and They're on Course for Global Domination," *The Conversation,* August 1, 2016, https://theconversation.com/parakeets-are-the-new-pigeons-and-theyre-on-course-for-global-domination-63244.

15. On zoo escapes and the ethics of zoos and zoo escapes, see Emma Marris, *Wild Souls: Freedom and Flourishing in the Non-human World* (New York: Bloomsbury, 2021).

16. For more information, see the Born Free USA website, https://www.bornfreeusa.org/.

17. Ron Magill, interview with the author, Miami, March 8, 2019; Adriana Brasileiro, "Activists Lose Last Legal Battle to Protect Rare Miami Forest from Walmart Development," *Miami Herald,* June 19, 2019.

18. Kisling, *Zoo and Aquarium History.*

19. E. Mullineaux, "Veterinary Treatment and Rehabilitation of Indigenous Wildlife," *Journal of Small Animal Practice* 55 (2014): 293–300.

20. Mullineaux, "Veterinary Treatment."

21. Peter Singer, *Animal Liberation* (New York: Random House, 2015), 8.

22. Peter Singer, interview with the author, February 11, 2019.

23. Jaclyn Cosgrove, "Firefighters' Fateful Choices: How the Woolsey Fire Became an Unstoppable Monster," *Los Angeles Times,* January 6, 2019.

24. Jenna Chandler, "Evacuation Orders Lifted as Tally of Buildings Destroyed by Woolsey Fire Swells to 1,500," *LA Curbed,* November 19, 2018, https://la.curbed.com/2018/11/9/18079170/california-fire-woolsey-evacuations-los-angeles-ventura.

CHAPTER 12. DAMAGE CONTROL

1. M. Nils Peterson et al., "Rearticulating the Myth of Human–Wildlife Conflict," *Conservation Letters* 3, no. 2 (April 2010): 74–82; Jacobellis v. Ohio, 378 U.S. 184 (1964), at 197 (Stewart, J., concurring).

2. Terry A. Messmer, "The Emergence of Human–Wildlife Conflict Management: Turning Challenges into Opportunities," *International Biodeterioration and Biodegradation* 45, no. 3 (2000): 97–102.

3. See the Internet Center for Wildlife Damage Management's website, https://icwdm.org/.

4. Robert Snetsinger, *The Ratcatcher's Child: The History of the Pest Control Industry* (Cleveland: Franzak and Foster, 1983).

5. Snetsinger, *Ratcatcher's Child,* 20.

6. Robert Sullivan, *Rats: Observations on the History and Habitat of the City's Most Unwanted Inhabitants* (New York: Bloomsbury, 2005), 97.

7. Thomas G. Barnes, "State Agency Oversight of the Nuisance Wildlife Control Industry," *Wildlife Society Bulletin* 25, no. 1 (1997): 185–88.

8. Dawn Day Biehler, *Pests in the City: Flies, Bedbugs, Cockroaches, and Rats* (Seattle: University of Washington Press, 2013); Colby Itkowitz, "Trump Attacks Rep. Cummings's District, Calling It a 'Disgusting, Rat and Rodent Infested Mess,'" *Washington Post*, July 27, 2019.

9. Sullivan, *Rats*, 145.

10. David E. Davis, "The Scarcity of Rats and the Black Death: An Ecological History," *Journal of Interdisciplinary History* 16, no. 3 (Winter 1986): 455–70; John T. Emlen, Allen W. Stokes, and David E. Davis, "Methods for Estimating Populations of Brown Rats in Urban Habitats," *Ecology* 30, no. 4 (October 1949): 430–42; David E. Davis, "The Characteristics of Rat Populations," *Quarterly Review of Biology* 28, no. 4 (December 1953): 373–401.

11. Snetsinger, *Ratcatcher's Child*, 44–55.

12. 7 USC 8351, Predatory and Other Wild Animals; for information on USDA APHIS Wildlife Services programs, see the reports at https://www.aphis.usda.gov/aphis/ourfocus/wildlifedamage/sa_reports/sa_pdrs.

13. Seth P. Riley et al., "Anticoagulant Exposure and Notoedric Mange in Bobcats and Mountain Lions in Urban Southern California," *Journal of Wildlife Management* 71, no. 6 (August 2007): 1874–84.

14. Clark E. Adams and Kieran J. Lindsey, *Urban Wildlife Management*, 2nd ed. (Boca Raton, FL: CRC Press, 2010), 98, 267.

15. For more information, visit the FAA Wildlife Strike Database, at https://wildlife.faa.gov/home, and the State Farm data-tracking webpage "How Likely Are You to Have an Animal Collision?," https://www.statefarm.com/simple-insights/auto-and-vehicles/how-likely-are-you-to-have-an-animal-collision.

16. Adams and Lindsey, *Urban Wildlife Management*, 37.

17. Carl D. Soulsbury et al., "Red Foxes (*Vulpes vulpes*)," in *Urban Carnivores: Ecology, Conflict, and Conservation*, ed. Stanley D. Gehrt, Seth P. D. Riley, and Brian L. Cypher (Baltimore: Johns Hopkins University Press, 2010), 74; Paul D. Curtis and John Hadidian, "Responding to Human-Carnivore Conflicts in Urban Areas," in ibid., 207.

18. Riley et al., "Anticoagulant Exposure," 1875–81; Courtney A. Albert et al., "Anticoagulant Rodenticides in Three Owl Species from Western Canada, 1988–2003," *Archives of Environmental Contamination and Toxicology* 58, no. 2 (2010): 451–59; Monica Bartos et al., "Use of Anticoagulant Rodenticides in Single-Family Neighborhoods along an Urban-

Wildland Interface in California," *Cities and the Environment* 4, no. 1 (2012): article 12.

19. David A. Jessup, "The Welfare of Feral Cats and Wildlife," *Journal of the American Veterinary Medical Association* 225, no. 9 (2004): 1377–83.

CHAPTER 13. FAST-FORWARD

1. J. D. Summers-Smith, "Decline of the House Sparrow: A Review," *British Birds* 96 (2003): 439–46; A. Dandapat, D. Banerjee, and D. Chakraborty, "The Case of the Disappearing House Sparrow (*Passer domesticus indicus*)," *Veterinary World* 3, no. 2 (2010): 97–100.

2. Ted R. Anderson, *Biology of the Ubiquitous House Sparrow: From Genes to Populations* (New York: Oxford University Press, 2006).

3. S. R. Palumbi, "Humans as the World's Greatest Evolutionary Force," *Science* 293, no. 5536 (September 7, 2001): 1786–90; A. P. Hendry, K. M. Gotanda, and E. I. Svensson, "Human Influences on Evolution, and the Ecological and Societal Consequences," *Philosophical Transactions of the Royal Society B* 372 (2017): article 20160028. For an example of evolutionary optimism, see Chris D. Thomas, *Inheritors of the Earth: How Nature Is Thriving in an Age of Extinction* (New York: Penguin, 2018).

4. Anderson, *Ubiquitous House Sparrow,* 9–12.

5. Anderson, *Ubiquitous House Sparrow,* 9–12.

6. M. P. Moulton et al., "The Earliest House Sparrow Introductions to North America," *Biological Invasions* 12, no. 9 (2010): 2955–58; C. S. Robbins, "Introduction, Spread and Present Abundance of the House Sparrow in North America," *Ornithological Monographs* 14, no. 14 (1973): 3–9; Anderson, *Ubiquitous House Sparrow,* 23.

7. Robin W. Doughty, "Sparrows for America: A Case of Mistaken Identity," *Journal of Popular Culture* 14, no. 2 (Fall 1980): 214–15; F. E. Spinner, "An Earnest Appeal to 'Young America,'" *Audubon Magazine* 1, no. 10 (November 1887): 232; Frank Chapman, editorial, *Bird-Lore* 10, no. 4 (July–August 1908): 178.

8. Anderson, *Ubiquitous House Sparrow,* 426–29; W. B. Barrows, *The English Sparrow (Passer domesticus) in North America, Especially in Its Relation to Agriculture,* U.S. Department of Agriculture, Division of Economic Ornithology and Mammalogy Bulletin 1 (Washington, DC: Government Printing Office, 1889).

9. Hermon C. Bumpus, "The Variations and Mutations of the Introduced Sparrow, *Passer domesticus*," in *Biological Lectures Delivered at the Marine Biological Laboratory of Wood's Holl, 1896–1897* (Boston: Ginn, 1898), 1–15.

10. Hermon C. Bumpus, "The Elimination of the Unfit as Illustrated by the Introduced Sparrow, *Passer domesticus*," in *Biological Lectures Delivered at the Marine Biological Laboratory of Wood's Holl, 1899* (Boston: Ginn, 1900), 209–26.

11. Richard F. Johnston and Robert K. Selander, "House Sparrows: Rapid Evolution of Races in North America," *Science* 144, no. 3618 (May 1, 1964): 548.

12. Adam G. Hart et al., "Evidence for Contemporary Evolution during Darwin's Lifetime," *Current Biology* 20, no. 3 (2010): R95; James William Tutt, *British Moths* (London: Routledge, 1896), 307; Arjen E. van 't Hof et al., "The Industrial Melanism Mutation in British Peppered Moths Is a Transposable Element," *Nature* 534 (June 2, 2016): 102–5.

13. A. L. Melander, "Can Insects Become Resistant to Sprays?," *Journal of Economic Entomology* 7 (1914): 167–73; Nichola J. Hawkins et al., "The Evolutionary Origins of Pesticide Resistance," *Biological Reviews* 94 (2019): 135–55.

14. J. A. Endler, *Natural Selection in the Wild* (Princeton: Princeton University Press, 1986).

15. Menno Schilthuizen, *Darwin Comes to Town: How the Urban Jungle Drives Evolution* (New York: Picador, 2018).

16. Gail L. Patricelli and Jessica L. Blickley, "Avian Communication in Urban Noise; Causes and Consequences of Vocal Adjustment," *Auk* 123, no. 3 (2006): 639–49; Erwin Nemeth and Henrik Brumm, "Birds and Anthropogenic Noise: Are Urban Songs Adaptive?," *American Naturalist* 176, no. 4 (October 2010): 465–75; Jesse R. Barber, Kevin R. Crooks, and Kurt M. Fristrup, "The Costs of Chronic Noise Exposure for Terrestrial Organisms," *Trends in Ecology and Evolution* 25, no. 3 (2009): 180–89; Marina Alberti et al., "Global Urban Signatures of Phenotypic Change in Animal and Plant Populations," *Proceedings of the National Academy of Sciences* 114, no. 34 (August 22, 2017): 8951–56.

17. Niels J. Dingemanse et al., "Behavioural Reaction Norms: Animal Personality Meets Individual Plasticity," *Trends in Ecology and Evolution* 25, no. 2 (February 2010): 81–89; Ulla Tuomainen and Ulrika Candolin, "Behavioural Responses to Human-Induced Environmental Change," *Biological Reviews* 86, no. 3 (2011): 640–57.

18. Maggie M. Hantak et al., "Mammalian Body Size Is Determined by Interactions between Climate, Urbanization, and Ecological Traits," *Communications Biology* 4 (2021): 972.

19. Schilthuizen, *Darwin Comes to Town*, 9.

20. Arne Jernelöv, *The Long-Term Fate of Invasive Species: Aliens Forever or Integrated Immigrants with Time?* (Cham, Switzerland: Springer, 2017), 55–70.

CHAPTER 14. EMBRACING THE URBAN WILD

1. J. L. Laake et al., "Population Growth and Status of California Sea Lions," *Journal of Wildlife Management* 82, no. 3 (April 2018): 583–95.

2. U.S. Army Corps of Engineers, *Passage to the Sea: History of the Lake Washington Ship Canal and the Hiram M. Chittenden Locks* (Seattle: Northwest Interpretive Association, 1993); Matthew Klingle, *Emerald City: An Environmental History of Seattle* (New Haven: Yale University Press, 2009).

3. Anders Halverson, *An Entirely Synthetic Fish: How Rainbow Trout Beguiled America and Overran the World* (New Haven: Yale University Press, 2010); Peter S. Alagona, "Species Complex: Classification and Conservation in American Environmental History," *Isis* 107, no. 4 (December 2016): 738–61. Most steelhead die at sea, and even of those that survive long enough, not all return to their natal streams: some wander, interbreeding with other stocks.

4. Tamara Jones, "Freeloading Sea Lions Wear Out Welcome, Face Eviction," *Los Angeles Times*, January 29, 1990, A15; Associated Press, "The Steelhead Skunk Sea Lions and Take a Lead—Removal of 3 Big Eaters Cited," *Seattle Post-Intelligencer*, September 18, 1996, B1.

5. Carlton Smith, "Lethal Injection for Herschel? 'Jury' to Decide," *Seattle Post-Intelligencer*, September 30, 1994, A1; Katia Blackburn, "Protected Sea Lions Endangering Rare Fish in the Pacific Northwest," *Los Angeles Times*, November 13, 1988, p. 4.

6. Associated Press, "Bill Paves Way to Kill Sea Lions at the Locks," *Seattle Post-Intelligencer*, April 29, 1994, C2; Kim Murphy, "Officials Approve Killing of Problem Sea Lions," *Los Angeles Times*, March 14, 1996, 3.

7. Will Anderson and Toni Frohoff, "Humans, Not Sea Lions, the True Culprits in Steelhead Decline," *Seattle Post-Intelligencer*, March 29, 1996, A13.

8. "Trout Hapless Prey at Fish Ladder: Net to Protect Steelhead from Seals to Be Deployed," *Los Angeles Times*, January 18, 1988, 24; Jones, "Freeloading Sea Lions"; Scott Sunde, "Big Splash for Fake Willy—Decoy Put into Service against Sea Lions," *Seattle Post-Intelligencer*, October 17, 1996, B1; Gil Bailey, "Activist Chains Self to Sea-Lion Cage," *Seattle Post-Intelligencer*, February 2, 1995, B3; Don Carter, "Tribe May Harvest Sea Lions," *Seattle Post-Intelligencer*, December 6, 1994, A1; Tracy Wilson, "Proposal to Relocate Sea Lions Rejected," *Los Angeles Times*, February 18, 1994, 1.

9. "Hondo, Bully of Locks, Is Finally Captured," *Seattle Post-Intelligencer*, May 24, 1996, C2; Associated Press, "Trout-Devouring Sea Lion Trio Begin Life Sentence at Sea World," *Washington Post*, July 6, 1996, A15.

10. Jack Hopkins, "Refugee Sea Lion from Ballard Locks Dies in Florida," *Seattle Post-Intelligencer*, September 3, 1996, B1; ENN Staff, "Sea Lion Problem Solved in Seattle," *Environmental News Network*, April 8, 1998.

11. Jim Sterba, *Nature Wars: The Incredible Story of How Wildlife Comebacks Turned Backyards into Battlegrounds* (New York: Broadway, 2013); David Baron, *The Beast in the Garden: A Parable of Man and Nature* (New York: W. W. Norton, 2010); Nathanael Johnson, *Unseen City: The Majesty of Pigeons, the Discreet Charm of Snails and Other Wonders of the Urban Wilderness* (New York: Rodale Books, 2016); Lyanda Lynn Haupt, *The Urban Bestiary: Encountering the Everyday Wild* (New York: Little, Brown, 2013).

12. Timothy Beatley, *Biophilic Cities: Integrating Nature into Urban Design and Planning* (Washington, DC: Island Press, 2010).

13. Catherine E. Newman et al., "A New Species of Leopard Frog (Anura: Ranidae) from the Urban Northeastern US," *Molecular Phylogenetics and Evolution* 63, no. 2 (2012): 445–55.

14. Frank Kummer, "Philly's Skyline to Get Dark at Midnight to Protect Migrating Birds," *Philadelphia Inquirer*, March 31, 2021.

15. Winifred Curran and Trina Hamilton, eds., *Just Green Enough: Urban Development and Environmental Gentrification* (London: Routledge, 2018).

16. Heather Swanson, City of Boulder ecological stewardship supervisor, interview with the author, Boulder, CO, September 22, 2017.

17. Karina Brown, "A Federal Bird Kill in the Columbia River Did Nothing to Save Salmon," *Willamette Week*, February 6, 2019; Lynda V. Mapes, "Hundreds of Sea Lions to Be Killed on Columbia River in Effort to Save Endangered Fish," *Seattle Times*, August 13, 2020; Ben Goldfarb, "For Sea Lions, a Feast of Salmon on the Columbia," *High Country News*, July 6,

2015,https://www.hcn.org/articles/on-the-columbia-river-what-do-you-do-with-a-hungry-sea-lion.

18. Karl Marx, *The Eighteenth Brumaire of Louis Bonaparte*, trans. Daniel De Leon (Chicago: C. H. Kerr, 1913), 9. Quoting J. R. McNeill, Elizabeth Kolbert also referred to Marx's quote along these lines in her book *Under a White Sky: The Nature of the Future* (New York: Crown, 2021), 88, 148.

CODA

1. For an example from Africa, see Tess Vengadajellum, "Life in the Time of Lockdown: How Wildlife Is Reclaiming Its Territory," *South African,* April 23, 2020, https://www.thesouthafrican.com/lifestyle/environment/life-in-the-time-of-lockdown-how-wildlife-is-reclaiming-its-territory/; from Asia, Melina Moey, "Animal Crossing: Wildlife in Asia Come Out to Play during Lockdown," *AsiaOne,* April 29, 2020, https://www.asiaone.com/asia/animal-crossing-wildlife-asia-come-out-play-during-lockdown; from Europe, Becky Thomas, "Coronavirus: What the Lockdown Could Mean for Urban Wildlife," *The Conversation,* April 3, 2020, https://theconversation.com/coronavirus-what-the-lockdown-could-mean-for-urban-wildlife-134918; from North America, Louis Sahagún, "Coyotes, Falcons, Deer and Other Wildlife Are Reclaiming L.A. Territory as Humans Stay at Home," *Los Angeles Times,* April 21, 2020; from Oceania, Sarah Bekessy, Alex Kusmanoff, Brendan Wintle, Casey Visintin, Freya Thomas, Georgia Garrard, Katherine Berthon, Lee Harrison, Matthew Selinske, and Thami Croeser, "Photos Showing Animals in Cities Prove That Nature *Always* Wins," *Inverse,* April 18, 2020, https://www.inverse.com/culture/animals-in-cities-photos-covid-19; from South America, "Wild Puma Captured in Deserted Chile Capitol," *Yahoo! News,* March 24, 2020, https://news.yahoo.com/wild-puma-captured-deserted-chile-capital-155944794.html.

2. Since 2000, some films—including *Wall-E* (2008), *Interstellar* (2014), and *Mad Max: Fury Road* (2015)—have suggested that nature would take longer to recover in a postapocalyptic world.

Selected Bibliography

This selected bibliography lists major works cited in the notes. Works with less direct relevance are not included here.

Adams, Clark E., and Kieran J. Lindsey. *Urban Wildlife Management.* 2nd ed. Boca Raton, FL: CRC Press, 2010.

Adams, Lowell W. "Urban Wildlife Ecology and Conservation: A Brief History of the Discipline." *Urban Ecosystems* 8 (2005): 139–56.

Alberti, Marina, et al. "Global Urban Signatures of Phenotypic Change in Animal and Plant Populations." *Proceedings of the National Academy of Sciences* 114, no. 34 (August 22, 2017): 8951–56.

Anderson, Ted R. *Biology of the Ubiquitous House Sparrow: From Genes to Populations.* New York: Oxford University Press, 2006.

Atkins, Peter J. *Animal Cities: Beastly Urban Histories.* Farnham, Surrey: Ashgate, 2012.

Barber, Jesse R., Kevin R. Crooks, and Kurt M. Fristrup. "The Costs of Chronic Noise Exposure for Terrestrial Organisms." *Trends in Ecology and Evolution* 25, no. 3 (2009): 180–89.

Baron, David. *The Beast in the Garden: A Parable of Man and Nature.* New York: W. W. Norton, 2010.

Barrow, Mark V., Jr. *Nature's Ghosts: Confronting Extinction from the Age of Jefferson to the Age of Ecology.* Chicago: University of Chicago Press, 2010.

Beatley, Timothy. *Biophilic Cities: Integrating Nature into Urban Design and Planning.* Washington, DC: Island Press, 2010.

Benson, Etienne. "The Urbanization of the Eastern Gray Squirrel in the United States." *Journal of American History* 100, no. 3 (2013): 691–710.

Biehler, Dawn Day. *Pests in the City: Flies, Bedbugs, Cockroaches, and Rats.* Seattle: University of Washington Press, 2013.

Bilger, Burkhard. "Swamp Things: Florida's Uninvited Predators." *New Yorker,* April 20, 2009.

Blair, Robert B. "Land Use and Avian Species Diversity along an Urban Gradient." *Ecological Applications* 6, no. 2 (1996): 506–19.

Bolster, W. Jeffrey. *The Mortal Sea.* Cambridge, MA: Harvard University Press, 2012.

Booker, Matthew. *Down by the Bay: San Francisco's History between the Tides.* Oakland: University of California Press, 2020.

Bradley, Catherine A., and Sonia Altizer. "Urbanization and the Ecology of Wildlife Diseases." *Trends in Ecology and Evolution* 22, no. 2 (2007): 95–102.

Brown, Frederick L. *The City Is More Than Human: An Animal History of Seattle.* Seattle: University of Washington Press, 2016.

Bumpus, Hermon C. "The Elimination of the Unfit as Illustrated by the Introduced Sparrow, *Passer domesticus.*" In *Biological Lectures Delivered at the Marine Biological Laboratory of Wood's Holl, 1899,* 209–26. Boston: Ginn, 1900.

Bush, Emma R. "Global Trade in Exotic Pets, 2006–2012." *Conservation Biology* 28, no. 3 (June 2014): 663–76.

Coates, Peter. *American Perceptions of Immigrant and Invasive Species: Strangers on the Land.* Berkeley: University of California Press, 2007.

Côté, Steeve D., et al. "Ecological Impacts of Deer Overabundance." *Annual Review of Ecology, Evolution, and Systematics* 35, no. 1 (2004): 113–47.

Cranz, Galen. *The Politics of Park Design: A History of Urban Parks in America.* Cambridge, MA: MIT Press, 1982.

Cronon, William. *Nature's Metropolis: Chicago and the Great West.* New York: W. W. Norton, 2009.

Crooks, Kevin R., and Michael E. Soulé. "Mesopredator Release and Avifaunal Extinctions in a Fragmented System." *Nature* 400 (August 5, 1999): 563–66.

Curran, Winifred, and Trina Hamilton, eds. *Just Green Enough: Urban Development and Environmental Gentrification*. London: Routledge, 2018.

Davis, David E. "The Characteristics of Rat Populations." *Quarterly Review of Biology* 28, no. 4 (December 1953): 373–401.

Decker, Ethan H., et al. "Energy and Material Flow through the Urban Ecosystem." *Annual Review of Energy and the Environment* 25 (2000): 685–740.

DeStefano, Stephen. *Coyote at the Kitchen Door: Living with Wildlife in Suburbia*. Cambridge, MA: Harvard University Press, 2010.

DeStefano, Stephen, and Richard M. DeGraaf. "Exploring the Ecology of Suburban Wildlife." *Frontiers in Ecology and the Environment* 1, no. 2 (March 2003): 95–101.

Dingemanse, Niels J., et al. "Behavioural Reaction Norms: Animal Personality Meets Individual Plasticity." *Trends in Ecology and Evolution* 25, no. 2 (February 2010): 81–89.

Douglas, Mary. *Purity and Danger: An Analysis of the Concepts of Pollution and Taboo*. London: Ark Paperbacks, 1984.

Endler, J. A. *Natural Selection in the Wild*. Princeton: Princeton University Press, 1986.

Evans, K. L., et al. "What Makes an Urban Bird?" *Global Change Biology* 17, no. 1 (January 2011): 32–44.

Fitter, R. S. R. *London's Natural History*. Collins New Naturalist Library, Book 3. London: HarperCollins, 2011.

Flores, Dan. *Coyote America: A Natural and Supernatural History*. New York: Basic Books, 2016.

Forman, Richard T. T., and Lauren E. Alexander. "Roads and Their Major Ecological Effects." *Annual Review of Ecology and Systematics* 29, no. 1 (1998): 207–31.

Foster, David R., et al. "Wildlife Dynamics in the Changing New England Landscape." *Journal of Biogeography* 29, nos. 10–11 (October 2002): 1337–57.

Gehrt, Stanley D., et al. *Urban Carnivores: Ecology, Conflict, and Conservation*. Baltimore: Johns Hopkins University Press, 2010.

Gilfoyle, Timothy J. "White Cities, Linguistic Turns, and Disneylands: The New Paradigms of Urban History." *Reviews in American History* 26, no. 1 (1998): 175–204.

Grier, Katherine C. *Pets in America: A History*. Chapel Hill: University of North Carolina Press, 2010.

Grooten, M., and R. E. A. Almond, eds. *Living Planet Report—2018: Aiming Higher.* Gland, Switzerland: World Wildlife Fund, 2018.

Haensch, S., et al. "Distinct Clones of *Yersinia pestis* Caused the Black Death." *PLOS Pathogens* 6, no. 10 (2010): e1001134.

Hall, Peter. *Cities of Tomorrow: An Intellectual History of Urban Planning and Design in the Twentieth Century.* 3rd ed. Oxford: Blackwell, 2002.

Halverson, Anders. *An Entirely Synthetic Fish: How Rainbow Trout Beguiled America and Overran the World.* New Haven: Yale University Press, 2010.

Hardin, Scott. "Managing Non-native Wildlife in Florida: State Perspective, Policy, and Practice." *Managing Vertebrate Invasive Species* 14 (2007): 43–52.

Haupt, Lyanda Lynn. *The Urban Bestiary: Encountering the Everyday Wild.* New York: Little, Brown, 2013.

Hawkins, Nichola J., et al. "The Evolutionary Origins of Pesticide Resistance." *Biological Reviews* 94 (2019): 135–55.

Herzog, Hal. *Some We Love, Some We Hate, Some We Eat: Why It's So Hard to Think Straight about Animals.* New York: HarperCollins, 2010.

Jackson, Kenneth T. *Crabgrass Frontier: The Suburbanization of the United States.* Oxford: Oxford University Press, 1987.

Jernelöv, Arne. *The Long-Term Fate of Invasive Species: Aliens Forever or Integrated Immigrants with Time?* Cham, Switzerland: Springer, 2017.

Johnson, Benjamin Heber. *Escaping the Dark, Gray City: Fear and Hope in Progressive-Era Conservation.* New Haven: Yale University Press, 2017.

Johnson, Nathanael. *Unseen City: The Majesty of Pigeons, the Discreet Charm of Snails and Other Wonders of the Urban Wilderness.* New York: Rodale Books, 2016.

Johnston, Richard F., and Robert K. Selander. "House Sparrows: Rapid Evolution of Races in North America." *Science* 144, no. 3618 (May 1, 1964): 548–50.

Jones, Bryony A., et al. "Zoonosis Emergence Linked to Agricultural Intensification and Environmental Change." *Proceedings of the National Academy of Sciences* 110, no. 21 (May 21, 2013): 8399–404.

Karesh, William B., et al. "Ecology of Zoonoses: Natural and Unnatural Histories." *Lancet* 380, no. 9857 (2012): 1936–45.

Kellert, Stephen R. "American Attitudes toward and Knowledge of Animals: An Update." *International Journal for the Study of Animal Problems* 1, no. 2 (1980): 87–119.

Kiechle, Melanie A. *Smell Detectives: An Olfactory History of Nineteenth-Century Urban America.* Seattle: University of Washington Press, 2017.

Kisling, Vernon N., ed. *Zoo and Aquarium History: Ancient Animal Collections to Zoological Gardens.* Boca Raton, FL: CRC Press, 2001.

Klingle, Matthew. *Emerald City: An Environmental History of Seattle.* New Haven: Yale University Press, 2009.

Koeppel, Gerard T. *Water for Gotham: A History.* Princeton: Princeton University Press, 2001.

Kolbert, Elizabeth. *Under a White Sky: The Nature of the Future.* New York: Crown, 2021.

Krysko, Kenneth L., et al. "Verified Non-indigenous Amphibians and Reptiles in Florida from 1863 through 2010: Outlining the Invasion Process and Identifying Invasion Pathways and Stages." *Zootaxa* 3028 (2011): 1–64.

Laake, J. L., et al. "Population Growth and Status of California Sea Lions." *Journal of Wildlife Management* 82, no. 3 (April 2018): 583–95.

Lawrence, Henry W. *City Trees: A Historical Geography from the Renaissance through the Nineteenth Century.* Charlottesville: University of Virginia Press, 2008.

Leopold, Aldo. *Game Management.* New York: Charles Scribner's Sons, 1933.

Longcore, Travis. *Ecological Consequences of Artificial Night Lighting.* Washington, DC: Island Press, 2005.

Lutts, Ralph H. "The Trouble with Bambi: Walt Disney's *Bambi* and the American Vision of Nature." *Forest and Conservation History* 36, no. 4 (October 1992): 160–71.

Marra, Peter, and Chris Santella. *Cat Wars: The Devastating Consequences of a Cuddly Killer.* Princeton: Princeton University Press, 2016.

Marris, Emma. *Rambunctious Garden: Saving Nature in a Post-wild World.* New York: Bloomsbury, 2011.

———. *Wild Souls: Freedom and Flourishing in the Non-human World.* New York: Bloomsbury, 2021.

Martin, Justin. *Genius of Place: The Life of Frederick Law Olmsted.* New York: Hachette Books, 2011.

Mazur, Rachel. *Speaking of Bears: The Bear Crisis and a Tale of Rewilding from Yosemite, Sequoia, and Other National Parks.* Guilford, CT: Rowman and Littlefield, 2015.

McCleery, Robert A., Christopher E. Moorman, and M. Nils Peterson, eds. *Urban Wildlife Conservation.* New York: Springer, 2014.

McHarg, Ian L. *Design with Nature*. New York: J. Wiley, 1992.

McKinney, Michael L. "Urbanization, Biodiversity, and Conservation." *BioScience* 52, no. 10 (2002): 883–90.

———. "Urbanization as a Major Cause of Biological Homogenization." *Biological Conservation* 127 (2006): 247–60.

McNeur, Catherine. *Taming Manhattan: Environmental Battles in the Antebellum City.* Cambridge, MA: Harvard University Press, 2014.

McShane, Clay, and Joel A. Tarr. *The Horse in the City: Living Machines in the Nineteenth Century.* Baltimore: Johns Hopkins University Press, 2007.

Meagher, Sharon M., ed. *Philosophy and the City: Classic to Contemporary Writings.* Albany: State University of New York Press, 2008.

Messmer, Terry A. "The Emergence of Human–Wildlife Conflict Management: Turning Challenges into Opportunities." *International Biodeterioration and Biodegradation* 45, no. 3 (2000): 97–102.

Mooallem, Jon. *Wild Ones: A Sometimes Dismaying, Weirdly Reassuring Story about Looking at People Looking at Animals in America.* New York: Penguin, 2014.

Mullineaux, E. "Veterinary Treatment and Rehabilitation of Indigenous Wildlife." *Journal of Small Animal Practice* 55 (2014): 293–300.

Nagel, Thomas. "What Is It Like to Be a Bat?" *Philosophical Review* 83, no. 4 (October 1974): 435–50.

Newman, Catherine E., et al. "A New Species of Leopard Frog (Anura: Ranidae) from the Urban Northeastern US." *Molecular Phylogenetics and Evolution* 63, no. 2 (2012): 445–55.

Ostfeld, Richard. *Lyme Disease: The Ecology of a Complex System.* Oxford: Oxford University Press, 2011.

Palumbi, S. R. "Humans as the World's Greatest Evolutionary Force." *Science* 293, no. 5536 (September 7, 2001): 1786–90.

Parker, Simon. *Urban Theory and the Urban Experience: Encountering the City.* New York: Routledge, 2015.

Pergams, Oliver R. W., and Patricia A. Zaradic. "Evidence for a Fundamental and Pervasive Shift Away from Nature-Based Recreation." *Proceedings of the National Academy of Sciences* 105, no. 7 (2008): 2295–300.

Peterson, M. Nils, et al. "Rearticulating the Myth of Human–Wildlife Conflict." *Conservation Letters* 3, no. 2 (April 2010): 74–82.

Pickett, Steward T. A., et al. "Evolution and Future of Urban Ecological Science: Ecology in, of, and for the City." *Ecosystem Health and Sustainability* 2, no. 7 (2016): e01229.

Pickett, S. T. A., et al. "Urban Ecological Systems: Linking Terrestrial Ecological, Physical, and Socioeconomic Components of Metropolitan Areas." *Annual Review of Ecology and Systematics* 32 (2001): 127–57.

Pimentel, D., R. Zuniga, and D. Morrison. "Update on the Environmental and Economic Costs Associated with Alien-Invasive Species in the United States." *Ecological Economics* 52, no. 3 (February 15, 2005): 273–88.

Pollak, Daniel. *Natural Community Conservation Planning (NCCP): The Origins of an Ambitious Experiment to Protect Ecosystems*. Sacramento: California Research Bureau, March 2001.

Quammen, David. *The Song of the Dodo: Island Biogeography in an Age of Extinctions*. New York: Random House, 2012.

———. *Spillover: Animal Infections and the Next Human Pandemic*. New York: W. W. Norton, 2012.

Revels, Tracy J. *Sunshine Paradise: A History of Florida Tourism*. Gainesville: University of Florida Press, 2011.

Robichaud, Andrew A. *Animal City: The Domestication of America*. Cambridge, MA: Harvard University Press, 2019.

Rome, Adam. *The Bulldozer in the Countryside: Suburban Sprawl and the Rise of American Environmentalism*. Cambridge: Cambridge University Press, 2001.

Rosenberg, Kenneth V., et al. "Decline of the North American Avifauna." *Science* 366, no. 6461 (October 4, 2019): 120–24.

Rosenzweig, Roy, and Elizabeth Blackmar. *The Park and the People: A History of Central Park*. Ithaca, NY: Cornell University Press, 1992.

Sanderson, Eric W. *Mannahatta: A Natural History of New York City*. New York: Abrams, 2009.

Schilthuizen, Menno. *Darwin Comes to Town: How the Urban Jungle Drives Evolution*. New York: Picador, 2018.

Sellars, Richard West. *Preserving Nature in the National Parks: A History*. New Haven: Yale University Press, 1999.

Shelford, Victor E., ed. *Naturalist's Guide to the Americas*. Baltimore: Williams and Wilkins, 1926.

Singer, Peter. *Animal Liberation*. New York: Random House, 2015.

———. *The Most Good You Can Do: How Effective Altruism Is Changing Ideas about Living*. New Haven: Yale University Press, 2015.

Snetsinger, Robert. *The Ratcatcher's Child: The History of the Pest Control Industry*. Cleveland: Franzak and Foster, 1983.

Spotswood, Erica N., et al. "The Biological Deserts Fallacy: Cities in Their Landscapes Contribute More Than We Think to Regional Biodiversity." *BioScience* 71, no. 2 (February 2021): 148–60.

Sterba, Jim. *Nature Wars: The Incredible Story of How Wildlife Comebacks Turned Backyards into Battlegrounds.* New York: Broadway, 2013.

Sullivan, Robert. *Rats: Observations on the History and Habitat of the City's Most Unwanted Inhabitants.* New York: Bloomsbury, 2005.

Surls, Rachel, and Judith B. Gerber. *From Cows to Concrete: The Rise and Fall of Farming in Los Angeles.* Los Angeles: Angel City Press, 2016.

Thomas, Chris D. *Inheritors of the Earth: How Nature Is Thriving in an Age of Extinction.* New York: Penguin, 2018.

Tuomainen, Ulla, and Ulrika Candolin. "Behavioural Responses to Human-Induced Environmental Change." *Biological Reviews* 86, no. 3 (2011): 640–57.

Tutt, James William. *British Moths.* London: Routledge, 1896.

Walker, Richard A. *The Country in the City: The Greening of the San Francisco Bay Area.* Seattle: University of Washington Press, 2013.

Warren, Louis S. *The Hunter's Game: Poachers and Conservationists in Twentieth-Century America.* New Haven: Yale University Press, 1999.

Zallen, Jeremy. *American Lucifers: The Dark History of Artificial Light.* Chapel Hill: University of North Carolina Press, 2019.

Index

Founded in 1893,
UNIVERSITY OF CALIFORNIA PRESS
publishes bold, progressive books and journals
on topics in the arts, humanities, social sciences,
and natural sciences—with a focus on social
justice issues—that inspire thought and action
among readers worldwide.

The UC PRESS FOUNDATION
raises funds to uphold the press's vital role
as an independent, nonprofit publisher, and
receives philanthropic support from a wide
range of individuals and institutions—and from
committed readers like you. To learn more, visit
ucpress.edu/supportus.